# Chicken Soup for the Soul.

# Let It Go

*Chicken Soup for the Soul: Let It Go*
*101 Stories of Forgiveness & Freedom*
Amy Newmark

Published by Chicken Soup for the Soul, LLC www.chickensoup.com
Copyright ©2025 by Chicken Soup for the Soul, LLC. All Rights Reserved.

No part of this publication may be reproduced, stored in a retrieval system or transmitted in any form or by any means, electronic, mechanical, photocopying, recording or otherwise, without the written permission of the publisher.

CSS, Chicken Soup for the Soul, and its Logo and Marks are trademarks of Chicken Soup for the Soul, LLC.

The publisher gratefully acknowledges the many individuals who granted Chicken Soup for the Soul permission to reprint the cited material.

Front cover photo created by Daniel Zaccari using Adobe Firefly from the prompt "Two young girls with yellow flower seated on green field background"
Back cover and interior photo image courtesy of iStockphoto.com (©Boonyachoat)

Photo of Amy Newmark courtesy of Susan Morrow at SwickPix

*Cover and Interior by Daniel Zaccari*

Publisher's Cataloging-in-Publication Data

Names: Newmark, Amy, editor.
Title: Chicken soup for the soul : let it go , 101 stories of forgiveness & freedom / Amy Newmark.
Description: Cos Cob, CT: Chicken Soup for the Soul, LLC, 2025.
Identifiers: LCCN: 2025936956 | ISBN: 978-1-61159-123-1 (paperback) | 978-1-61159-357-0 (ebook)
Subjects: LCSH Forgiveness--Literary collections. | Forgiveness--Anecdotes. | Happiness--Literary collections. | Happiness--Anecdotes. | Conduct of life--Literary collections. | Conduct of life--Anecdotes. | Self help. | BISAC SELF-HELP / Motivational & inspirational | SELF-HELP / Personal Growth / Happiness | SELF-HELP / Self Management / Stress Management
Classification: LCC BF637.F67 C45 2025 | DDC 155.9/2/02--dc23

Library of Congress Control Number: 2025936956

PRINTED IN THE UNITED STATES OF AMERICA
on acid∞free paper

30 29 28 27 26 25         01 02 03 04 05 06 07 08 09

# Chicken Soup for the Soul.

# Let It Go

## 101 Stories of Forgiveness & Freedom

### Amy Newmark

Chicken Soup for the Soul, LLC
Cos Cob, CT

Changing lives one story at a time®
www.chickensoup.com

# Table of Contents

## ❶ Put the Past in the Past

1. A Second Chance, *Kathleen Chamberlin* ................................. 1
2. Who Do You Think You Are? *Tracy Farquhar* ...................... 4
3. Choose Love, *Lori Fuller* ............................................................ 8
4. The End, *Sandy Anderson* ........................................................ 10
5. The Scar, *Kitty Chappell* .......................................................... 13
6. She Flies with Her Own Wings, *Ruth Kephart* ..................... 16
7. Moving Past the Past, *Charles Earl Harrel* ............................ 18
8. Silencing the Boom, *Melissa Cronin* ...................................... 22
9. Life Lessons, *Suzy Ryan* ............................................................ 26

## ❷ Understand Their Actions

10. The Apology, *Kathleen Birmingham* ....................................... 30
11. Sympathy Flowers, *Casey McMullin* ....................................... 34
12. Mom's Wisdom, *Eugene Mead* ................................................ 37
13. The Joy Ride, *Mary Elizabeth Laufer* ..................................... 40
14. The Kaleidoscope Effect, *Lillie Houchin* ................................ 44
15. Emotional Shackles, *Jessica Loftus* ......................................... 48
16. Pop, *Paul Lyons* .......................................................................... 51
17. My Mantra, *Kathy Dickie* .......................................................... 54
18. Even a Cold Fish Needs Love, *Wendy J. Hairfield* ................ 56

## ❸ Use the Power of Forgiveness

19. Love Restored, *Jeannette E. Nott* ..................................60
20. Spreading Sunshine, *Jill Anne Berni* ............................64
21. Dirty Little Fingers, *Melissa Face* ................................67
22. Don't Drink the Poison, *Nancy Emmick Panko* ...............70
23. The Still, Small Voice, *D. Lincoln Jones* .......................74
24. Auntie Beast, *Carly Sutherland* ...................................77
25. The Phone Call That Changed My Life, *Denise R. Fuller*......80
26. Why I Choose Gratitude, *David A. Grant* .....................83
27. From Revenge to Peace, *Susan Boltz* ..........................86

## ❹ Let Compassion Heal You

28. The Teddy Bear, *Judith Ann Hayes* ..............................90
29. Midnight Grace, *Shawnelle Eliasen* .............................93
30. Don't Bruise the Petals, *April Knight* ..........................97
31. Circle of Prayer, *Cathi LaMarche* ................................99
32. Sharing My Friend, *Kathryn Lay* .................................103
33. I Lubbyou, *Catherine Shavalier-Chernow* ....................105
34. Once Upon a Time, *Dale Mary Grenfell* .....................108
35. Daddy's Little Girl, *Linda Bruno* .................................111
36. Dragonflies, *Celeste Bergeron Ewan* .........................114

## ❺ Be Open to Family

37. Painted Nails, *Barb McKenna* .....................................118
38. The Power to Heal, *David A. Grant* ............................123
39. The First "I Love You" *Miranda Lamb* ........................126
40. The Strength of Forgiveness, *Kim Carney* ..................129
41. At First Sight, *Jeanie Jacobson* ..................................132

42. Tasting Forgiveness, *Priscilla Dann-Courtney* ............... 136
43. Three Christmas Miracles, *Connie Nice* ............... 139

### ❻
### Just Let Them…

44. No Shame in My Game, *Melissa H.B. Bender* ............... 143
45. Worth the Effort, *Suzy Ryan* ............... 147
46. Changing More than Diapers, *Jenny Pavlovic* ............... 149
47. Grab Bag, *Cathi LaMarche* ............... 152
48. The Empty Room, *Mindi Susman Ellis* ............... 156
49. Can't Is a Four-Letter Word, *Brenda Beattie* ............... 159
50. The View from the Back Seat, *Joan M. Borton* ............... 162
51. The Curvy Sister, *Debra Mayhew* ............... 164

### ❼
### Accept that Parents Are Not Perfect

52. The Ritual, *Diane Caldwell* ............... 168
53. Thoughts on Love and Forgiveness, *Becky Povich* ............... 172
54. Better Late Than Never, *Leigh Smith* ............... 175
55. Finding Our Beat, *Nicholas R.* ............... 178
56. The Gift of Forgiveness, *Beverly A. Golberg* ............... 183
57. The Trouble with Dad, *Alma Barkman* ............... 186
58. No Fault, *Christy Heitger-Ewing* ............... 190
59. Fudge and Fathers, *Mark Musolf* ............... 194
60. Mary's Girl, *Ruth Logan Herne* ............... 197

### ❽
### Move Forward after an Apology

61. Losing Sophie, *Jennie Ivey* ............... 201
62. The Polar Bears, *Lainie Belcastro* ............... 205
63. A Wink from the Universe, *Heidi Allen* ............... 208

64. You're Forgiven, *Lee E. Pollock* ............................................. 212
65. These Things Take Time, *Melissa Crandall* ........................ 215
66. Forgiveness Practice, *Rita Billbe* ....................................... 217
67. Learning My Lesson, *Rosanna Micelotta Battigelli* ............ 220
68. The Pilgrim's Wife, *Eva Carter* .......................................... 223

## ❾
## Forgive Yourself

69. The Support of a Family, *Janet Hartman* .......................... 228
70. The Fire Within, *John Apel* ................................................ 230
71. A Story of Forgiveness, *S.R.* ............................................... 234
72. The Angels on the Train, *Ryan Freeman* ........................... 237
73. A Walk with Thelma, *Jill Burns* .......................................... 240
74. His Messenger, *Sandra Wood* ............................................ 242
75. No Need for Goodbye, *Arturo Guajardo IV* ....................... 246
76. Empowering Humiliation, *Diana Bauder* .......................... 248
77. Reservation for One, *Dana D. Clark* .................................. 251

## ❿
## Make an Ex-Spouse an Ex-Enemy

78. Ex's and Oh's, *Natalie June Reilly* ..................................... 262
79. Close Encounter of the Healing Kind, *Jenna Romano* ...... 265
80. Baking Away Bitterness, *Linda Fitzjarrell* ......................... 268
81. Define Normal, *Natalie June Reilly* ................................... 271
82. Chicago Peace, *Teresa Curley Barczak* .............................. 274
83. I'm Not Going to Hate You, *Dustin Urbach* ....................... 277
84. Guess Who Came for Dinner? *Linda LaRocque* ................ 281
85. The Gift I Needed, *Yvonne Curry Smallwood* ................... 284

## ⓫
## Liberate Yourself by Letting It Go

86. The Blueprints, *Cindy Golchuk* ............................................. 288
87. Shredding Sadness, *Susan Maddy Jones* ............................ 292
88. Walking in Another Direction, *Susan Yanguas* ................. 296
89. Let It Go, *Tamara Bell* ......................................................... 299
90. Take Center Stage, *Violetta Armour* ................................... 303
91. Forgiveness Is a Choice, *Katherine Van Hook* ................... 306
92. Return to Heart Mountain, *Jessie Miyeko Santala* ............ 308
93. Recipes for Healing, *Steve Coney* ...................................... 312
94. Relief Within My Heartache, *Kellie Burley* ....................... 314

## ⓬
## Make Marriage Work

95. Repairing Brokenness, *Jody Fuller* .................................... 317
96. What Dreams May Come, *Lindsay Shirley* ........................ 321
97. Our First 5K, *Lisa M. Bartelt* .............................................. 323
98. Mud Pie and Coffee, *Marianne L. Davis* ............................ 326
99. Anything for a Buck, *Karen O'Keeffe* ................................. 330
100. Brown and White Butterflies, *Melissa Harding* ............... 334
101. Sleepless Nights, *Jean Davidson* ....................................... 337

Meet Our Contributors ................................................................. 340
Meet Amy Newmark ..................................................................... 353
About Chicken Soup for the Soul ............................................... 355

# Chapter 1

# Put the Past in the Past

# A Second Chance

*If you are still breathing, you have a second chance.*
*~Oprah Winfrey*

My mother and I had a relationship that could be described as "difficult" at best. We couldn't seem to get along or agree about anything. When we spoke on our weekly phone calls, she would push my buttons, and I would find myself annoyed and impatient. To compound the estrangement, my mother was beginning to show evidence of memory loss and would repeat her most offensive comments.

Then, a call came one Sunday morning with the heart-wrenching news that my father had suffered a fatal heart attack. I spoke to the police officer and my bewildered mother, who asked when I was coming over. I reassured her that I would be there as soon as I could, and arranged for someone to stay with her until I could make the four-hour drive from my home to hers.

The next week was a harrowing experience for both of us as I made funeral arrangements and endless phone calls, and prepared to bring my mother to live with us. She and I would have to find a way back to each other but in reversed roles. I would be the caretaker, showering and dressing her; I would be the cook, preparing all her meals; and I would be her chauffeur, driving her to the many doctors she had to see. I would also be her accountant and have her power of attorney, paying all the bills on her house, hiring painters and working with a Realtor now that the house would have to be sold.

When she first came to live with me, she fought like the lioness of old, snarling and striking out with razor-sharp claws. I would respond in kind — that is, until she would ask me in a timid and uncertain voice where my father was and if he was all right. Her vulnerability and disorientation dissolved my anger, and I would explain that he had passed. I realized she was hearing these words as if for the first time, and her sobs would break out again, as would mine.

I learned not to do that and, instead, when she asked, I would say that he was fine, he was golfing or bowling or at a meeting. These answers seemed to satisfy her, especially when I told her he would be home by dinner.

Lying went against everything I had been taught and every principle that structured my life. But these lies were less damaging than the harsh truth. So, I told them with less of a twinge of conscience with each telling because they provided her with something familiar, recognizable and comforting.

Gradually, she became accustomed to living with me and underwent a transformation. Even the smallest gesture was received gratefully and acknowledged with a thank-you or a compliment. I would look at her, bewildered. Who was this woman, and what had she done with my mother?

I had had to retire from my job to care for her, which meant long hours in her company. She would talk about her parents and her childhood, coming more alive as I asked questions about her past that she could answer.

Another way I came to enjoy her company was through music. Having grown up in a family where music was valued and singing along with the radio was encouraged, I knew the lyrics of nearly every song she did. I had a fairly good singing voice, but my mother sang like an angel. So, after dinner, we would sit by the living room fireplace and sing. It gave her such pleasure because music, for some reason, is untouched by Alzheimer's disease. She could relive some of the former joy she had taken in performing with the senior choral group. She had frequently sung solos. It was a special bonding time as we sang our duets.

Eventually, it was no longer possible to keep her with me. She would awaken at all hours, calling for me to dress her, insisting that people were waiting outside. Or I would awake to her calling for help and find her in the walk-in closet in a bedroom down the hall instead of in the bathroom across from her room. Making the decision to move her to the structured and safer environment of the care facility, while necessary, was difficult. I visited her at the times she would be most alert, and we would talk and sing together, drawing a small audience of fellow clients and aides who would join in our mini concerts.

While the music remained strong, her memories became more clouded. She no longer asked about my dad, thought she was a twenty-year-old, and forgot she had ever married or had children. Because I saw her every other day, I remained present in her mind longer than the rest. But one day, she no longer knew me as her daughter, and I was very sad indeed. Trying not to cry, I asked her, "Who am I if I am not your daughter?" Without hesitation, she said, "You're my friend."

I realized what a great compliment she had paid me with those three words, as powerful as if she had said "I love you." I was more than family to her. We can't choose our family. We love them despite our conflicts. But we choose our friends, and we choose to love and value them. I reached out and squeezed her hand and said, "You're my friend, too."

It's strange to be thankful for a disease as devastating as Alzheimer's, but I found the silver lining in it. It may have robbed my mother and me of some things, but it paved the way for us to find something deeper. It allowed us to find each other. It gave us a second chance.

— Kathleen Chamberlin —

# Who Do You Think You Are?

*Gratitude turns what we have into enough, and more.
It turns denial into acceptance, chaos into order,
confusion into clarity...*
~Melody Beattie

The 23andMe DNA test that my ex-husband had gifted me for my sixtieth birthday sat on my desk for several weeks before I finally opened it. I spit the required saliva into the tube, registered online, and sent off the sample. Over the next few weeks, I got periodic e-mail updates on the progress of my specimen, and I was invited to participate in some surveys, which I would sometimes do when I had some free time.

When I opened the online results I found nothing that startling. I was shown to have 44% French and German and 37% British and Irish ancestry, with a bit of Scandinavian, Spanish, Portuguese, and Eastern European thrown in. There was an option to create an account and connect with possible relatives in their database, but I decided to put that off for a while.

Then, late one night, I went for it. I created the account and clicked the "DNA Relatives" button. When the list of names popped up, I stared at it, confused. All of my four siblings are sisters, but the first name on the list was a name I didn't recognize. It was labeled "half brother." The second unidentifiable name was labeled "aunt."

I struggled to make sense of what I was seeing for several minutes before I clicked on my half-brother's name to see his profile. It said he was born two years before me, was from a town very close to where I was born, and was adopted. He had found his mother's name, which he shared, but his father's name was left blank on his birth certificate, which had just become available to him a few years earlier.

So, the logical conclusion, once I was able to form one, was that my father had had a dalliance before I was born, which resulted in the birth of this child who was given up for adoption. It was a startling revelation, but not really all that surprising since my parents divorced when I was fifteen because my dad had found someone else. I sent a brief note to this newly found brother and thought how strange it would be to tell him about his father and our family.

The next day, I received an excited message back from my brother, and we exchanged e-mail addresses to continue the conversation. He let me know that he had learned his birth father's name not that long ago, so I sent him a brief outline of my family, thinking it would fill in some of the blanks for him. After a few exchanges, he said, "It is apparent that your birth father is [name] as he is my birth father." The name that filled in that blank was not my father's name but the name of a close family friend who was my godfather.

This second shock derailed me. I spent the rest of the day swimming through a vast sea of emotions. I reached out to some friends who helped to hold my head above water as I floundered around with the enormity of this new truth. I talked to my sisters (whom I now know are half-sisters), and we sorted through what this all meant.

By the end of the day, I was calmer but still reeling. Thoughts filled my head. How does this affect my identity, my sense of self, the very foundation of my life? How could my mother withhold this from me her whole life? We were very close, and I thought we shared everything. Did the birth father know? Did they make a pact to keep it a secret forever? Or did she really believe that her husband was my father? I don't look that much different from my siblings, which I'm sure was a relief to her. But she must have suspected, perhaps until the day she died at age eighty in 1997.

In fact, they're all dead now (except for that second name on the list, my birth father's elderly sister whom I don't intend to contact). My father died in 1990, and my birth father died in 2016. This means that the story behind my birth will remain a mystery, and there's no one left to blame — which is truly a blessing in many ways.

In fact, when I woke up the next morning, I decided to see the whole thing as a blessing.

One of the most profound things I've learned in my sixty years is that everything that shows up in our life's path offers a gift, an opportunity, or a blessing. Usually, though, these events appear as challenges, sometimes even tragedies and shocks. And there is no way to understand them as anything other than immense challenges when we are immersed in the necessary emotions surrounding them. The grief, sadness, anger, disappointment and other powerful reactions must be fully realized and expressed for as long as it takes to wade through them. Eventually, we will find that we're able to make decisions again about how to proceed, what to do with what has shown up, and how to start to move toward a better place.

The next day, I still felt the swirl of conflicting emotions, but I realized that I was still *me,* that the father who raised me was still my father, and that whatever happened sixty years ago and led to my arrival here on this Earth was truly a blessing, no matter how it happened or what was kept hidden. I decided that my life was still my life, and that this truth has always been. It's just that now I know it, and I also know that shining light on a truth can offer tremendous healing and growth. I realized that I had found this new brother, who amazingly shares many similar views on life and spirituality, and that if he has come into my life at this particular time, there must be something for us to experience together as brother and sister.

I still periodically find myself in that swirling vortex of emotions, but those moments are becoming less frequent as I choose to focus on the opportunities that I know will continue to emerge from this situation. My newly found brother and I communicate via e-mail regularly. Although we live far apart, I know we'll arrange to meet in person soon. He is getting to know my children as their uncle, and we continue to be amazed at the similarities we are discovering in each other. And, just recently, I had a dream that my father (the one who raised me) communicated to me that he's still my father, that he loves me and that all is well. And I truly believe they were the words of his spirit.

Here, in this experience, is the true opportunity to consider who I really am. I can truly live my life in a state of gratitude and peace.

— Tracy Farquhar —

# Choose Love

*All, everything that I understand,
I only understand because I love.*
~Leo Tolstoy

Because I volunteer with an animal rescue, friends and co-workers frequently give me donations for the animals. One evening, as I was delivering gifts to the shelter, I looked up to see a Pit Bull charging across the parking lot with her handler in tow. I quickly assessed the situation and bent down to greet the medium-sized blue Pit Bull. She lunged toward me as she stood on her hind legs and threw her front paws around my neck, showering me with kisses. I rubbed her head as her butt wiggled and her tail wagged furiously.

"Do you know her?" the handler asked me.

"No, I've never seen her before." I stood up and walked with the dog (I believe her name was Suede) and her handler into the kennel. In the lobby, where there was more light, I noticed that Suede had a lot of scars and had obviously given birth to many litters of puppies.

"Was she a fighting dog?"

"No," came the curt reply. "She was bait." My heart sank as Suede ran excitedly between her handler and me, asking for love from one and then rushing to the other for more.

Every Saturday for weeks, Suede went to the adoption shows in hopes of finding her forever home. Each week, she happily greeted anyone who walked by. People shopping in the pet store stopped to play with her, or just sat on the floor and petted her as her tail wagged non-stop. She was a favorite of kids and adults alike because of her willingness to love everyone she met. Her handlers shared her story with anyone who stopped. She amazed everyone with her tremendous heart and courage to love. Suede's scars kept some people from considering her, and others feared her breed. But one wonderful Saturday, Suede got adopted! After a thorough home inspection (they couldn't let her go with just anyone), her new home was approved.

She is now in a home where she is safe and spreads love to everyone she meets. She will never again be abused or have reason to be afraid of people.

I think about Suede sometimes. Before she was rescued, her only interactions with people resulted in abuse. Despite that, she happily greeted every stranger she came across and still expected nothing but love. She had every reason to be angry and afraid. Instead, Suede chose love.

My challenge to myself and to you: When the divisiveness and anger of the world get you down, remember Suede. Choose love.

—Lori Fuller—

# The End

*Sometimes it's better to end something and try
to start something new than imprison yourself
in hoping for the impossible.
~Karen Salmansohn*

I was married over twenty years: it was rough. There seemed to be no end to the poverty and abuse. It was far from what I had grown up with. Then I never saw violence, prescription drug abuse or fraud in my family or with the people I was around.

Years went by, and no matter what I did, the abuse and poverty got worse. I was cut off from my family. I wasn't allowed to drive. My children were suffering. It was very scary, but I really believed in marriage and wanted it to work.

One cold night in January, I had a vivid dream. I usually slept very lightly, listening for my children, and also because my husband had taken to sleeping with a loaded shotgun by my pillow. He said he didn't want me to leave. I just wanted him to be normal, get a job and support his family — something he had never done and would never do.

Perhaps I was just really tired that night or had ceased to care. I had had nightmares but not dreams before. But this was a real dream, and it went like this:

*My husband and I were standing in the middle of a good-sized empty room in an old building. It had a scuffed wood floor and woodwork. It seemed to be on an upper floor, so one had to go out into the hall and down the stairs* to get outside. The windows were open as it was a warm, sunny day. There were no window coverings on the two large windows. The floor had a raised wooden threshold, so the door closed tight without much space under it.

We were talking close to the door, but the conversation wasn't pleasant. Suddenly, my husband had a can of stain for the floor and a brush in his hand. I stepped back, out of habit, to avoid a blow. He got down on one knee close to my feet and started to brush stain on the floor, back and forth, unknowingly moving away from me. His conversation got meaner and more frightening while he was very serious about soaking the floor with stain. Back and forth he went, covering the floor with stain and making threats. I didn't move but watched him and his brush. Sometimes, I would answer a question, but mostly I watched as he worked on the floor.

Slowly, he moved away from me toward the wall between the windows. It seemed like forever, but then he bumped into the wall. He stood up with the can in one hand and a brush in the other, still threatening me. His words had no love. It seemed then that there had never been any love or even a marriage. He looked at me and then the floor. He was up against the wall, and the entire floor was wet... a sea of stain. His words became rage. He just kept spewing hate.

I realized in that moment that I was done. There was no marriage and no future. I reached over, grabbed the door handle and started to pull it shut. He just kept talking and threatening.

I slowly kept moving until I was standing on the raised threshold of the door. I backed into the hall and finished closing the door behind me, firmly and quietly. I could still hear violence and hate coming from his mouth. He must not have even noticed I was gone.

In that moment, I was free. All the crap he threw at me all those years slid off me like water. I knew what was right, what I had to do, and I wasn't afraid. It was the end!

Then I woke up very clear-headed. It was still a cold January night, but I was done. I slept well the rest of the night.

My kids and I left in April. Only then would I see the full extent of his wrath. He could no longer physically hurt me, but he could make my life even more miserable. He filed bogus complaints with the cops, who would stop me for drugs, alcohol and weapons. I was dragged out of my church on one of his complaints. My bosses and co-workers were harassed. I had to keep changing jobs. He stalked me. My friends were threatened. He told his parents I had cheated on him, so he was leaving me. I found out he had taken loans out in my name. He faked a disability. He got government benefits for me when I wasn't living with him. The fraud was extensive, and I discovered that it had been going on for a long time.

The divorce was final some years later. Every time I would get weak from the unending battle, I would see myself (again) stepping over the threshold of that empty room and pulling the door shut as I stepped into the hall.

— Sandy Anderson —

# The Scar

*Fun fact: Cats don't actually "sharpen" their claws. When they scratch on furniture, they are stripping away worn layers from the claw to reveal a fresh layer.*

"Since this is such a beautiful day and it's Saturday," Jerry said, reaching for the hairdryer, "why don't you fix a picnic lunch while I run a few errands, and then we can drive up into the mountains? Maybe toss our lines in the lake and catch a few fish for dinner?"

As my husband and I planned our day, our large tuxedo cat, El Gato Gordo, purred softly in my arms, gazing lazily at the lush green trees through our upstairs master bath window.

When Jerry turned on the dryer, Gato bolted in panic. In his hurry to escape, Gato's claws ripped the soft flesh on the underside of my lower left arm. The cut was deep and bled profusely. After stopping the bleeding and inspecting it closely, we decided no stitches were required. Jerry helped me treat and dress the wound while I insisted no amount of discomfort would interfere with our day's plans. He left, and I began searching for Gato.

"Gato!" I called, several times, but there was no answer. Since cats are so intelligent and sensitive to human emotions, I wondered if perhaps he felt my shock at being scratched and feared I was unhappy with him.

Finally, I found him huddling beneath the stairwell, wide-eyed and trembling. I picked him up gently, favoring my bandaged arm. As

I held Gato close, I felt the wild thumping of his heart. Kissing him on the head, I whispered, "It's okay, sweetheart. It was just an accident. I know you didn't mean to hurt me." I sat on the stairs holding and stroking him in my lap until he relaxed. Finally satisfied that he was over his trauma, I released him and started preparing for our afternoon outing.

I dashed to the store for some chips and dip, and while waiting in the checkout line I met the husband of a neighbor who lived at the end of our street.

"What happened to your arm?" he asked, noting the bandage.

After I explained, he responded with raised brow, "I tell you one thing, if that had happened to me, that would be one dead cat!"

Horrified, I said, "It was an accident! He didn't deliberately hurt me — he was just frightened."

"I don't care whether it was an accident or not, I'd get rid of that cat!"

Driving home, I thought angrily, "Well, it's obvious he's no cat lover!"

Several weeks later, the wound was completely healed, but in its place was a prominent white curved scar — almost three inches in length.

Early one morning as Jerry and I sat enjoying our freshly ground vanilla-nut coffee, he glanced at my arm and said, "I'm so sorry, honey. Maybe the scar will fade with time, and you won't even be able to see it."

I surprised him with my response. "I hope it never goes away! I want to always have this scar — as a reminder."

"Why on earth would you want to remember that Gato scratched you? Are you mad at him?" he asked, eyes wide. Gato, dozing in the corner, raised his head at hearing his name.

"Of course not!" I responded, blowing Gato a kiss.

Then I related the comments made by our neighbor's husband and how it got me to thinking.

"Seeing this scar will remind me that, yes, I suffered a minor injury, but it wasn't about me — it was about Gato and what prompted his action. Gato would never deliberately hurt me. His lashing out at me was a reaction — not a malicious intent — because he was suddenly frightened and felt threatened. People can do the same."

I refreshed my cup, inhaling its sweet aroma. After adding more half-and-half with sweetener, I took another bite of my cinnamon roll.

"How so?" Jerry asked, eyeing the last doughnut on the plate.

"Cutting remarks can sometimes be made by those closest to us — someone we trust and feel safe with — and I want to remember that. Shouldn't a friend be given the same compassionate understanding as a pet? Just as I wouldn't think of getting rid of Gato because he hurt me, neither should I immediately react by getting rid of a friend."

Jerry nodded as he gave in and took the doughnut.

"Rather than taking offense," I continued, "wouldn't it be better to learn what prompted their out-of-character action? Maybe their response was due to something totally unrelated to us, and they simply reacted out of fear, insecurity or pent-up frustration — by lashing out at whoever was the nearest."

Setting down his cup, Jerry reached for my hand and clasped it gently. "You mean like the other day when everything had gone wrong at the office, and I came home and rudely lashed out at you? Oh, I know I later apologized, but it had to have cut you deeply at the time — it was so unlike me," he said, eyes watering. Releasing my hand, he took my arm and gently caressed the scar. With a boyish grin, he said, "I noticed how you looked at your scar after my inconsiderate comment, and I wondered why — after all, it was healed. You never retaliated or lashed back at me in response, but the tears in your eyes said it all. Now I know why."

That was decades ago, and since that time both Gato and my husband have passed on. But just as I wished, my scar still remains. I thank God that although it has faded, it is still visible. It is an ever-present reminder that validates an old proverb, "A friend loves at all times."

And since I am a friend lover as well as a cat lover, it helps me to resist the temptation to kill a friendship over a self-defensive swipe or an unintentional wound.

— Kitty Chappell —

# She Flies with Her Own Wings

*Keep up your faith to go high and fly, even after so
many pains and sorrow. You can turn from a caterpillar
to a butterfly. Life gives you a second change:
a call to grow.*
~Ana Claudia Antunes

For many years, he held her back
He told her not to dream
He was like a river wild
She like a gentle stream
She craved love and happiness
But kept it all inside
Spent her days in quiet fear
Tethered by his side
She watched the sky with wishful eyes
And dreamed of when she'd fly
Cried herself to sleep at night
As life just passed her by
Caged by life's own cruelty
She was captured in his grasp
While he raised his hands in anger
Hers in prayer she clasped
One day her prayers were answered

For she left him far behind
Released the chains of hurt and hate
And all the ties that bind
Now she flies with her own wings
In skies pearlescent white
Loosed from the bounds of all her fears
She soars in graceful flight
Where she lands will still be seen
The world's an open slate
She'll write a story all her own
For now she holds her fate
At last she's free, no longer caged
And no matter where she'll roam
Those injured wings, now greatly healed
Will guide her safely home

— Ruth Kephart —

# Moving Past the Past

> *Forgiveness means letting go of the past.*
> ~Gerald Jampolsky

"I gave you one with Melvin's signature on it. You remember, don't you? The oil painting with a goat in it."

"Sorry, Nita, but you never gave me such a painting or any painting for that matter." I looked at my wife and she nodded in agreement. "And we don't have any with goats on them." Uncle Melvin was an accomplished artist, especially with oils, and Laura and I had always wanted one of his fabulous landscapes. That's why I commissioned him to paint one, a western scene with relatives around a campfire.

"Well, you probably lost it then," Nita replied, "or gave it away to someone."

"No, we never lost it or gave it away because we never had it in the first place." The bickering with my sister escalated tensions in the room and pushed my patience to the limit.

"Well, all I know is that you had one."

"That's it, Nita! I'm done!" There was no reasoning with her. My stomach hurt and I had a headache. Disagreeing with each other had become part of every family holiday gathering since Mom died. I stormed out of Nita's front door on Thanksgiving Day. Arguing over whether I ever owned a certain painting from my uncle had turned from ridiculous to impossible, dredging up past hurts. "I'm out of here, and I'm not coming back."

As I drove home that afternoon, my mind played back the unresolved issues from our childhood. There were many of them: some silly, others serious. Fighting over seating positions in our car was a little of both. Thinking they could settle the problem, our parents assigned us to opposite sides in the back seat. Beads of vinyl divided the sections. My section was on the right, hers on the left. The middle area served as a demilitarized zone to separate enemy combatants. We were not allowed to cross it.

Nita would sit as close as possible to her boundary and then move her little finger across the forbidden zone. When I yelled that Nita had crossed the line, Mom and Dad would turn around to catch the culprit. However, just before they did, my sister would move her finger back as if nothing had happened. She would look at them with those innocent eyes, and swear, "I've been on my side the whole time." That was a lie, of course, or at least a half-truth. All I knew was that I needed to even the score. Our foolish confrontations escalated year after year — and so did my resentment.

I suppose one should be thankful on Thanksgiving, but I didn't feel that way. After the big upset with my sister, I just wanted to get home, fast. Fortunately, I only encountered one stoplight — at the light rail crossing on SE Burnside Avenue. While waiting for the MAX train to clear the station, I turned on the radio, trying to drown out my thoughts. Maybe it was the music or seeing the train, but something jogged my memory, taking me back to the week our sibling rivalry had turned ugly.

Nita had received a gift that week, a new GE clock radio. From then on, she played her obnoxious rock music constantly. It bugged me and she knew it. According to the house rules, she needed to shut down her music at bedtime — but that seldom happened. If I yelled for the parental police, she would turn the radio off before they entered the playroom, adjacent to our Jack and Jill bedrooms.

One night, I heard static on her radio when I switched off my desk lamp. Then I tried it again — more crackling. I soon realized that if I turned the lamp switch halfway on, the flickering light bulb would create static on her radio. The tables had turned now and Nita became the victim, complaining that I had somehow jammed her radio. I guess I'm not a good liar, because I was deemed guilty and grounded for two weeks. Nita, of course, received no punishment at all. No matter, a payback plan was in the works.

Two nights later, I lay awake in bed, waiting for Nita to finally turn off her radio and fall asleep. Slowly, I slipped out of bed and tiptoed to my closet. Underneath the laundry box was my Lionel train set. Working quietly, I opened the box and pieced the O gauge track together, section by section, and eased it out my door into the playroom. I had just enough track to reach my sister's room on the other side.

Leaving the other freight cars in the box, I placed my Steam Locomotive #2018 on the track and attached the coal car, my whistling tender. I plugged in the transformer and made sure the wires were connected correctly. With everything set, my engine left the station in my room and slowly moved down the line to Nita's room. Then, with the electrical power at full throttle, I hit the whistle lever on the transformer. The sound pierced the silence. I heard Nita scream and jump out of bed. I tried to reverse the engine and bring it back before she knew what had happened. However, the extra power derailed my engine in the middle of the playroom. My train, of course, was confiscated and given to charity.

The retribution was sweet, but I had allowed something much worse to take root. As the years passed, our sibling relationship grew cold. Resentment and animosity lay just below the surface. I became offended at almost everything she said or did. Our once loving relationship became one of contention and ill will. The root of the problem was lack of forgiveness. Although neither of us would admit it, we were both infected with it.

I avoided family gatherings after the Thanksgiving Day fiasco. I made up excuses, but everyone knew the real reason. I had grown frustrated with all the bickering, fabricated stories, and endless conflicts. Trying to deal with the issues just brought old wounds to the surface again. I needed a solution that would help restore our relationship.

After some serious prayer and contemplation, I suggested a new strategy — that we take each other out to dinner on our birthdays — no gifts, no rehashing past issues, no teasing, just a pleasant dinner and some friendly conversation. The first time was a little awkward for both of us, but each year it became a little easier. Now we look forward to it.

I think forgiveness is a commitment to move beyond the past and start fresh. By establishing our new tradition, my sister and I made a similar commitment. It helped us reconnect, experience forgiveness, and find healing for our relationship. Forgiveness is a powerful force. It can release people from a prison of bitterness, resentment, or whatever else that holds them captive. And it doesn't take two to forgive. One is enough to begin the process. I never asked my sister to reciprocate. I simply forgave her and offered a long overdue apology.

My lack of forgiveness is gone now. Knowing the damage it can cause, I will never give it a foothold again.

—Charles Earl Harrel—

# Silencing the Boom

> *It's not an easy journey, to get to a place where you forgive people. But it is such a powerful place, because it frees you.*
> ~Tyler Perry

I woke from a September nap to a voice on the radio. "George Russell Weller has not been charged with a crime," the National Public Radio commentator said. Two months earlier, the eighty-six-year-old man had confused the gas pedal for the brake and sped through the Santa Monica Farmer's Market. He struck seventy-three people. Ten pedestrians died. I suffered severe injuries: multiple fractures, a ruptured spleen and a brain injury.

The commentator was interviewing an eighty-nine-year-old man who admitted he did not do well on the written test in a recent driver's safety class, but would continue driving. "I've been driving for seventy-five years and I've been careful," he said. "It's other people's turn, let them be careful." I glared at the radio's red blinking light as if I could stun the arrogance out of the old man's grating voice.

His disregard for the tragedy ignited my resentment toward Russell Weller. If he hadn't been driving, I'd still be working as a nurse. But in order to return to nursing, I had to focus my energy on healing. So I let my resentment ferment.

Six years later, it still fermented. I unearthed the news articles I had collected about Russell Weller, hoping to discover something that would allay my resentment. I read a bystander's account of what he heard at the scene: boom, boom, boom. Metal slamming into people. I desperately wanted to forgive Russell Weller, otherwise boom, boom, boom would continue to haunt me. But I didn't know how to forgive him. How do you forgive someone you've never met?

The more I read about Russell Weller, the more confused I felt. A reporter quoted him saying, "If you saw me coming, why didn't you get out of the way?" Why would someone who mowed down a bunch of people say that? Other articles referenced his friends' claims that he was a gentle and concerned person. His attorney said his client was "deeply sorry." My eyes stung from all the reading, from all the searching for answers as to why Russell Weller had been driving when he had a history of accidents. I wanted to ask him why he had insisted on driving to the post office that day to mail a letter, rather than listening to his wife, who begged him to stay home and wait for the postman to pick it up.

I realized I couldn't forgive Russell Weller by reading words on paper. I needed to see him in person, up close. I needed to hear a genuine apology from Russell Weller.

I decided I would return to Santa Monica with my husband to visit Russell Weller. I had tried calling him, but his number was disconnected. I called his pastor, who asked his family for permission for us to meet. They said he was too ill. I believed them, but I did not give up. I called a private investigator. "If you insist on going to his house you should hire a police escort," he advised.

On Valentine's Day, my husband and I rolled up to Russell Weller's house. I couldn't think of a better day to forgive him. I cautiously walked up the long driveway to the front door, holding a sweetheart rose plant. I crouched down and placed the plant on the step. I did not leave a note. I believed Russell Weller would know that the plant came from me. As I stood up, I glimpsed bright red letters pasted across the black mailbox: NO SOLICITORS.

I ran back to the car, my heart pounding. "You did it!" my husband yelled. Tears fell down my cheeks. "Do you think you can let go now?" he asked.

"I don't know." I wished I could have said yes. I wished I could have said I forgave Russell Weller.

Ten months later he died.

The boom, boom, boom still haunted me. I tried convincing myself that I had forgiven him. I told my therapist it was an accident, and that Russell Weller must have suffered too. I told family and friends that I had forgiven him. "You're so strong," a friend said. "I'm not sure I could forgive someone who brought so much harm to so many people."

A year passed, and I still struggled to truly forgive Russell Weller. After coaxing from a friend, I called the head deputy of The Santa Monica Farmer's Market. Within a week, I received a videotape of Russell Weller speaking to police investigators one hour after the crash.

I slid the disc into the DVD player. Silver specks blotted the screen for many seconds before he shuffled, with his cane, into the fluorescent-lit room. He sat down, tapped his cane and picked at his bruised arm — the only injury he sustained in the accident. He scanned the faded white walls, then gazed at the peeling ceiling. He raised his arm up and said, "Can you imagine?" Who did he think he was addressing?

An investigator walked into the room, and Russell Weller immediately said, "I'll tell you everything that happened." He spoke with urgency, as if he needed to make sure the investigator knew the accident wasn't his fault. He did not cry. Somehow, crying leads you to believe that someone is truly sorry so I wished he had cried. He spoke about his work as a food broker, and his time served in Korea. Shouldn't he have asked about the pedestrians he had rammed into an hour earlier? I found myself disliking him. Then he looked straight ahead, his voice loud and clear, and said, "All of a sudden the car accelerated." It was as if he believed the car was to blame. His speech slowed, and his southwestern twang lowered to a whisper: "I'm in trouble with my heart and soul." I scooted closer to the television. A long moan rose from his throat. "God almighty, those poor, poor people. What a tragic ending, and I contributed to it."

In that moment, I forgave Russell Weller.

More than a decade later, I still feel the swelling on his bruised arm. I still hear sorrow seep from the steady tap of his cane. But I do not hear, boom, boom, boom.

—Melissa Cronin—

# Life Lessons

*Forgiveness is a funny thing. It warms
the heart and cools the sting.*
~William Arthur Ward

Toward the end of the school year, a student library aide tried to hook up a DVD player in my seventh grade social studies class. From the start, he impressed me with his helpful and positive can-do attitude. Though he worked diligently to set up the system, after fifteen minutes, he saw that the brackets wouldn't allow the cord to slip into the socket. "You've worked so hard," I encouraged. "The library is blessed to have you helping them; I'm so impressed with you. What is your name?"

He beamed with joy at the compliment. "Kevin. Kevin Smith." Immediately my expression changed to one of shock and disbelief! After a long pause, he whispered, "Are you Trent's mom?"

"Yes. Yes I am."

Fear and embarrassment distorted his face. "Oh, please forgive me."

At once, my mind replayed the last six months of my son, Trent's, eighth grade year at the local public school. Since he'd attended a Christian school where I'd taught since kindergarten, changing to a public one was a new experience for both of us. I decided I'd try to get a job there, too, because I wanted to teach where Trent attended. A couple of months before, Trent had decided to enroll in a video production class offered at his new school.

To my relief, the public school maintained strict discipline; they held students to high standards. We both fit right in and enjoyed our year. Then around springtime, Trent changed. He no longer wanted to go to school. He begged to change back to our private one. Every morning I battled, threatened, and cajoled him. We'd arrive at school with him whining, "I just can't do it mom. I just can't go to school. Don't make me. Don't you understand, I just can't do it?" However, he refused to share his reasons for making such a scene before school. Many days as I prepared to face my 170 students, I thought I'd pass out from the exhaustion of the morning.

Then Trent started hanging out in my classroom and wouldn't go out to lunch with his friends. His sweatshirt hood pulled tight on his head made his melancholy look even scarier. His grades spiraled down, and he lost the special connection to his old school buddy. Unfortunately, that friend dropped Trent for another friend — it crushed him. My husband and I didn't know what to do, but we knew we needed some help.

Over the next month, we met with Trent's P.E. teacher, his youth pastor, and a church counselor. During the first session with the therapist, Trent broke down crying about a bully from school who wouldn't leave him alone. To our shock, Trent shared that he'd been kicked, thrown down, and called filthy names. The session ended with Trent feeling better equipped to handle the bully at school. If that didn't work, my husband and I were prepared to inform the principal about the situation.

Somewhat skeptical, we agreed to give Trent some time to handle the problem. It didn't take long because the bully struck the next day. His P.E. teacher saw the incident and came down hard on him, but the next day, the bully struck again in the same class. The savvy teacher said, "We're done," and she sent the offender to the principal, who suspended the student.

We all breathed a long sigh of relief. The drama, however, continued. The bully became even more belligerent to Trent. The principal took harsher action with the punishment, and finally, the bullying stopped. As the offender suffered the consequences of his actions, Trent gradually returned to his old self. The hood came down, the scowl left, and he started hanging out with his friends again.

Before I met Kevin that day in my classroom, I envisioned grabbing him by the shirt and saying, "If you touch my son again, watch out, because I'm going to put on my boxing gloves!" The Mama Bear in me itched to take action. But when I realized that the helpful young man before me was the bully, my heart hurt for Kevin. For him to lash out so brutally, he must have his own dark struggles. He seemed to be just another student trying to find his way through the labyrinth of middle school.

"Please forgive what I did to Trent." With pain in his eyes, Kevin stared at me. "I don't know what got into me. I'm not like that! I think I just didn't have enough sleep. I acted in a way that just wasn't me. I don't know what happened. I'm so sorry."

"Kevin, we all make mistakes." I comforted him and gently touched his shoulder. "Trent and I forgive you. We know you never wanted to act like that. Now, make a change. Go down the right path and never do that again. I know you can do it."

He flashed me a grateful smile. "Thank you, Mrs. Ryan"

"No, thank you, Kevin. I'm so glad we've had the chance to meet."

When I saw Trent later that day, he told me, "Mom, when I saw Kevin in P.E., he said you were chill."

Graduation from the eighth grade is in six days and Trent and Kevin's middle school days will be a memory. I'm proud of Trent, who so willingly forgave his abuser, but wouldn't allow it to continue. He even picked Kevin to be on his P.E. team. I'm also proud of Kevin. It takes a mighty man to admit when you're wrong. Let's hope neither one of these middle school students will forget these life lessons. I know I never will.

— Suzy Ryan —

# Understand Their Actions

# The Apology

*Could a greater miracle take place than for us to look through each other's eyes for an instant?*
*~Henry David Thoreau*

I moved to the Phoenix area in my early twenties, and to expand my social life I joined a young adult group at my church. At every gathering I met new friends who helped me to feel more accepted and at home. Because I love music, I started singing in the choir, where I met Lisa. We were about the same age, both a little on the geeky/nerdy side. No matter, our voices blended well together, and soon we began composing songs. Finding people with similar interests helped ease my feelings of loneliness after moving to a new city.

"Are you going to go on the retreat?" Lisa asked. Once or twice a year, the young adult group put on a retreat.

I hesitated. I had little experience with retreats and I still felt like an outsider.

"Come on," Lisa said. "Everyone goes."

"Okay." I reluctantly agreed. After all, some cute guys were in the group. Perhaps I would have an opportunity to get to know one of them better.

As the retreat weekend approached, I learned that the theme was forgiveness. My experience with forgiveness could pretty much be summed up with a heartfelt "I'm sorry!" when I bump someone in the grocery store, or a reluctant non-apologetic "Sorry." This forced apology I learned around the age of four. I hadn't grown much since then.

In my twenties, the world revolved around me and what I wanted. What I feared. What I dreamed. What I hated. I liked being around other people. And, as most people do, I learned how to be pleasant enough without giving in and having to apologize any more than necessary. In short, the forgiveness theme made me uncomfortable. I would attend the retreat, but I planned to sit quietly in the background and watch.

The retreat was held at a camp in Prescott, Arizona, a gloriously wooded paradise that emanated peace and solitude. The first night we gathered in the common room where we also ate our meals. According to plan, I found a spot in the back where I could watch, unobserved. Lisa sat at the front, ending up across from me as we were in a rather disjointed circle. I finger-waved at her, but pretended not to see when she indicated I should sit by her.

The leader, a deacon at our church, got up and spoke about the healing power of forgiveness. His words were motivating and touching.

"Now comes the hard part," he said. "I want to invite you to look into your hearts and if you feel moved to do so, go to a person here in the room and ask to be forgiven for something you've done."

Initially, there was total silence.

Was he kidding?

Who was going to publicly acknowledge that they'd screwed up?

Everyone got busy. Picking their nails. Tying their shoes. Evading the glances of others.

Then Lisa stood up.

We all watched, secretly glad someone else was going first in front of forty witnesses. I was impressed.

My admiration turned to embarrassment, however, as Lisa made her way through the crowd toward me.

Lisa planted her feet firmly in front of me.

I looked down. I couldn't meet her eye.

"Kathleen, I'd like to ask your forgiveness."

I shook my head. Then nodded, not sure how to respond. I felt the heat rise into my cheeks. I could hardly breathe knowing that everyone could hear and see all this. I had no idea what I was forgiving her for.

I wanted her to just go away.

"I have been jealous of you and how easily you joined our group. Even though you became my friend when we worked on music together, I still thought you were doing it for yourself. I've held that against you and I'm sorry."

"It's okay," I choked out. Stunned, I stood up, gave her an awkward hug and then sat back down. Lisa turned and went back to her seat.

Applause broke out and the tension in the room evaporated. All except mine.

Lisa's bravery broke the ice and everyone started to ask forgiveness for various injuries, some big, some small. Echoes of "I'm sorry," and "please forgive me," laughter, and tears floated around as I sat in a fog of incomprehension.

What had just happened?

I mentally reviewed experiences I'd had with the group. Lisa was usually there, and she laughed and joked with the group. But there was a difference. More reserved than I, Lisa always joined the periphery of the group. I hadn't notice her loneliness.

But why had she asked my forgiveness?

I was the one who had neglected to see the situation through anyone's eyes but my own. I was the one who hadn't once thought about what it must be like to be the shy one, the one left out. It had never occurred to me she had a different experience than I did.

Then it hit me.

She needed to ask my forgiveness in order to forgive herself for holding something against me I hadn't even intended. My lack of empathy and compassion had created a dissonance between us.

The world began to change for me. I learned empathy the day that Lisa asked my forgiveness. I had read *To Kill a Mockingbird* by Harper Lee several times. But I realized that I had never understood the message Atticus Finch taught his children: "You never really know a man until you stand in his shoes and walk around in them."

Soon the weekend was over, and my life gained momentum. I wish I could say I had instant empathy. My journey, however, was longer. At first I avoided Lisa because I felt so uncomfortable with the knowledge that I'd hurt her enough that she needed to apologize in order to feel better. How messed up is that? After an uncomfortable apology on my part we reconnected, but our friendship was never the same.

I met and married a man from the group and we moved away from Phoenix. I lost touch with Lisa after I moved, but her actions and words stuck with me. Life's funny in how many chances it gives you to learn a lesson. Each time I found myself unable to sleep, or found myself alone and angry because I couldn't let go of a perceived injury, I would remember.

Lisa's bravery became my salvation.

Through the years my friendships were better, stronger, deeper. I learned compassion and empathy. I apologized and forgave quickly. I watched carefully, ensuring that I never overlooked someone in the same way again.

Lisa allowed me the gift of friendship because her example taught me to forgive.

— Kathleen Birmingham —

# Sympathy Flowers

*Flowers always make people better, happier,
and more helpful; they are sunshine,
food and medicine for the soul.
~Luther Burbank*

The first morning after the fog of grief rolled in, my friends dropped by and surprised me, bringing gifts to my door. They brought me candy, hot-chocolate mix, a card, and, most curiously, a gift box filled with white flowers.

I didn't know what to make of it all at first, other than offering a distant thank-you for stopping by. It was a forty-minute drive for a two-minute conversation, with me standing awkwardly on the front step in ugly, loose sweatpants and a white button-up. I had been staring blankly at my computer screen for hours, trying to write something vaguely coherent for my senior capstone paper without much success. When they asked me how I was, I made some half-hearted, self-deprecating joke about my outfit, something about the shirt feeling put-together but tight and the pants feeling depressing but comfortable.

The joke did not land, settling with a sad chill in the cold and quiet January air.

"Be gentle with yourself," one friend told me. Some bitter part of myself raised its hackles, telling me I didn't know how to do that, but I told her I would anyway. At least, I thought, I could try.

Thinking back, those were probably the most important things they could have given me. Candy was a gentle reminder to eat. Hot chocolate was for the heavy moments of silence, to have something warm to hold onto. The card, of course, was obvious: a reminder that they were there and loved me, that this was real and happening. That sometimes words are wholly inadequate, but they're all we have.

For the longest time, I got stuck on the flowers. They sat in their little, open-air gift box with the wrapping that obscured their base, staring back at me.

I thought they were a bouquet at first. Yet another thing I would have to watch wither and die. Having just put down my dog, I was certain of one thing: the idea of letting something die is horrifying because we feel we are responsible for killing it. When there is nothing we can do, the first place that blame turns is the mirror. Even if it is not true, even if it is horribly unkind, it is the only place we know we can turn to and take control over. I was already overwhelmed, not ready to accept even that meager responsibility.

I didn't mention the flowers for the longest time. I tried hard to ignore them and got angry when I couldn't. Then I felt stupid for feeling angry about it, asking myself why I couldn't just be grateful, why I had to stew over something that felt so inconsequential. They hadn't done anything wrong. They hadn't done anything, really, except look nice while I dressed myself yet again in sweatpants and barely brushed my hair.

*Be gentle with yourself,* my friend had reminded me. *Take a step back and be gentle with yourself.*

Eventually, I realized that the gift box didn't actually contain a cut bouquet at all. It was a perennial ready for planting, sitting patiently in that box with its dirt obscured by the wrapping. It was not dying, not plastic, yet living and breathing all the same.

Still, it confused me. I wracked my brain for why they could have brought it. In my grief, I was tired of trying to make everything beautiful, of trying to make pain poetic and consumable. I wanted to just feel it.

I sat at the dining-room table and stared at the plant, hearing the clock tick away the seconds. I became increasingly frustrated with my inability to string together words like I used to. With the dog dying, the time passing, the semester coming to a close, and my inability to sit down to write about existentialism in postmodern literature only worsening, I couldn't pretend that time moved as it normally did.

After a while, I gave up trying to think it through. I scurried to my room with my card and chocolates. I cried knowing they had thought of me long enough to buy these things, long enough to make the forty-minute drive up and back. I think what hit me hardest was that they had thought about me longer than I had thought about me.

The plant was a staple on the dining room table. My mother would tell me when she watered it, how nice it was, how it needed more sunlight. The white buds greeted me through the days, reminding me to eat, reminding me to take my time, reminding me I was loved. Slowly, setting the plant by the front window in the sunspot, seeing how it looked brighter than it had the morning they brought it, I finally figured it out.

Even in the harsh and desperate ticking of time moving forward, perennials are always in a state of growing. The flowers may wither and turn brown, crunch and die, but there's the promise that, should they be tended to, they will return next spring. They endure the cold and the dark for each thin beam of light, roots stretching carefully under the surface. And should they be granted the care they need, they will grow beautiful once again, exhaling fresh air with the new beginnings that spring provides.

— Casey McMullin —

# Mom's Wisdom

*An ounce of mother is worth a pound of clergy.*
*~Spanish Proverb*

School mornings were always hectic. The first sentence I usually heard was, "It's time to rise and shine!" It was Mom's loudest voice, and there was no way I could ignore it or hide from it.

"Okay, Mom. I'm getting up and dressed!" I would manage to call back, although my morning voice sounded like a bullfrog.

Mom's loudest voice blared out again as she announced, "Breakfast is ready!"

By then, I could smell the heavenly aromas of breakfast, and I couldn't get to the kitchen fast enough. In fact, it was a race between my sister, my brother, and me. We usually slid into our seats at the same time, sometimes knocking each other out of our places.

"Yum! Thanks, Mom! This is my favorite," I panted, as I gobbled down the scrambled eggs, bacon, and mile-high fluffy pancakes, and guzzled down both the orange juice and hot chocolate.

"You're welcome, dear," Mom sang out. "Now, grab your lunches and books, and let's get going. The school bus will be here any minute!"

We all skedaddled out to the bus stop as we grabbed our lunch bags that contained a sandwich, fruit, and dessert — usually our favorite cookies or cupcakes.

Then, one day, much to my horror, there was no dessert in my lunch! I looked through every nook, cranny, and space of my lunch bag, and even turned it upside-down, dumping everything out. My dessert just wasn't there! What could have happened to it? Did Mom forget to make or buy it? Or was she too busy? *Oh, well,* I thought. *It's only one time, so it's no big deal.* But, for the next several days, my lunch contained no dessert! So one day, as soon as I got home from school, I bellowed out, "Hey, Mom! Why haven't you been putting a dessert in my school lunches?"

Mom stood up and responded, "Why, Eugene, I have been including a dessert in your lunch every day. In fact, this whole week I have put your favorite cookies in your lunches — chocolate chip! If you're not getting them, then who is?"

So then we reviewed my activities and schedule, and what I did with my lunch each day. As soon as I arrived at school, I always put my lunch in the classroom closet along with all of the other lunches. And that brings us to Carl — the terror of the third-grade classroom. The teacher did not like him in class and would send him to the closet, where he would spend most of each day.

Carl lived in a group foster home. He was loud, rough, and somewhat of a thief; he would take just about anything that wasn't fastened down. Mom and I concluded that with nothing else to do, and time on his hands, Carl was probably going through the lunches and eating what he liked.

My mother and I talked about ways to resolve this problem. She explained to me that Carl didn't need to be chastised; he needed, more than anything, a friend. So Mom said, "I'm going to put two packages of goodies in your lunch: one for you and one for Carl." That's what Mom did, and then I put my lunch bag in the school closet as usual.

I said nothing about the lunch goodies to Carl, but one day out on the playground, he stopped me and asked, "Why are there always two packages of goodies in your lunches?"

So I told him, "My mother put one in my lunch bag for me and one in for you."

Another day, Carl asked me if he could come to my house and meet my mother. I told him, "That will be fine, but there are certain conditions you will have to abide by."

He asked, "Such as?"

I explained, "You will be welcome at our house as long as you don't take something that doesn't belong to you, and do not fight or swear." He was agreeable.

After that, Carl would come to our house every day after school. He always obeyed our house rules, and we enjoyed our time together playing marbles and other games.

Before the school year was out, Carl was transferred to another group home and another school district. I still think of Carl and wonder what happened to him. I know what happened to me. Because of my mother's example, I learned a lifelong lesson about how to recognize need and show compassion for others.

—Eugene Mead—

# The Joy Ride

*When someone you love becomes a memory,
the memory becomes a treasure.*
~Author Unknown

Every time the Navy transferred my husband to a new duty station, the small wooden cradle his father had made for our son moved with us. Yet whenever Mark brought up the subject of having another child, I refused.

"It was different when Brian was born," I said. "You were in training, and the Navy gave you a couple days off to coach me through labor and help with the new baby. Now you're on a submarine for months at a time. I'm not going to do it alone! I already feel like a single mother."

Mark knew it was no use arguing. He couldn't guarantee that his sub would be in port when I needed him.

The year Brian was nine, I turned thirty. A girlfriend sent me a Christmas card with a photo of her smiling kids. On the bottom of the card, she wrote, "I'm due again in June!" I felt a twinge of jealousy.

"Are you having second thoughts?" Mark asked. We were getting ready to move to Charleston, South Carolina, where he'd been assigned to a sub with a predictable schedule. "If you get pregnant now, I'll be home when the baby is born," he promised.

That's all he needed to say. We weren't even settled in Charleston when I found I was expecting. Mark missed the holidays, but knowing he'd be back for our baby's birth made it easier to live with. The days passed, and my abdomen grew round, as if I'd stuck Brian's basketball under my shirt.

A couple of months before the big event, my in-laws offered to drive down from New York and stay with Brian when it came time for his father to help me at the hospital. Mark returned from sea excited to hear his parents were coming. "There's going to be an overnight trip for fathers of the crew," he said. "It's the week after you're due, so my father will still be here."

I made a face. Brian had been two weeks late. What if this baby was late, too? But Mark's father had recently survived a heart attack. He might not be with us much longer. How could I say no? The chance of the two events coinciding was low.

Mark phoned his dad. "How'd you like to take a ride on a submarine?" he asked. Of course, his father said yes.

My in-laws arrived a few days before my due date, but a week went by with no sign of labor. The cradle and layette were ready, but apparently the baby wasn't.

On the day of the cruise, Mark and his father packed their underwear and toothbrushes while I waddled around the house uneasily. What if our baby chose that night to come?

"Don't worry," Mark said. "We'll be back first thing tomorrow."

The men kissed us all goodbye and left. That evening at dinner, my stomach felt queasy. I thought I was just upset about Mark leaving. But in the middle of the night, a strong contraction woke me. I began my Lamaze breathing and held off calling the doctor. After all, I was in labor fifteen hours with my son, and Mark said he'd be home in the morning.

The contractions shortened to a minute apart. I pounded on my mother-in-law's bedroom door and yelled, "This baby isn't going to wait for Mark!" She drove me to the hospital and stayed in the waiting room with Brian while a nurse listened sympathetically to my rants.

"My husband and I planned carefully so that he'd be home when our baby was born," I told her. "He promised me! And where is he now? Taking a joy ride on a submarine with his father!"

At 5:26 that morning, I gave birth to a baby girl and named her Emily. The doctor sang "Happy Birthday" as he cut the umbilical cord.

My husband had missed it. All the other times Mark had missed special occasions, I couldn't be mad. Going to sea was his job; it paid the bills. But this time he didn't have to go!

When the sub pulled into port, Mark received his mother's message that the baby had arrived. He and his father rushed into my hospital room as I was holding Emily. Mark kissed me on the cheek. "I'm sorry I wasn't here."

"It's okay," I lied. It wasn't okay at all. His parents were standing beside him, so I didn't tell him how abandoned I'd felt. I looked into my infant's big brown eyes, grateful that she was healthy and my labor was over.

Eventually, Mark retired from the Navy and took a civilian job. One day, our daughter came home from school and set her books down on the kitchen table. A sheet of paper sticking out of her English book caught my eye. I smiled when I saw the title: "The Story of My Life." Emily was only in fifth grade. Her life story so far had to be pretty short.

I pulled out the paper and cringed. In careful cursive, she'd written, "My mother has never forgiven my father for not being with her when I was born."

Oh, no! What had I done? More than a few times, I'd mentioned to Emily that her father had missed her birth, that she came later than we'd expected while her dad was on a submarine deep in the ocean with Grandpa. Mark's absence stood out from my memories of that day. Had I really said that I'd never forgiven him, or did she sense it?

I tucked the paper back into her book. That night, I explained to Emily how her father had always wanted another baby. Not being present at her birth didn't mean she wasn't important to him. Although I tried to sound forgiving, it was still a sore spot for me.

More years passed, and we lost Mark's father. At the funeral service, the minister asked my husband if he'd like to say a few words. Mark edged his way out of the pew and stepped up to the altar. Staring out at the congregation, he began, "My best memory of my dad was when I was in the Navy, and we went on a father-son submarine cruise."

My stomach tightened. It all came back: how he'd left me alone with his mother, and I'd gone through labor with a nurse. After all this time, I hadn't let go of the hard feelings.

"My father was the happiest I'd ever seen him," Mark continued. "He wanted to know how all the equipment that I operated worked. I could tell he was proud of me." He pushed tears off his cheeks. "I'd made something of myself without going to college." Mark looked in my direction. "And though I regret missing my daughter's birth, that cruise was the best experience I shared with my dad." His shoulders heaved with silent sobs.

Tears came to my eyes. Finally, I understood why that cruise was so important to him. When he sat down beside me, I pressed my hand into his. He squeezed mine back, and any lingering resentment melted away.

—Mary Elizabeth Laufer—

# The Kaleidoscope Effect

*Life is like an ever-shifting kaleidoscope —
a slight change, and all patterns alter.*
~Sharon Salzberg

I stood at the altar next to my husband-to-be and said, "I do," not fully comprehending that I was also saying "I do" to two ex-wives and three stepchildren, the youngest of whom was five years old. Although I was thirty-one, I knew little about being a wife and even less about being a stepmother. But I loved Bill and accepted the circumstances willingly, confident I'd figure it out along the way.

Days after our honeymoon, my husband's second wife called, insisting Brené, the youngest, spend part of her summer with us. "We can do that," Bill said without hesitation.

Just like that, the honeymoon was over. My wedding-day confidence nose-dived, and my stomach shifted uneasily as I suddenly faced the reality of an ex-wife's demands on our lives.

"You okay with this, sweetheart?" Bill asked after the fact.

"Sure," I said cheerfully, keeping the anger and disappointment from my voice. "I want you to have a relationship with your daughter." I readied our spare bedroom for Brené, shoving aside my feelings of resentment toward Bill's ex-wife while contemplating how to establish my own relationship with a little girl.

The next day, Bill and I picked up Brené. She was an energetic, petite girl complete with blond pigtails. My heart melted as she placed her tiny hand in mine, allowing me to escort her to our car. During her visit, Brené and I spent lots of time together, feeding ducks at the park, making cupcakes for her daddy, and giggling while watching kiddie movies. She was the daughter I couldn't conceive, and my heart was full of love for her. But I reminded myself that Brené wasn't my daughter and I could only hope that she'd accept me as a mother figure in her life.

During subsequent visits, Brené acted lovingly and was comfortable in my company. By Christmas, her attitude and behavior toward me shifted. "You can't tell me what to do!" she shrieked.

I froze. "Brené," I said softly, regaining my composure, "don't you want to go to the Christmas party?"

"No!" she replied, shaking her head fiercely. "You can't make me. Mommy says so." She stormed into the bathroom, slamming the door.

"Let me talk with her," Bill said. "She's probably just tired."

He disappeared into the bathroom, emerging moments later cradling a teary-eyed Brené. "We're not going to the Christmas party," he said curtly. "It seems that Shannon has filled Brené's head with the notion that you're like the evil stepmother in *Cinderella*. Now she's afraid of you."

"What? Why would Shannon do such a thing?"

"Honestly, I don't know, but I'll talk with her," Bill answered, his eyes blazing with anger.

The following day, Bill confronted Shannon. "Why did you tell Brené that Lillie's like the evil stepmother in *Cinderella*? What an awful thing to say!"

"That's what Lillie gets for stealing my daughter from me!"

"Lillie doesn't want to steal Brené from you."

"Yes, she does!" Shannon shouted, her face reddening. "You just don't see her for the wicked person she is."

"What?" His eyebrows drew together in a scowl. "Why would you think such a dreadful thing?"

"Well, all I know is that every time Brené visits you, all she talks about is 'Lillie and I did this. Lillie and I did that.' Lillie can't have her own children, so she wants mine. No one can be Brené's mother but me."

"You're crazy," Bill snapped back, putting Shannon on the defensive.

Hoping to diffuse the situation, I turned toward Shannon. "You make a valid point. Perhaps I was overzealous, but I certainly had good intentions. I wanted Brené to feel welcome in our home. I never intended to infringe on your relationship with Brené. I apologize."

"I don't believe you, not for a second. You're evil!" Shannon's lips twisted with scorn. "No one gets to be Brené's mother but me. No one. I'll see to that! Now both of you get out of my house!"

As we scurried toward the front door, Brené stopped us. "Daddy, when will I see you and Lillie again?"

Bill collected himself and knelt down, looking directly into Brené's eyes. "That's up to your mother. She'll call us when you're ready to visit."

"I'll be ready very soon!" Delight rang in her voice.

I choked back the tears, feeling as if I was somehow responsible for Shannon's outrage. "You've done nothing wrong," Bill assured me. "Try not to fret about it. We'll work with the situation as best we can."

Shannon called eventually, and Brené visited with us regularly throughout her childhood and teen years. Not wanting to be further misconstrued, I spent little time alone with Brené. But the evil stepmother label was firmly planted in Brené's mind, and any hopes I had of having a relationship with her had been vanquished. "You've always been and always will be the evil stepmother," Brené said frequently. Even now, some thirty-five years later, those same hurtful words fly from her mouth when I don't meet her expectations or demands.

For years, Shannon for the shattered relationship between Brené and me, harboring disdain and contempt toward her for villainizing and diminishing me. I saw Shannon as the enemy, and I was her helpless victim. The dark side of me wanted to lash out at her and exact some form of revenge. But I just couldn't be that ruthless. Being vengeful would've hurt Bill's relationship with his daughter and only worsened the situation.

I decided to step back and look at the situation in a different light. Shannon was playing an illogical story inside her head, one that she truly believed. With that false narrative, I was the villain she feared would destroy her mother-daughter relationship, and she had no option other than to diminish me in order to protect that relationship. She used her fear creatively to place a wedge between Brené and me while at the same time striking out at her ex-husband. Oddly, that same fear became the heart of their mother-daughter dynamic. By adulthood, Brené had too much vested interest in the story she'd been fed; she couldn't let go of the evil stepmother label for fear of losing her relationship with her mother.

Although I couldn't change or influence the situation, I understood it better. With that understanding, my perspective shifted in much the same way the patterns shift in a kaleidoscope when it's held to the light and the cylinder's turned. Something new was created in me — a feeling of compassion and forgiveness for Shannon and Brené. The shift from feeling like an angry victim to being a compassionate and forgiving person was profound. Shannon and Brené were no longer my enemies, only frightened, fragile, and flawed women. More importantly, I realized that we're all a kaleidoscope of complexity — thousands of different facets of light and dark yearning to be understood.

— Lillie Houchin —

# Emotional Shackles

*To give vent now and then to his feelings, whether of pleasure or discontent, is a great ease to a man's heart.*
~Francesco Guicciardini

"Just don't let it bother you," my father advised after I broke into tears while reporting that my third attempt at infertility treatment had failed.

"But, Dad, this was our last chance," I sobbed. "We will never have children. I will never be a mother!"

"Well, there is nothing you can do about it. You just have to get over it and move forward," he responded mechanically before changing the subject abruptly.

My mouth dropped. For months, I had tended to my father's grief over my stepmother's death. As a dutiful daughter, I called him daily and visited him twice a week. How could he so carelessly dismiss the important benefits of having a child?

Weeks later, when we sat down to a special dinner I had prepared for his birthday, the subject of my not having children came up. Once more, I started to cry.

"What's your problem?" my father asked coldly as he heaped a second serving of beef stroganoff and wild rice onto his plate. "I wouldn't have cared if I never had children."

Again, my mouth dropped as his words seared through my mind and stabbed through my heart. Shocked at hearing such a pronouncement, I said little for the remainder of our dinner. After he left, I ran to my bedroom and wept uncontrollably for over a half-hour. Not only did my father fail to offer any comfort for my devastating loss, but he completely invalidated me as his daughter—his only child. *Certainly, he could not have meant his hurtful words, I thought hopefully. Maybe he will apologize after he reflects on his words more carefully.*

But that apology never came. In fact, my father's demeanor grew colder toward me during our visits and phone calls. Consequently, my contacts with him decreased as my resentment increased. For months, I harbored anger much of the time, even about issues that had nothing to do with having children or my father. Then my body reacted to my anger with migraine headaches and digestive troubles. In my unwillingness to forgive, my regular practices of prayer and meditation went by the wayside as I struggled with my faith in God.

Then a miracle happened. In the middle of a deep sleep, I had a profound dream about my mother who had died twenty years before. In this dream, she said, "Well, your father didn't listen to me for twenty-seven years. What makes you think he would listen to you?" I woke up laughing. Suddenly, I realized how silly my expectations of my father were. He's a great "fixer," but not a good "consoler." All this time, I had been trying to get a rich outpouring of blood out from a dry, empty turnip.

For weeks, I laughed heartily every time I thought of my mother's words in my dream. At times, I could even imagine her laughing with me. Gradually, I released my anger and unrealistic expectations as I found gratitude for the things my father could give (like fixing my thermostat, driving me to a repair shop when my car broke down, and keeping me informed of the latest news and technological developments). In short, I forgave him.

As time passed, my father still made comments that struck me as insensitive. However, I reminded myself of his good qualities and my decision to lower my expectations of his emotional capabilities. Instead, I turned to compassionate friends and a professional counselor to support me in my grief over never having children. Although my grief lingered a long time, my father and I got along better. I stopped being so angry, my headaches and stomachaches subsided, and I started practicing my faith again.

About two years later, another miracle happened. Amazingly, my father started to express his emotions much more deeply. For example, he tearfully related painful stories from his early childhood in which his siblings teased him for being a sissy when he cried. He also described how he learned to follow his parents' unhealthy teaching that it is best to ignore your feelings. Later, he would tell sad stories about his golf friends with a good deal of empathy. Finally, he even told me the reason why he was so insensitive about my inability to have children. "I felt that my world was falling apart after your stepmother died, and I couldn't handle hearing about your loss, too."

After my father died, I reflected on his lifelong struggle with expressing his feelings and his later success in freeing himself from the emotional shackles of his childhood. When I valued him for who he was and where he was on his life journey, he was able to find his inner resources to heal. Now, when I struggle with forgiveness, I remember how I forgave my father. As a result, it becomes a little easier each time I need to forgive.

—Jessica Loftus—

# Pop

> *Gratitude bestows reverence, allowing us to encounter everyday epiphanies, those transcendent moments of awe that change forever how we experience life and the world.*
> *~John Milton*

When I was seventeen, Dad gave me a compliment. I remember it because I think it was the first one. Until that point, nothing I had done seemed good enough for Dad.

When I was young, he would take us — his seven sons — down to help with his janitorial business at St. Thomas Grade School, the same school I attended. The other students lived in big houses, but our family of nine lived in a three-bedroom duplex. I always thought we lived in half a house.

One night at the school, Dad threw his keys at me and said, "Damn you! Look at all the spots you missed! Why don't you wake up? You're not going to amount to anything!" And I wondered what he thought he had amounted to. He was the one cleaning toilets.

At seventeen, I wrote and performed a show that was a huge success. It sold out the high school theater two nights in a row. Dad said, "Paul, I've never been so proud in my life! Nothing John did could compare to this." John, my older brother, was the star of the family — football hero, MVP. John even called our father "Pop," another thing that made me feel he was much closer to him than the rest of us who called him "Dad."

Why did he have to bring up John? Why couldn't he just acknowledge me? I decided that my father couldn't even give a compliment the right way.

For years, Dad was a disappointment. His Hallmark birthday cards were too generic, as if he wasn't even willing to celebrate with me or show he cared. Meanwhile, I was paying a therapist so I could talk about him. I wanted an apology for the times he had yelled at me.

I find it easy to apologize to most people. I pride myself on it. In fact, years ago when I was teaching, my seventh-grade students got sick of me apologizing to them for losing my temper. I never understood why they would tell me there was no need to apologize. Maybe they thought it was appropriate to lose one's temper when students throw things at you.

Up until I started teaching, I had always seen anger as wrong and Dad as wrong. Period. But while teaching and experiencing a classroom of crazed adolescents, I finally understood what it was like for my dad to be dealing with seven sons. My anger wasn't a mistake — it was part of the passion of wanting to make a difference in their lives. And, yes, it was a fear of losing control, of not being respected. In his commitment to me, Dad risked being enraged and disliked. I was out to be better than him; he was out to make me better. Beneath his temper was an intense concern for what he thought was best for me. We all have good intentions, but not always the best delivery.

When I turned thirty-nine, I decided I needed to forgive him. He had been doing his best, and again… seven sons! So, I went back to my old school where he had berated me.

As I stood outside the window, I realized that Dad was not who I had to forgive. I needed to forgive myself for all the years I had bottled up my anger toward him. I was so critical of myself that I couldn't enjoy my life.

I couldn't view anything in a positive light. Rarely did I permit myself to enjoy a movie or a ballgame without a nagging sense that I should be doing something productive. Sunsets stood for disappointment, showing me that the day was over and I hadn't gotten enough done.

As much as I wanted Dad to apologize, I realized I owed him an apology for the anger I had carried for so long. His anger occurred in occasional outbursts; my anger was rooted deep. Apologizing to him was extremely difficult: I'd be changing who I was. When I apologized to the class, I was honoring my ideal of never losing my temper. But apologizing to Dad would mean letting go of what made me better than him. It would mean seeing myself for the self-righteous jerk I had been.

The next time we had breakfast, I told Dad that I was sorry he had to deal with the chip on my shoulder. He said I didn't have to apologize for anything. I told him it meant a lot to me after he saw my first show in high school and said he had never been prouder in his life. For the first time, thirty years after he said it, I let the words in. It moved me deeply.

"Well, I knew how much it hurt you that year not to get a chance to play quarterback," he added.

As he said that, I realized why he had brought up John in his compliment all those years ago. He knew how devastated I was not playing quarterback. He wanted me to know that football wasn't as important as my writing and performing. It wasn't that Dad couldn't give a compliment right; I was the one who had taken his compliment the wrong way and turned something nice into something insulting.

I began seeing past the slights I kept collecting to realize that this man — a stranger to me for so many years — was my biggest ally. Dad was never against me; the world was not against me. My world was dark because I kept turning out the light.

My mom's love was always obvious, pure and simple. Dad's love was clumsy, complicated, critical. His love snuck up on me like an avalanche. We have a lot in common, especially our faltering, expanding hearts.

I looked up at Dad, the man whose features I have inherited: his strong nose, pale pink skin, blue eyes and thinning white hair. Even our crooked smiles matched.

"Well, there is something I do have to say." And as tears welled up, I said, "Thank you, Pop." And he has been "Pop" ever since.

— Paul Lyons —

# My Mantra

*Empathy is about standing in someone else's shoes,
feeling with his or her heart,
seeing with his or her eyes.
~Daniel H. Pink*

When my children were teenagers, I purchased a magnet with what was said to be a First Nations or Native American prayer. I placed it on the door of our refrigerator in full view. I found the words to be thought provoking and hoped they would teach my children to have more patience and be more forgiving of others.

> *Oh, Great Spirit, grant that I may not criticize my neighbor
> until I have walked a mile in his moccasins.*

Although my children are adults now, with homes of their own, I've kept the magnet on our fridge door for the past twenty-five years. During that time, I've often found that the message has helped me see situations from a different perspective.

For example, a number of years ago, I was on my way to a farewell function with several colleagues. A popular department manager was retiring. As we were leaving the office, we bumped into our colleague, Wendy, who had previously planned to attend the event with us. I asked Wendy if she wanted us to wait for her, and she responded in a fairly rude manner, declining our invitation. One of my other colleagues was quite annoyed and clearly resented Wendy's behavior. "I don't know why you even bothered to invite her," she said.

Reflecting on how frazzled Wendy appeared as she rushed away from us, I commented that perhaps we should just give Wendy a break and forgive her for declining at the last minute. She was obviously having a bad day, and it wasn't worth holding a grudge against her if we weren't aware of what provoked her unusual behavior.

A week later, I learned that when we bumped into Wendy, she was returning to the office from a medical appointment where she was told she had pancreatic cancer. She died a year later. Wendy wasn't being rude to us; she had just received a very traumatizing diagnosis. On reflection, I'm amazed she was able to respond at all.

Whether it's a family member who let me down, a friend who betrayed a confidence, or a difficult colleague, the quote on my fridge guides me. Although it's not always easy to forgive, I've been able to shed a lot of resentment over the years by focusing on my mantra.

— Kathy Dickie —

# Even a Cold Fish Needs Love

*Never forget the three powerful resources you always have available to you: love, prayer, and forgiveness.*
~H. Jackson Brown, Jr.

Have you ever felt as if someone hated you before you were even introduced? That's how I felt about a co-worker named Carolyn who I met when I was promoted to a new position in a new department.

On my first morning, every person was welcoming except Carolyn. Her cubicle was next to mine, and she was the last one I met.

I extended a hand and smiled. "It's nice to meet you, Carolyn."

She didn't smile. She unenthusiastically shook my hand and then squirted sanitizer into her palm. "Hi," she said.

The next day, my supervisor, Ben, told me that one of my first assignments was to write a brochure about a project that would help salmon. A culvert under a road was blocked, so when salmon tried to swim back to the stream where they were born to lay eggs, they hit a barrier.

I was excited to work on the salmon project until Ben said, "Carolyn has the folder with all the background information. You'll need to get it from her."

All afternoon, I stalled. Finally, I asked her for the folder.

"I handle anything to do with salmon," she said. "If you need a brochure, I can write one."

"Actually, the brochure is my first assignment from Ben."

She didn't look up.

I waited for her to say something. I noticed a sign on her wall that said: "Even cold fish need love."

"I like your sign," I said.

She glanced at it and then kept working, as if I weren't there.

I walked back to my cubicle. *Cold fish Carolyn*, I thought. *How appropriate. Well, she's not going to get any love from me!*

The next day, as much as I hated taking this matter to Ben, I didn't know what else to do. He shook his head and walked into Carolyn's cubicle. "Can I see you in my office?" She followed him, and he shut the door. I heard him talking to her in a raised voice. When she came out, she got the folder and plopped it onto my desk.

"Thanks," I said.

She glared at me.

For the next few weeks, the tension between us grew. For the most part, we avoided each other. If we did pass in the hallway, we huffed or sneered.

Initially, I felt I had won a small victory by securing the folder, but as time passed, I dreaded coming to work. I had always gotten along with people, and this situation gave me a nervous stomach each morning.

When I finished the brochure, I gave it to Ben.

"Good job," he said later that day. "Why don't you run it by Carolyn to see if she has any comments?"

*Run it by Carolyn? No way. She'll rip it apart.* I went home without giving it to her.

Unable to eat dinner, I took out a book I often consulted: *There's a Spiritual Solution to Every Problem*, by Wayne Dyer.

I found one section where he talked about how holding onto pain and seeking revenge against someone would keep one stuck in pain. "Practice letting go of injured feelings with love and pardon… Let go, and let God."

I knew that as hard as it was going to be, I needed to make peace with Carolyn if I wanted peace at work. I started by treating her in a friendly way the next morning.

"I know you've been working on these types of projects for a long time," I said, handing her the brochure. "Could you take a look at this and let me know what you think?"

She looked surprised.

*Let go and let God,* I thought.

She took the brochure from me. "Okay," she said.

The next day when I came in, the brochure was on my desk. She had made some suggested changes in red, but not as many as I had expected. I actually agreed with some of them.

I poked my head around her cubicle. "Thanks, Carolyn," I said.

No response.

I continued saying "Good morning" when I came in, and I smiled when I ran into her during the day. It was hard, because she continued to ignore me. I felt like a salmon trying to swim upstream. But each time, I would say to myself, "Let go, and let God."

Carolyn's birthday was coming up. I found a nice card with a fish on the cover and put it on her desk. Around noon, she stuck her head around the corner and said, "Thanks for the card."

As time went on, we began getting to know each other and talking. I learned that she had been at this job for a long time and no longer felt appreciated. She had been trying to find another job closer to where her family lived and wasn't having any luck.

After the new culvert was installed, we went to the stream together to see if we could spot any salmon. The sun was out, and it was hard at first to see through the stream's current.

"There's one!" she said, pointing.

"There's another over there!" I shouted.

The new culvert was working — and so was our friendship.

— Wendy J. Hairfield —

# Chapter 3

# Use the Power of Forgiveness

# Love Restored

*Love makes your soul crawl out from its hiding place.*
~Zora Neale Hurston

When I told my mother I was pregnant, she told me I had to leave town so no one would find out. She found a maternity home run by the Salvation Army in Omaha, Nebraska.

The drive to Nebraska was long, made even longer because my mother refused to talk to me about what she called "my situation." When we pulled up in front of the home, I remember thinking it looked so cold and foreboding. Once inside, an older woman came in and sat across from us. My mother answered her questions about me as if I wasn't there.

There was no talk of options. It was taken for granted that because of my actions, I was not fit to bring up a child, and the baby would have a better life without me.

After my mother left, I was shown to my room, which I would share with another girl. There were two beds and one chest of drawers. There were no mirrors or artwork on the walls.

We were assigned jobs ranging from cleaning toilets to clearing dishes from the tables in the dining hall.

One of the social workers told me about an opportunity to leave the home and live with a family until it was time for me to give birth. In exchange for looking after their three young children, cleaning, cooking, doing the laundry and ironing, I was given my own room and bath. I was much happier there than at the home. At night, I would lie in bed and talk to my baby. I'll never forget the first time I felt her move.

I was not prepared for labor, delivery or how I would feel emotionally. When the labor pains started, I was very scared. I had no idea what to expect, and the pain was intense. I remember lying on a gurney outside the delivery room. I was crying out, "I'm hurting so badly!"

A nurse came over to me and said, "Well, it serves you right."

The next thing I remember is waking up from the anesthesia and being told to sign the relinquishment papers on the clipboard in front of me. I asked to see my baby and was told I couldn't see her until I signed. Years later, I found out that was a lie.

On September 19, 1970, I saw my newborn daughter for the first time through the window of the hospital nursery. She was beautiful, and I wanted to etch that moment in my mind forever. Tears filled my eyes, as only minutes before a nurse had told me it would be the last time that I'd see her.

There was no counseling for unwed mothers back then. I was told that if I loved my baby, I should give her up so she would have two parents. The nurses told me I would get on with my life and forget the entire experience.

I left the hospital a totally different person than when I entered it. My heart was hardened, and a part of me was missing.

I always hoped that my daughter would contact me one day, but I never really thought it would happen. As much as I wanted to search for her, I never felt I had the right, and I was afraid to disrupt her life.

I never returned to New Jersey to live, even though all my family was back there. I moved to Denver two years later, attended the Paralegal Institute and worked as a paralegal for almost twenty years.

In September 1994, I received a letter from the Nebraska Children's Home that simply stated, "We have a matter of extreme importance to discuss with you," and provided a phone number. That call changed my life.

I was told that my daughter, Stacey, was looking for me and had asked if I wanted to be in touch with her. When I said yes, they proceeded to tell me all about her. My daughter was twenty-four, married and worked as a social worker. On October 3rd (my birthday), I received my first letter from her. It was a long letter, and she included her college picture. She told me all about her family. I'll never forget her exact words: "I've had a great life with wonderful parents, but I always wanted to find you just to say thank you for having me."

I called my mother in New Jersey and told her that my daughter had found me. She was very quiet, and as usual, I took her silence as shame. I could not hold it in anymore, and I told her, "I know you are ashamed of me, but I really need to talk to you about this."

Through her tears, I heard my mother say, "For twenty-four years, you thought I was ashamed of you? I was ashamed of myself for making you give up that baby."

My first phone call with my daughter lasted three hours. In January 1995, I flew to Nebraska. It was the most wonderful weekend of my life. I told her what I had held in my heart for so many years. I told her that I loved her, and I was sorry I had given her up. She told me, "You didn't give me up. You gave me a better life."

In 2001, Stacey was pregnant with her first child. I remember sitting with her and looking at baby books. She told me how much she loved being read to as a child. I told her how I missed having the chance to read to her. Stacey picked out a book, handed it to me and said, "It's never too late. Why don't you read a story now to me and my baby?" She stretched out on the couch and put her head in my lap. I read the book — through tears, of course!

Daniel Jacob was born on April 27, 2001. When D.J. was two months old, I flew to Nebraska to see him. Stacey asked if I wanted to hold him. Without hesitation, I reached out, and she placed him in my arms. As I held him close, I felt a warmth come over me that I had never before experienced, and I was transported back to that moment when I saw my baby for the first time. This time, however, I was given the chance to hold my grandchild.

Five years later, Stacey and her husband adopted a three-week-old baby girl. Her name is Kierstin, and I've been a part of her life, too. When I flew to Omaha to see her when she was just a few months old, Stacey greeted me at the airport. Standing alongside her was a woman holding my new granddaughter. Stacey introduced her. It was Kierstin's birth mother. It was a very special moment for all of us.

The first Mother's Day after Stacey found me, Stacey sent me a beautiful card and signed it, "Thank you for giving me the greatest gift — The Gift of Life."

—Jeannette E. Nott—

# Spreading Sunshine

*Dogs don't rationalize. They don't hold anything against a person. They don't see the outside of a human but the inside of a human.*
~Cesar Millan

I finally received the call. My therapy-dog mentor was on the line, ready to give me our first assignment. "Jill, I'm hoping that you'll consider taking a difficult assignment. It's for a long-term-care home in a tough, low-income neighborhood. These people really need to have a therapy dog in their facility, and I'm having a difficult time filling this position. Will you do it?"

I looked down at my dog, Sunshine. She looked up at me, her tail wagging. I didn't hesitate. "Yes," I said. "We'll do it."

Three years before that fateful phone call, Sunshine was found outside the city pound one cold morning. Her eyes were swollen shut from infection. When a dog rescue was notified that a beautiful Golden Retriever was on death row, they came to pick her up and take her to a veterinarian for surgery. One of the rescue volunteers told me, "Sunshine never stopped wagging her tail. She knew we were there to help her."

I had called the rescue looking for a dog, and that's when I heard about Sunshine. When we went to the rescue to see her, she ran to my husband and sat down beside him. He looked up at me and smiled. "I guess she's coming home with us!" After all she had been through — being abandoned and suffering — Sunshine was eager to forgive and move forward.

When Sunshine and I started our therapy-dog sessions, I soon discovered that walking with her through the halls of the long-term care facility was like being in the presence of a movie star. The residents adored her, and she reciprocated. Once, when we were leaving, a caregiver came up to me with a lady in a wheelchair and asked if we could visit. The lady saw Sunshine, and her eyes lit up. With her hands shaking, she cupped Sunshine's head and began to whisper to her. The caregiver was stunned. "Amazing," she said. "Ethel hasn't spoken to anyone in years." Yet, we could distinctly hear her telling Sunshine how lovely she was.

Beautiful miracles like that happened all the time. One instance occurred with a new arrival at the home, a gentleman who was once a farmer. When he saw Sunshine, tears started to roll down his cheeks. "You don't know what this means to me," he said. "I never thought I would see a dog again." He then began to reminisce about the dogs he had in the past. As we were leaving, his wife mouthed a tearful "thank you."

The residents wanted to give back, too. The majority of them had very little — they lived in a home with the barest of amenities. But these people would save sandwiches or cookies from their plates and offer them to Sunshine. One resident in particular tried to give me a quarter to "help pay for Sunshine's food." It touched me deeply. Perhaps these folks didn't have a lot, but they wanted to give what they could because they were so appreciative that we visited them.

We were also assigned to the Alzheimer/dementia floor in the long-term care facility, and this is where I witnessed Sunshine's forgiveness once again. A gentleman was patting her and humming to her. Suddenly, he struck her hard across her face. I was absolutely horrified and pulled Sunshine away, but she had other ideas. Calmly, she walked back over to the man and placed her head on his lap. He continued to stroke her head and hum. That was the power of Sunshine. She quickly forgave whatever horror befell her, whether it was being abandoned at the pound, blind and alone, or being hit by a stranger.

We volunteered for six years until Sunshine started to have difficulties with arthritis. I often think of the power of her love for humankind. She had been neglected and abandoned in her past, yet continued to give unconditional love and affection to everyone she met. Sunshine's lesson of forgiveness and her willingness to connect had a lasting impact on so many lives, especially mine.

—Jill Anne Berni—

# Dirty Little Fingers

*Holding resentment is like eating poison and waiting
for the other person to keel over.*
~Author Unknown

His name was Jeremy and everybody in the sixth grade class thought he was hilarious. That is, of course, except for our teacher. It was apparent that he had a true behavioral problem, but we were in a pre-Ritalin time period and it was still acceptable to punish children who had attention and hyperactivity issues.

Jeremy was a constant disruption to our class and he had been since the fourth grade. He called our teacher funny names, blurted out inappropriate comments, and threw objects across the room. Early on, he was reprimanded and sent out of the classroom. But that only enabled him to cause more of a ruckus by pressing his mouth against the window like a blowfish and writing bad words in the condensation of the glass.

Our teacher then tried other forms of punishment, such as placing him in a corner and tying him to his desk with a jump rope. Somehow, he always managed to make a scene and the punishment was usually more disruptive than the initial act.

Still, Jeremy was outrageously funny and his behavior was a welcomed distraction for the sixth grade class. It was much more enjoyable watching him spit paper at the ceiling or draw stick figures on his desk with a permanent marker than learning how to divide fractions. He completely exhausted our teacher but we were so thankful for him.

One of Jeremy's favorite hobbies was picking on people. He made fun of the overweight children, the boy who got braces, and the girl who was just beginning to develop. He picked on anything and anyone he could, and each time he did, his audience roared. He was a real comedian.

It was a Tuesday in March, and Jeremy had arrived at school in typical form. His outbursts were frequent and his comments were more lewd than ever before. And as usual, his fans were thoroughly entertained. We were about to go to art class when Jeremy turned around in his seat, pointed his dirty finger at me and shouted, "Look y'all! Melissa's picking her nose!"

Of course I wasn't. But try telling that to twenty-five hysterical twelve-year-olds. Red in their faces, they all stared, laughed, and pointed at me, even the ones I thought were my friends. I cried.

Jeremy said I was picking my nose so it had to be true. I even started questioning myself. Was I picking my nose and I didn't realize it? Maybe I had scratched my nose from an angle and made it appear that I was picking. I didn't know what had happened. But I did know that I felt humiliated, upset, and very, very alone.

The next day was nearly as tragic. At snack time, Jeremy announced, "What do you have for snack today, Melissa? Is it a Boogerfinger Bar?" I held back the tears and ate my granola bar while my classmates laughed at me. And for three more days, I endured ridicule from Jeremy and his twenty-four devotees.

Then, just as the teasing had begun, it suddenly stopped. Jeremy was easily bored and he had found another target. A new girl, Diane, entered our class and she had very curly hair. "You're a spaghetti head!" he laughed. "You've got oodles of noodles on your scalp!" Everyone roared, except for me. I didn't think Jeremy was funny anymore.

Jeremy left our school the following year and did not return until we were well into high school. He was very different from how I remembered him, perhaps more mature, or maybe just medicated. He was calm, well-mannered, and not at all funny.

After graduation, I heard he was earning a living by driving trucks across the country. I pictured him pointing his dirty finger and laughing at the other drivers. Sixth grade was long ago; but I couldn't help but remember him that way.

I somehow survived the traumas of my sixth grade year and have even forgiven Jeremy for the way he teased me. I haven't forgotten; I have forgiven.

Two years ago, I saw Jeremy. I had just moved back to my hometown and had accepted a position as a sixth grade teacher at my former school. I saw Jeremy after class one day making ice cream sundaes at his sister's restaurant. I recognized him when I watched him jokingly point his finger at a customer. It still looked a little dirty to me.

But when he walked to my car, he was so excited to see me that he gave me an enormous hug. I ordered a Butterfinger sundae and he brought it to my window. We caught up on the past ten years of our lives and reminisced about our middle school days. When I got ready to leave, Jeremy said, "It was so good to see you Melissa! I wish you the best in everything."

"You too," I replied. And I meant it.

— Melissa Face —

# Don't Drink the Poison

*When a deep injury is done us,
we never recover until we forgive.*
~Alan Paton

It had been a busy morning at the Health Services Center where I worked as the nursing supervisor when I got a life-changing phone call. A disembodied voice said, "Mrs. Panko, your son has been in a fight, and you need to come to the principal's office to get him."

I prayed as I raced to the parking lot, got in my car, and drove the eight blocks to the high school.

Finding my way to the principal's office, I encountered my son sitting in a straight chair, being verbally pummeled with questions from an agitated man whom I assumed was the principal. Something was off. The man seemed oblivious to Tim's disorientation.

Even without my nursing assessment skills, I could tell he was hurt. He was bruised about his head and face. Both eyes were bloodshot, and his pupils were unequal. Alarm bells went off in my head. While the overbearing principal droned on about the rules about fighting in school, I asked Tim to tell me how many fingers I was holding up. He couldn't get it right and was confused about the day, date, and time. Finally, I held up my hand to the annoying man in charge. "Quiet! He's hurt. I'm taking him to see a doctor, and I'm calling the police."

I led my son from the room. Tim just kept asking over and over, "Mom, did I eat lunch?" I felt like I was going to throw up.

Arriving at the offices of the large medical/surgical group for which I worked, I led Tim in through the back door and was greeted by one of the nurses I knew. I quickly gave her the rundown of his condition, and she led us into a suite where Tim could be assessed. Soon, the room was crowded with medical personnel, all of whom were my friends and co-workers. One took Tim's blood pressure; another got oxygen on him; another performed neurological checks while conveying information to someone on the phone. He turned to me and said, "We're calling an ambulance to take him to the hospital. Tim has a concussion, maybe even a brain contusion, and we don't have a pediatric neurologist in town. Nancy, we may have to Life Flight him to the trauma center."

I looked up at my friend, Olivia, and said, "Liv, get me a paper bag." I sagged to the floor while still holding onto my son's hand hanging limply at his side. Tim was in and out of consciousness even though we continued to beg him to "stay with us." Liv handed me the bag into which I breathed in and out, trying to slow my hysterical, rapid breathing.

The ambulance delivered Tim to the hospital, and my husband, George, met us there. The next thing we knew, our only son was lifting off in a helicopter from the hospital landing pad and being flown sixty-five miles away to the trauma center. We had to drive while the chopper was in the air. The only comfort we had was that Tim was accompanied by a trauma doctor and nurse.

When we arrived at the cubicle in which Tim was being evaluated, we couldn't believe our eyes. He was sitting up eating a Popsicle!

The doctor standing at his side explained, "His neuro signs are much better. He definitely has a brain contusion, but there's no bleeding. He has some amnesia, which may or may not clear up. You can take him home, but he's got to rest with absolutely no exertion for a few days."

We rushed to Tim, hugging him gently from both sides. "Thank God!"

"Can you tell us what happened, honey?"

He proceeded to tell us a story of a guy who saw his girlfriend talking to Tim at lunch. He became so enraged that he and his friends ambushed Tim outside the cafeteria, pummeling his head until he was semi-conscious. Finding him bleeding and crumpled in the hall, a friend took him to the nurse's office. Tim knew his assailant. That name became embedded in my consciousness as the embodiment of evil.

Tim recovered with the exception of the amnesia. However, I began having headaches and recurrent nightmares about this faceless young man beating my son. I'd wake up in a cold sweat.

Two years later, while working at the health services center on campus, I grabbed the sign-in sheet to attend to the next student. I couldn't believe my eyes — it was the name emblazoned on my brain, the kid who had assaulted my son and got off with only a year's probation. I put down the clipboard and turned to another nurse, telling her, "Donna, you'll have to take care of this one. I just can't." I went to the lounge and sat with my head in my hands, shaking.

Donna came to get me when the young man had left the building.

"He's here at the university. I can't believe he came to the infirmary."

Donna replied, "Maybe he didn't know you worked in Health Services."

"Oh, yes, he did. His father teaches on campus, and he knows where I work."

At our staff meeting the next morning, I asked all my co-workers for solutions to this situation. My friend Anne offered, "Maybe he won't come again."

Anne pondered the problem and offered some wise words. "Nancy, you've lived with this agony for two years. It's as if *you* have taken a poison and expected *him* to die. The only solution is to forgive him for what he did to Tim. It would be giving a gift to yourself."

I thought about Anne's words for weeks. It finally hit me during Lent. Could I give up my hatred toward someone for an evil act against my family? It was time.

I had been asked to speak at one of the fraternities on campus one evening. During my talk, I choked on my own saliva. I signaled for someone to get me a drink. A young man jumped up before anyone else had a chance to move, ran out of the room and came back with a bottle of cold water. Our eyes met. It was him. I said, "Thank you." He said, "You're welcome." Something in me softened.

The next day, I sat down with pen in hand and wrote a note to the young man telling him I was giving a gift to myself—a gift of forgiveness to someone who had hurt my family. It was not to excuse or condone the act. It was simply to say, "I forgive you." Putting a stamp on it, I sent it out. I felt like a huge weight had been lifted off my heart. I was done drinking the poison.

—Nancy Emmick Panko—

# The Still, Small Voice

*God turned the adversity into a blessing.*
*~Lailah Gifty Akita*

We were three strangers — Marcus, Jim, and me — meeting for the first time on the first day of a new job. We were all in our fifties — not always a good place to be. However, we found that we worked well together. And, after a year, we decided we could do better working for ourselves.

We set up our business in a one-room office furnished with used equipment in a rundown building. We had no customers and were dependent solely on our own efforts to make a go of it. With great resolve and more than a smidgen of panic, we went to work.

By the end of our first two weeks, we had enough money in the company account to ensure that we'd each receive a paycheck at the first of the month and that the rent, electricity and lease on the equipment would be paid. We breathed a little easier.

We worked hard, and the business grew. At the end of the first year, there were six of us filling our new, expanded office. Things were looking good indeed.

Along the way, differences in management philosophy resulted in Jim's interest being purchased, leaving Marcus and me to run the business. At the end of our second year, we'd grown to twelve employees and had again expanded our space. The world was looking rosy.

Marcus and I met each morning for an hour before the business opened to discuss the events of the previous day, both successes and potential problems, needs of the business, and our personal lives. Marcus kept me informed of the financial side of the business, which was his responsibility. I, in turn, charged with generating revenue, told him about sales, pending sales, and large deals that were in progress.

We formed a deep friendship, going well beyond being business partners. We had a similar sense of humor and shared the same political philosophy and moral values. In those casual meetings, we discussed personal problems and our families. We laughed, cried and shared our victories.

In our fifth year of business, Marcus came to me requesting that I fill out a financial report for the state. "Just fill in the blanks, sign it and send it in," he advised. As finances were his department, I found the request to be out of the ordinary. Still, I willingly complied.

While filling out the forms, I discovered severe financial problems in the business that Marcus had never told me about. When confronted with my discovery, he shrugged off my concerns, saying the problems were "inconsequential."

The state agreed with my assessment. Within days, our business was closed and all the employees were terminated. My world collapsed almost overnight. Everything we'd worked for was lost and gone. I also lost a friend — Marcus.

During the next period of my life, my emotions ranged from rage at the betrayal by my partner to sorrow for the employees who were suddenly out of a job, to despair as I struggled with the total loss. I felt guilty; I should have known of the problems. I quickly found it difficult to trust anyone. All this gelled into one emotion — anger. Anger at Marcus. Anger at myself.

My blood pressure skyrocketed, requiring larger doses of medication. Even the thought of Marcus sent my blood pressure off the chart, my temples pounding, and my head throbbing. My stomach burned.

I put all my efforts into starting another company in an entirely different field. I trusted no one. It was my company; no one else was welcome to share. Two years passed in which I wrested a living from a slowly growing list of clients. There was little joy. Headaches were always with me, and I knew why: Marcus! Anger always boiled below the surface. Blood pressure hovered in that area that warned: danger!

One day while driving to an appointment, a voice spoke in my ear as though another person was in the car with me. I recognized it immediately. It was that still, small voice that I'd heard on a few other occasions. The voice quietly whispered, "David, you can't live with this anger in your soul. You have to speak with Marcus. Clear the air of the problem between the two of you."

On two other occasions, that voice has spoken to me, once as a direct answer to prayer about a problem in my life. It gave me detailed instructions on how to solve the problem that I had prayed about.

The other occasion was on a trip to Nogales, Mexico. A man was racing down the street, chased by a squad of military men with rifles at port arms. I stared with open mouth at the spectacle passing by. As the military people rounded a corner, the still, small voice spoke, "David, Get out of here." I immediately crossed the border back to the United States. I've never been back to Mexico.

The admonition to clear the air of the problem with Marcus was still echoing when I turned the car around and drove directly to Marcus's home. He answered the door, saying, "I was hoping for a chance to talk with you. I'm so sorry for what happened." He ushered me into his living room, where we discussed the loss of our business, trust and friendship for the next two hours. At the end of that time, we agreed to meet for lunch within the next two weeks.

Early one morning, a week later, the phone rang. A friend was on the other end of the call. His words gave me chills. "Marcus had a heart attack last night and died."

I sometimes still struggle with thoughts of "what might have been," but the debilitating hatred that earlier infected me is gone. I find contentment with memories of holiday meals that my wife and I shared with Marcus and his family, of the high-fives we exchanged when things had gone well, and of the laughter over silly jokes. Such is the power of forgiveness. Thank God for that still, small voice that sent me to Marcus before it was too late.

— D. Lincoln Jones —

# Auntie Beast

*There are things that we don't want to happen
but have to accept, things we don't want to know
but have to learn, and people we can't live
without but have to let go.*
~Author Unknown

Aunt Janice was the kind of person who melted your heart with her smile, who warmed your entire being with her presence, who touched your soul when you thought nobody else could even get close. Her laughter was the kind that bubbled up, the contagious kind, a deep down, from the gut kind of laugh. She smelled of sweet flowers and something else, something I could never quite identify, but it smelled beautiful nonetheless. Something that I smelled every time she would reach down and whisper in my ear, secrets spent in soft, breathy undertones that were meant just for me. With her golden mane of hair and emerald eyes that dared anyone to mess with her, she was dazzling, understated, the epitome of beauty. How ironic it is, I think, years later, that I spent the entirety of my life calling her "Auntie Beast."

Auntie Beast was my father's youngest sister, the youngest of five children, the beloved aunt of ten nieces and nephews. It hardly matters now where the name Beast came from. What's important is that it was, that it still is, an affectionate nickname that reverberates throughout our family constantly. We talk about Auntie Beast's collectables, her outlandish outfits, and her crazy, cat-lady tendencies. We talk about her loves, her desires, her wishes, her dreams. And sometimes we talk about what she would have been like if she were still alive today.

When I was in grade ten, I learned that Aunt Beast was sick, and that she had been for some time. Not the kind of sick that I knew, not a cold or the flu or an upset stomach. Aunt Beast was depressed. I was 15, a hormonal teenager, and I didn't understand. Okay, she was depressed. So what? I got a 65 on my math test and had a huge fight with my best friend. I was depressed, too. After all, that's what my parents meant, wasn't it?

"Aunt Janice is sick. She has depression."

"Yeah," I thought. "Welcome to the club."

For two years I downplayed my aunt's illness, not to her or to anyone else in my family, but to myself. Surely, since I was younger, and I could pick myself up in tough times and move on with my life, couldn't everybody? Every time I saw Aunt Beast, she never looked sick, never acted sick, always profoundly expressed her love for me and constantly confirmed, despite my attempts to get her to confess otherwise, that there was nothing wrong with her.

"How are you, Aunt Beast?"

"Oh, I'm fine, sweetheart."

"Fine? Are you sure?"

"Oh, yes. I'm as Frazzled, Insecure, Neurotic, and Emotional as they come. I'm FINE."

The two of us laughed at her clever acronym, dismissing it as we always did, because by then I was used to her version of contentment, as puzzling as it could be. I left it alone then, because if she said she was okay, then I figured that she must be okay. She was always smiling and laughing and telling me that she loved me. Her definition of the word "fine" never fazed me. I was so much in denial that I always looked at the whole, the "fine" Aunt Beast, instead of taking apart the pieces and seeing what was really there.

I never got the chance to really look at those pieces of her soul. Auntie Beast died in November of my senior year of high school, at her home by the lake. She had committed suicide.

The days following her death were a blur. I know I was in shock.

My dad and his sisters tried to come to some kind of understanding, tried to piece together why it might have happened. I asked him if he had any idea, if he knew she was suffering, why we didn't do anything to help her.

"We knew she was sad. We knew she was depressed. We didn't think that she was going to do this."

And while I knew that she didn't lay it out for us, that I couldn't have solved her problems for her, I still felt guilty. I felt guilty for not being there, for not understanding. Mostly I felt guilty for being so naïve. I chose to look the other way when Aunt Beast said she was "fine." I didn't want to look any closer, to believe anything other than that she was strong and healthy and beautiful, and that she always would be.

With time that guilt subsided, and I know now that I can't blame myself for Auntie Beast's death. I know that she knows that I loved her with all my heart, that I love her still, that I will love her always. But I wish I had paid more attention, that I had looked at the pieces of her problem, of her depression, that I had taken it seriously. I miss her every single day of my life, but the pain is sporadic now instead of a constant ache. Her loves, her hopes, her wishes, her dreams… she will always be a part of me. I can still hear her voice, whispering in soft secrets, just for me….

"How are you, sweetheart?"
"Oh, I'm fine, Auntie Beast."
"Fine? Are you sure?"
On second thought… I'm good.

— Carly Sutherland —

# The Phone Call That Changed My Life

*To forgive is to set a prisoner free and discover that the prisoner was you.*
~Lewis B. Smedes

It was the phone call that no one ever wants to receive. The phone call that changes your life. The words on the other end of the phone echoed. "They shot him. He is dead." Who got shot? Who is dead? Silence.

My mother-in-law said that the police had shot and killed her son. My husband.

The day had started out like any other day in Miami. Sun, heat and humidity. Homework, cleaning the house, and errands. My husband was annoyed at it all. He decided to go to his parents' house to chill. His car wasn't working, so I drove him two hours north to what we thought was a quiet and vacant house. His parents had been on vacation and weren't expected to return for a couple of weeks. Little did we know that their plans had changed.

For the two-hour drive, no one said a word. I silently prayed. When we arrived at the house, he jumped out. No kiss, no goodbye, nothing. I sighed and started the drive back home to our daughters.

As I was driving away, a sinking feeling in the pit of my stomach started to grow. Anxiously, I called the house phone to check in. No answer. Did he go for a walk to calm down, take a nap, or what?

Later, I learned what had happened. His parents had arrived home early, and my husband burst through the door. Within minutes, he and his stepfather were exchanging words — which had never happened before. My husband respected and loved his stepfather, and the feeling was mutual. But that night was different. It was like someone had pulled a switch, and everything that could go wrong did. A gun was pulled. Police were called. In-laws were safely rushed out of the house and taken to a safe place. All the while, I was driving back home.

The police didn't know my husband. The situation quickly got out of hand.

I got a phone call from a lead officer explaining to me what was going on. He asked me questions: *Does my husband drink?* No, never. *Is he taking any medications? Drugs?* No. *Whose gun is it?* Not ours, but my in-laws did have guns in their house. My answers sounded hollow. The officer told me they didn't know where he was and to get my daughters and take them to a hotel or a safe place. I chose a hotel.

I called a friend. She told me later that I said this wasn't going to end well. I don't remember saying that, but the pit in my stomach continued to grow. I looked at my daughters. What should I tell them? Dad was having an off-day and needed a time-out? Little did I think that anyone would wind up dead. Maybe in a straitjacket but certainly not dead. After all, didn't the police have training for situations like this?

Then the call came. My mother-in-law said matter-of-factly that they had shot him. He was dead. There was nothing else to say.

The following week was a whirlwind of navigating work, going into my children's school to explain the situation, making funeral arrangements, and being questioned by the police.

At the funeral, we said goodbye. I drove toward the police station and found myself pulling into the parking lot. I thought that I wanted to demand answers. Instead, I suddenly felt an overwhelming sense of forgiveness for the officers who had called that night.

As if I was floating outside my body, I walked into the station and asked to speak to a lead officer. Whisked into an interrogation room, I sat in front of an officer, grasping for the words to explain who I was and why I was there. I knew that I had to forgive these officers. I choked out that my husband was shot the weekend before. The officer was aware of the ongoing case. All the police officers involved had been taken off duty until an investigation could be completed.

A million images flashed before my eyes. These officers didn't know my husband, the father of my children. We had had a bad day. My daughters would never see their dad again or have the honor of him walking them down the aisle at their wedding. Tears welled up, and my voice cracked. I looked at this officer and said, "Please just let the officers involved know that I forgive them. All of them."

He started to tear up and said, "It is never easy to take a life." He was deeply sorry for my loss. I believed him.

There were still more questions than answers, but I do know that by offering the gift of forgiveness, it gave me the chance to grieve without bitterness.

Choosing to forgive the officers that evening was just the first step. I had to take the steps to forgive my husband for putting himself and us in this situation. I had to forgive myself for working so much and not seeing the signs of desperation and illness in my husband. I had to give myself time to work through the stages of grief and remind myself that there is hope. We would not just survive but thrive.

—Denise R. Fuller—

# Why I Choose Gratitude

*The greatest discovery of all time is that a person can change [their] future by merely changing [their] attitude.*
~Oprah Winfrey

An endurance cyclist for many years, I was out cycling on a typical late fall day in central New England. It was one of those days that most likely inspired Robert Frost to write. In fact, I was only a few miles from his birthplace when my life took a bit of an unexpected turn.

Strike that. It was more of an unexpected crash.

No one gets up in the morning wondering if the day will wind down with an ambulance ride and a trip across state lines to the nearest trauma center.

But on November 11, 2010, that was to be my fate.

The local authorities estimated that the teenage driver who broadsided me was moving along between thirty and forty miles per hour when we met. The windshield of his car was pushed right into the passenger's seat. Luckily there was no one sitting there.

My injuries were extensive: broken bones, torn tendons, and head-to-toe bruises.

For the next several days, my wife pulled shards of glass from my head.

And the icing on this accident cake? A traumatic brain injury.

A full year after that November day, a medical professional let me know in no uncertain terms that my life would never be the same. In fact, he labeled me "permanently disabled."

It's been six years since that fated day — the most difficult years, the most glorious years, and the most unexpected years of my life. As predicted, my bruises faded from black to yellow to gone. My bones mended, and the visible signs of my accident faded from the public eye.

But living with a traumatic brain injury, well… to say that life has become a challenge would be an understatement of truly epic proportions.

A hale and hearty case of PTSD only added to the mix.

Many things that I used to take for granted, things like knowing the day of the week, what season we are in, or even how to read, have become challenges.

I hold no bitterness toward the young man who careened into me. To hold any bitterness or resentment would stop me from moving forward with my own life. Everyone has "stuff."

If you have a heartbeat, life has thrown you a curveball or two. It's part of our shared human experience. I've seen close friends lose parents. And children. I know many people who battle life-threatening or life-changing chronic illnesses.

And some of us get hit by cars in the prime of our lives.

The biggest question is this: Will I let this experience, no matter how painful, pull me down or lift me up?

I've seen many who choose to be beaten by life's hardships. They wander around, melancholy at what they've lost, telling their tale of woe to anyone who will listen.

Thanks, but no thanks. I choose to be grateful.

Life is indeed for the living. It has taken me many years to come to grips with the fact that life as I knew it is gone. This was not an overnight process. There were peaks and valleys, wonderful days and then months filled with thoughts of suicide.

My life is vastly different than I ever envisioned. Most of my time these days is spent advocating for those affected by traumatic brain injuries. From working with others who share my fate to multiple keynote presentations at medical conferences, the life that I live today simply astounds me.

I have emerged as a new person with a new mission. My experience as a brain injury survivor has made me uniquely qualified to serve others. I speak to many groups, large and small, about what I have learned. My written work about life as a true survivor has been read around the world, including in *Chicken Soup for the Soul: Recovering from Traumatic Brain Injuries*.

On occasion, I think about the young man who forever changed my life. I wonder how my life might have unfolded had I chosen to hold on to anger, to not forgive him.

Had I chosen that path, misery and discontentment would now define my life. This I know as surely as I breathe. I have seen others who have not been able to let go, to forgive, to move on. They live in constant misery.

And the young man who started me on this new, wondrous path of discovery, what ever happened to him?

I must admit that I tracked him down on Facebook a while ago. If his page is any reflection of his life, he is a student at a local college and moving forward with his life. It is my hope that he rarely thinks about that fall day so many years ago.

And the one time that I did meet him in the weeks following my accident? If you guessed that I gave him a hug, you are correct.

— David A. Grant —

# From Revenge to Peace

*Forgiveness is like faith. You have to keep reviving it.*
~Mason Cooley

"Aunt Rachel and Uncle Harold have been murdered," my mom said softly over the phone. "An employee who did their yard work beat them to death and has been arrested."

Immediately, shock and disbelief overwhelmed me. I didn't know his name and never asked. Knowing that would make it real. Since I lived 1,300 miles away from the publicity, I was shielded from the details but not the reality. At the funeral, the spicy sweet smell of carnations brought no peace or comfort as we buried my aunt and uncle.

Everyone has people they dislike or avoid, but I'd never had a reason before to hate someone. Nightmares plagued my dreams when I fell asleep. In the worst one, a hooded figure sat restrained in an electric chair. A large switch on the wall glowed as a judge encouraged me to pull the lever. At first, I hesitated. But as the dreams continued night after night, I gleefully yanked that bar, relishing the outcome. I'd wake up in a cold sweat, my heart pounding, and then I'd cry because I had become inside what I hated most — a killer.

I found it difficult to concentrate, and day-to-day tasks became almost unbearable as if I were trying to swim through mud. Any joy evaporated from my life, and nothing brought me peace or pleasure.

I'd grown up in a religious home, but this shattered everything I'd ever known about forgiving. He'd beaten my dear elderly loved ones to death with a baseball bat! How could I let someone off the hook for a crime so heinous? Trapped in misery, I only managed the prayer, "Oh God, I can't stand this!"

One day, my husband was cleaning the car with our two-year-old son playing in the front seat. Like a typical boy, he pushed every button and turned every knob he could find. Later, I crawled into the car for a trip to the grocery store. I started the engine, and the radio blasted at full volume: "MOST PEOPLE CONFUSE PARDON WITH FORGIVENESS." I turned down the volume and collected my wits as the preacher continued. "When someone is pardoned, the consequences for their crimes are removed. Unless you are a governor, the President of the United States or God, you can't pardon anyone!"

I backed out of the driveway and kept listening as I drove. "When you forgive, you give your right for revenge to God. The person who wronged you is still accountable for what they have done. The wrong is now between the wrongdoer and God. If you've been badly hurt and can't forgive, it's okay. Ask God to make you willing to forgive. That's enough for now."

I pulled over as tears streamed down my face. "God, I can't let go of this. You'll have to make me want to." I dried my eyes and went on with the day. That night there were no dreams, just sleep.

As weeks went by, a thought followed me around. Whose capacity for vengeance is greater, mine or God's? Who would a murderer fear more, Him or me? God could hurt this man more than I ever could, so I gave the Lord my right for revenge. It wasn't because I was being kind or loving—it was survival forgiveness. I forgave just for me, putting this situation in His hands. Even with my vindictive motive, the nightmares stopped completely.

When the court deliberated on the murderer's fate, I was at peace because his destiny was not in my hands. He was given a life sentence. Part of me was relieved because it was finished, and part of me wanted to be angry. He will live; they are dead. I placed it into the Lord's hands again. Peace returned. Joy and pleasure trickled slowly back into my life as my heart healed. I pushed it all out of my mind, relieved, thankful for normalcy, and ten years flew by.

When an offender is given a life sentence, he comes up for parole every ten years. Parole was denied him, but it brought me questions: What if God forgives him? What if someday I'm in heaven, he walks in and the Lord says that it's okay for him to be there? I decided that if the Lord lets him in, he must have changed. I gave up my right for revenge, so if my Father says it's okay, then I'll trust Him. At that point, I thought forgiveness was completed, but it resurfaced again a few years later.

Our church started participating in a new prison ministry, and they needed people to bake cookies for the prisoners. Baking the cookies included praying for the inmates who would eat them. So as I baked, I prayed that the Lord would change their lives. I asked that they would become new people who would know and love God. And then He whispered in my heart, "Pray for that other prisoner you know."

"For him, Father? You want me to pray for him?"

Reluctantly I began. First, I prayed that someone would bake cookies for him. A power began to flow into me as I asked my Lord to change his life and make him a new person. Something began to break inside me, like a dam that first cracked, then leaked, and love broke through in a torrent. "Father, I want to meet him in heaven someday." Did I say that? And then I continued, "Please, it will be such a waste otherwise."

I used to worry about walking into heaven and facing the people there whom I've wronged or hurt. Praying for him made me understand that our Father pours love into all of our hearts, even for those who hurt us. Others will want me in heaven with them, just like I want him there. It's liberating to know that when I extend forgiveness and pray, my heart opens to receive more of it from the Lord, others and myself.

Forgiveness was a process for me. I needed God's help to even be willing to give up my right for revenge. Trust in the Lord's justice nurtured acceptance of whatever the outcome might be. I have grace in my life again and I received a love for a man I believe I'll meet in heaven. I'll keep praying for him.

— Susan Boltz —

# Chapter 4

# Let Compassion Heal You

# 28

# The Teddy Bear

*Forgive, not because they deserve forgiveness,
but because you deserve peace.*
*~Author Unknown*

Earl's crossed arms and permanent grimace told everyone in the room he didn't want to be there. Meanwhile, Kim wiped away tears as she expressed her desire for a happy marriage with a husband who managed his anger.

The couple was attending a Cleansing Stream seminar, led by Church on the Way in Van Nuys, California. Earl, sporting a two-day stubble on his chin, was a bear of a guy — an angry, burly man with an intimidating scowl. Kim, on the other hand, radiated warmth and faith.

During a portion of the seminar held at a hotel, Earl and Kim joined three other couples for informal counseling and prayer. I was part of the Cleansing Stream's leadership team and I began with routine questions: "Where did you meet? How long have you been married? What do you do for a living?"

Earl grunted a few answers between complaints about this "inquisition," but I could see right through his bravado. Something was bothering him.

Kim said that if Earl didn't get help soon, the marriage would be over. Years of belligerence and shouting had taken their toll.

The session concluded with a time of prayer. With my eyes closed, I kept seeing a fuzzy brown teddy bear with a plaid bow around its neck. I wondered if I hadn't gotten enough sleep the previous night. What did a teddy bear have to do with this guy and his deep-rooted anger?

As the meeting broke for lunch, a leader asked if Earl felt any differently. "I never believed in any of this prayer stuff anyway, so the answer is no," he replied. "I only did this for my wife."

I leaned over to my husband and said, "I know this sounds crazy, but the Lord wants me to buy Earl a teddy bear."

My husband rolled his eyes, but after twenty-nine years of marriage, he had learned that my spiritual antennae usually picked up the right signals. "Okay, let's go find one."

At a nearby market, which happened to be having a sale on teddy bears, I found the exact bear I envisioned: a furry brown bear with a plaid bow around its neck. I purchased the bear and found a gift card too. I wrote a note explaining that God had told me to give Earl the bear, although I didn't know why.

When the seminar regrouped in the hotel ballroom, I found Earl and Kim sitting toward the back. I walked over and handed Earl the brown paper bag holding the bear and card. When he lifted the bear out of the bag, Earl clutched it to his chest and his shoulders began heaving uncontrollably. Tears rolled down his cheeks. People couldn't help looking his way.

After pulling him aside for a few minutes, the seminar leaders asked Earl to approach the podium in the front of the room. He did, clutching Kim and his teddy bear.

"I would like to thank the group for praying for me today," he stammered. "Something happened here today, and it happened because a lady bought me this teddy bear. You see, no one in the whole world knows what this teddy bear means to me. When I was a little boy, I had a very cruel father who regularly beat me. One day I disobeyed him and, for my punishment, he took my favorite teddy bear to the back yard incinerator, where he burned it right before my eyes. I was so crushed, so hurt, that I never forgave him. I realize today that God knew my unforgiveness caused great anger in my marriage. Now that God gave me back my teddy bear, I can start healing."

Dabbing at my tears, I sat in awe of God's tender grace and unfailing love.

— Judith Ann Hayes —

# Midnight Grace

*A mom forgives us all our faults, not to mention one or two we don't even have.*
~Robert Brault, www.robertbrault.com

Mom and I stood in the hallway, nose to nose. Her hands were on her hips and her feet peeped out from her long robe. Even her toes looked curled and angry.

"I think you'd better go to bed now," she said. "I'll be talking with your dad when he gets home. He'll be in to give you your consequence."

I spun around and stomped to my bedroom. Then I yanked the curtains shut, flipped the light switch, and plopped down on my bed. 10:15. The green digital numbers reported that my dad would be home from second shift soon. Dad was a gentle man, but I knew that I'd be in trouble. Worst of all, I deserved it.

I'd had the worst day at junior high school. My best friend, Mary Ellen, decided to join forces with cool-girl Regina. So there was no room for me at the lunch table. I ate my turkey-on-wheat alone, in the library, pretending to be immersed in a book. Then we square danced in P.E. class. I was nervous about holding hands with a boy. The boy was unkind, refused to hold my cold, clammy hand, and called me Trout for the rest of the day.

Of course, none of this had anything to do with my mom, except that I'd been terrible to her that afternoon. Years later I'd learn the terminology — misplaced anger — but on that day I'd just been hurt and mad and Mom was the retaliation target.

I watched the numbers morph until 10:30. "Might as well lie down," I muttered. I pulled back the comforter and slid between flannel sheets. As I lay there, I replayed the day's events through my mind.

Mom had baked cookies and they'd been fresh, piled on a plate, when I got home from school. Peanut butter. Sprinkled with sugar and imprinted with the tines of a fork.

"Couldn't you have made chocolate chip?" I said.

Mom looked up from the table where she helped my sister with her homework. "I could have," she said. "But I made peanut butter. Why don't you pour a glass of milk?" Then she smiled.

Later that night, when she pulled chicken from the oven, I balked again. Never mind that Dad was at work and Mom still put a nice meal on the table. I wanted hamburgers. "No one even likes that kind of chicken, Mom. Why didn't you make hamburgers?"

Mom breathed deep and ran her fingers through her long blond hair. "I made chicken and I've never heard anyone complain about it before," she said.

And it went downhill from there. I growled and complained until Mom hit her limit, lost her cool, and we had a shouting match in the hall.

By the time I heard the garage door open, I felt pretty bad about the whole thing.

I lay in bed and listened. The creak of the door. Dad's boots squeaking on the tile. Muffled voices in the kitchen. Then silence.

I wondered what my consequence would be. After soaking in the dark for a while, I didn't really care anymore. I'd hurt my mom. I'd seen it in her green eyes.

Why had I taken my troubles out on Mom? I knew that if I'd come home and shared what had happened, Mom would've listened. She would have offered encouragement and compassion. Then she would've said something funny and we'd have ended up laughing.

But I hadn't done that.

Before long, I heard Dad's quiet, bootless footfalls pass back down the hall. Then I heard the bathroom door shut. Then the rush of water.

"Why is he taking his shower first?" I wondered.

The longer I waited, the heavier my heart felt. I considered getting up to apologize, but Mom didn't want to see me. I decided it was better to wait for Dad.

The sounds of the night were exaggerated in the dark. The rumble of the heater. The wind outside my window. Then a strange sound. A whirring from the kitchen. The clank of dishes. "What's going on?" I wondered.

The minutes stretched long, but finally my bedroom door creaked open. A shaft of light stretched across the room and stung my eyes. Soft footsteps to my bedside. Mom's hair slid past my cheek as she leaned over to whisper in my ear. "Why don't you come down to the kitchen?" she said.

I shimmied out of my bed and followed Mom through the bedroom and down the hall. As I passed the bathroom, I noticed the door was open. Dad had gone to bed. I was halfway to the kitchen when I smelled the thick, juicy scent of hamburgers.

I rounded the corner, puzzled, confused, and wondering if I'd fallen asleep and was dreaming. The kitchen table was set for two. "Have a seat," Mom said. She bent to lift a tray of French fries from the oven.

I sat.

Mom scooped the steamy fries to our plates and then poured thick, vanilla shakes into the tall glasses she'd set on the table. Then she slid two burgers from the griddle onto rolls and placed them on our plates. Then she sat down, too.

"Ketchup?" she asked. She tilted the bottle in my direction.

I reached out to grasp the bottle, but I couldn't. My eyes turned to my pajama-clad lap. "Mom, I've been awful to you today. I had a bad day at school and I came home and took it all out on you. You didn't deserve it. And I don't deserve this," I said. "I'm sorry."

I looked up.

Mom put the bottle down. She stretched her hand across the table. "You're in a tough spot, Shawnie. Halfway to being a woman. Halfway from being a girl. I remember those days." She smiled and tears welled in her eyes. "And I forgive you." She stretched her fingers toward me.

I reached out and took her hand, soft and comforting.

"Now," she said. "How about some ketchup for that burger?"

I wiped my own tears and nodded.

Mom and I sat in the kitchen and munched burgers while the night wrapped around our house. We slurped shakes, crunched fries, laughed and cried.

And I learned a lot about grace.

It's now twenty-seven years later, and I'm the mother of five sons. They are good boys, but there are many, many times when a hefty consequence is laid out for one of them. And rightly so.

But then there are the other times. The times when I remember that night. The silence of the dark broken by Mom's laughter. The warmth of her hand around mine. The sizzle of the burgers and the salty, crisp fries.

The night when I should've been served a consequence.

But instead, my precious mom pulled out the griddle, wiped the dust from the blender, and dished up a hearty portion of grace.

— Shawnelle Eliasen —

# Don't Bruise the Petals

*A grandma is warm hugs and sweet memories.
She remembers all of your accomplishments
and forgets all of your mistakes.*
~Barbara Cage

Flowers are one of God's most extravagant gifts. He created millions of beautiful flowers and scattered them over the earth for us to enjoy. I love flowers and have a large flower garden inside the stone foundation of an old house that tumbled down a hundred years ago.

One of my favorite times is when my four-year-old grandson, Peter, comes to visit. His eyes are as blue as Bachelor Buttons and his hair is as yellow as the petals on a sunflower. He often helps me plant seeds or pull weeds and sometimes when he "hugs" the flowers I tell him to be gentle because flowers are tender and we shouldn't bruise the petals or they can't grow and be beautiful.

One day I used the hoe to make a long trench in the garden and I crawled along on my hands and knees dropping the seeds two inches apart in the soft, damp soil. When I got to the end of the row, Peter was standing there waiting for me. His hands were filled with all the seeds I'd just planted.

"Look Grandma, you dropped all of your seeds! Aren't you lucky I was there to pick them up for you?" he asked proudly.

"I'm very lucky, indeed!" I said and put the seeds back into the envelope. I'd plant them tomorrow when he wasn't there to "help" me.

My Dahlias are my favorite flowers and for the past nine years they've taken the blue ribbon for the Best of Show at the Flower Club Competition. This year the rain and temperature had been perfect and my Dahlias were more beautiful than ever and larger than dinner plates. I had no doubt they were going to win the Best of Show for the tenth year in a row. I'd get a silver plaque and my picture in the paper and most likely would be elected the next president of the garden club.

One evening I noticed my flowers were looking a little droopy and wilted and thought it might be the heat so I gave them a little extra water. By morning they looked even worse. I couldn't imagine what I'd done wrong but it was obvious they'd be dead before the flower show.

I examined the leaves and stems looking for bugs that might have killed the flowers and I discovered their stems had been broken and then taped back together with bandages. "Peter," I called. "Do you know what happened to Grandma's flowers?"

"I was walking on the stone wall and I fell on them," was his answer, "but I know when I skin my knee, you put a sticky bandage on it and then I get better so I bandaged the flowers so they'd get better."

"Flowers don't get better," I said.

"I'm sorry, Grandma, I know how much you love your flowers." His blue eyes filled with tears.

"Don't cry. I do love my flowers," I said and hugged him, "but I love you a thousand times more than all the flowers in the world."

"I love you too, Grandma," he smiled.

"I think it's time for some milk and cookies," I said and led him to the house.

It didn't bother me one bit that someone else's flowers would win the Best of Show this year and that I wouldn't get the silver plaque or that I might not be president of the garden club.

I have a grandson who loves me and my most important job is helping him grow and bloom without bruising his petals.

— April Knight —

# Circle of Prayer

*Prayer is not eloquence, but earnestness; not the definition of helplessness, but the feeling of it; not figures of speech, but earnestness of soul.*
~Hannah More

Most likely, the doctor found the first birthday card startling. I pictured him pausing, trying to pinpoint my motivation, before tossing the correspondence in the wastebasket, only to lift the card back out and place it on his desk. There, he'd glance at it whenever he passed by, recalling that he nearly took my life, only to save it two days later. He probably thought it odd that I remembered the day he was born. But how could I forget?

At thirty, I needed a tonsillectomy. Years of strep throat and failed antibiotics necessitated their removal. I read the risks and possible complications listed on the surgical consent form. But like most patients, I signed without much thought to the medical warnings and envisioned nothing more than a soothing Popsicle in the recovery room, followed by moderate pain for a couple of weeks. I could not have been more wrong.

After the surgery, I went home feeling as though I'd swallowed shards of glass. My five-month-old son Holden needed my attention, so I rested in between caring for him. The next day, a warm, thick liquid trickled down my throat, followed by the distinctive taste of copper. I called the surgeon's office as instructed for post-operative bleeding.

"Gargle with ice chips," he said.

"Excuse me?" I asked, believing that I'd misheard him.

The doctor explained that a blood clot might be holding a vessel open and, if knocked off, the bleeding would subside. I gargled the ice, and it worked… for a while. The next bout of bleeding — heavier and faster — increased my worry, and I called the office. I gargled with ice chips once again as instructed, and the bleeding stopped. Later in the day, I headed to the hospital without calling the doctor because the bleeding had increased. Shortly after my arrival in the ER, the bleeding eased.

"It looks like the problem has corrected itself," the doctor said as he looked around in my throat. "I'd hate to stir things up. I think we'll let it be and send you home."

The thought of leaving the safety of the hospital frightened me, but I didn't object. The doctor appeared to be a bit rushed. I noted his dress clothes. "Going somewhere fancy?" I asked.

"Oh, it's my birthday today. We were out to dinner. In fact, my wife's still at the restaurant waiting."

I had interrupted his birthday dinner. Probably made him leave before the arrival of his cake adorned with candles. I suddenly felt stupid for rushing to the hospital without calling for his advice. He instructed me to go home and rest and to call the office if a problem arose.

The next day, I actually felt better throughout the day. I went to bed with a sense of relief, but I soon found myself in a dreamlike state. Swallowing. Dreaming. Swallowing. Dreaming. Gulping. I shot up in bed to find my pillow soaked with blood. I shook my husband awake. The next fifteen minutes consisted of a speeding car, the running of stoplights, and my husband's pleas for me to stay upright. Soon, back in the ER, a hose dangling from my mouth transported my life sustaining blood to a nearby canister.

A nurse stood at my bedside, holding my hand and brushing the hair back from my face. "We're waiting for anesthesia to arrive. They're on call this time of night. We've paged them, and they should be here soon."

"How long?" I managed, watching my life travel down the hose.

"Fifteen minutes."

"I don't think I have that long." Her silence confirmed my fear.

The surgeon paced outside the room and glanced at his watch every few seconds, failing to mask his worry. My husband cradled our baby in the corner of the room as the nurse continued to hold my hand amidst the unspoken yet palpable panic. The nurse anesthetist from the Labor and Delivery Unit stood nearby, as a substitute, if the anesthesiologist didn't arrive shortly. The gurney suddenly lurched forward and clipped down the hallway as a strange man in scrubs arrived and placed a mask over my mouth, telling me to breathe deeply.

I awakened to the sounds of distant beeps, hisses, and whispers. Too weak to talk, I could only listen as the surgeon stood at my bedside. This time, he wasn't rushed and looked a tad disheveled.

"We were all praying for you in there," he said. "The surgical team formed a circle around you, holding hands while we prayed. We nearly lost you at one point." I nodded, somehow knowing there'd been a higher intervention.

"I need to tell you something," he said, his voice thinning.

He must've noticed my questioning glance. "During the initial surgery, I nicked your facial artery, and it weakened over time. That's why you've been bleeding on and off."

I knew that he risked repercussions by telling me the truth. Perhaps he told me out of fear that I'd later discover his wrongdoing. Or, perhaps, he did so because it was the right thing to do. Either way, I respected him for admitting his error.

He then explained the harrowing night in the surgical suite: the tricky cauterization of the artery the size of a pencil tip, too short to tie off; the impending need to cut my throat from the outside in order to repair the damage if the cauterization failed — a procedure he had never performed before; the lavage to rid my stomach of the large amount of blood; and the prayers over my body as they painfully watched the clock and waited to see if the cauterization would hold.

"I kept thinking about your baby," he said. "How would I tell your husband that you didn't pull through and that your son had lost his mother?"

With the mention of Holden, the realization struck that I'd been so close to death.

"God listened today, and I'm thankful. I pray that you can forgive me for my mistake." He squeezed my hand before leaving the room.

I drifted off to sleep, low on blood and energy. But I was alive. Over the next six weeks, the risk of bleeding still lurked until I had completely healed, but I knew God would not fail me now.

I forgave the doctor for the near fatal mistake during my tonsillectomy and for rushing me out of the ER the following day to return to his birthday celebration. He had stood before God, asking for His help in saving my life, knowing the burden he'd carry if I didn't survive. Knowing my husband would lose a wife, and that my son would grow up without a mother. If God could see fit to answer the doctor's prayers and grant him mercy, I could grant him his wish of forgiveness.

In the years to follow, my appreciation arrived at his office in the form of a birthday greeting. After all, he had saved my life when given a second chance, and he had asked for God's help that night to ensure my survival. And each day, I'm thankful the medical team believed in the power of prayer.

— Cathi LaMarche —

# Sharing My Friend

> *Forgiveness is not an occasional act,*
> *it is a constant attitude.*
> *~Martin Luther King, Jr.*

Cindy was my best friend. My mom called her a nuisance, but to me, she was a dog with a personality. At eleven, I fell in love with the tiny, curly-haired dog. Cindy was smart, too. I taught her tricks. She would sit by my feet and when I put a stick or piece of carrot by her mouth, I'd say "chew" and she would stand and obey. She loved going for walks with my friends and me. She danced around us as if listening to our conversations about school and clothes and movies we'd seen.

Sometimes, I sat with her in the front yard, letting her explore the soft grass. I'd tell her about my friends, the boys I liked, the test I was about to take in History. Cindy would sit and stare at me as if listening to everything I told her.

Then my uncle, my mother's younger brother, came to live with us. He and his wife slept in my room and I slept on the couch. My mom didn't want Cindy's curly fur all over the living room furniture, so she slept in the utility room in her plush bed. Instead of being beside my bed as usual, she was out of my aunt and uncle's way. I resented their presence and kept Cindy outside with me as much as possible.

But one afternoon, I went to get her from the back yard and she wasn't there. The back gate was partly open. Had Cindy been searching for me?

Let Compassion Heal You

I looked everywhere around the neighborhood, knocking on doors and asking everyone if they'd seen her. I called her name, my friend who always came to me. This time she didn't come.

"Sorry," my uncle said. "I guess when I went through the gate to check something in my car, I forgot to close it completely."

I didn't want his apology. I cried and searched.

I prayed for her safe return. Then one morning, two days later, my uncle left after breakfast. An hour later he was home, Cindy in his arms.

"She'd been picked up by the pound. I thought I'd check and there she was. Must've pulled her collar off somewhere," he said.

Mom let me keep her beside me all night. I hugged her and told her about everything I'd done since she'd been gone. She licked my hand and listened.

It was two days later before she'd leave my side. She limped a bit, though we couldn't find anything wrong. But she was home.

My uncle felt bad and offered to buy me another dog to keep Cindy company outside. I knew he and my aunt were having a hard time. They didn't have much money. I wanted to hate him, but I knew it wasn't his fault he was living with us.

One day, I came home and found him sitting with Cindy in his lap and talking to her. I listened a moment and wondered how long he'd been telling her his troubles. I guess he was smarter than I thought. Cindy stared at him, looking into his face as she'd always done with me when I talked to her.

I watched them. I thought that maybe Cindy and I could give him another chance.

"Want to feed her?" I asked.

He nodded. I gave him the box of her favorite treats. He fed her and stroked her small head.

"She's a good listener," he said.

I smiled. I already knew that. I guess if Cindy forgave him, I could too.

—Kathryn Lay—

# I Lubbyou

*To love is nothing. To be loved is something.*
*But to love and be loved, that's everything.*
*~T. Tolis*

My parents left Puerto Rico, my mother's home, soon after they were married. My father was in the military, so they moved from base to base as they had their children. Shortly after World War II, they lived in Japan for three years. During the boat trip home across the Pacific, a typhoon hit the boat. That was when my mother, pregnant with me and terrified by the storm, began her descent into mental illness.

Stateside, once I was born, my mother refused to take care of me or my sisters. She was hospitalized, drugged and physically survived several electric shock treatments, but her spirit was broken, and she never fully recovered. She continued to be hospitalized on and off throughout my youth.

At the age of seventeen, I was off into the world. I found a job as a secretary at the Buffalo Psychiatric Center. As I stepped off the bus and walked toward the campus, I remembered that my mother had been a patient there when I was a child. I saw the road that tunneled under a walkway connecting two massive brick buildings, the same walkway I had viewed long ago with childlike wonder. I remembered the coffee shop above the tunnel, where my mother sat smoking cigarette after cigarette, eyes cast down, subdued by medication and shock treatments.

Dismay swept over me when I realized that the office was in

the same building where my mother had been housed, the one with the large concrete porch and bars from floor to ceiling. I recalled my father lifting me up to kiss my lifeless mother goodbye through those same bars.

For several years, I worked in the mental-health system, which enabled me to understand and even help my mother through her last psychiatric hospitalization. I was in my late twenties when my mother had her final breakdown. This time, the hospital didn't rely on heavy medications and shock therapy. Instead, my mother was given a new drug through injections. She could not refuse to take the meds. Slowly, she became more coherent, able to engage in short conversations, and show concern for herself and her children.

For the first time in my life, I could have lucid talks with my mother. At around this time, my youngest sister and her husband decided to tell their siblings and parents that they loved them. For our family, this was monumental. Kind words were rarely spoken in our home and we were not accustomed to displays of affection.

After being released from the hospital, my mother started phoning me at home. I'd never pick up the phone. She would always leave the same message: "Es mama from Nee-a-gra Falls." My husband and I laughed at this, as if her accent didn't give her away. Besides, what other mama would be from Niagara Falls? Then she would call again, leaving the same message, "Es mama from Nee-a-gra Falls." Still laughing, I'd return her call. We'd have a short exchange.

One time, she ended the call with "I lubbyou."

I froze. And then I said, "Huh?"

She repeated it.

"Okay, goodbye." I hung up, almost dropping the phone.

Again, a month later, she phoned and left the same message; I returned the call and had a short talk. It ended with her saying, "I lubbyou." This was too much to bear.

It took many months before I could say, "I love you too, Ma," but the way I said it was just in lieu of saying goodbye—a kind of casual "I love you."

I was confused about this new feeling. I decided that every time my mother said she loved me, I would use those words to heal myself. I let them wash over me and repair the jagged hole in my heart. I started telling her I loved her just so she would say those words back to me. Sometimes, I'd murmur "Huh?" to make her repeat the words. She never refused. She knew. She'd let those comforting words wrap around my heart and soul.

Through our discussions, I could see her life's circumstances and her personality more clearly. I came to understand and appreciate her fortitude, strength and faith. I was able to forgive her.

As she lay dying years later, I sat by her bedside. She confided she was afraid to die. I told her that she had loved God so much throughout her life, it was time to let him wrap his arms around her and to melt into his love. She closed her eyes. Her body relaxed.

It touches my heart and consoles me that my last words to my mother gave her comfort. Those words — "I love you" — can heal a lifetime of wounds.

— Catherine Shavalier-Chernow —

# 34

# Once Upon a Time

*It doesn't matter who my father was;
it matters who I remember he was.*
~Anne Sexton

Having spent a large part of my life putting as much distance as possible between myself and my abuser, the last thing I imagined was that I would be at his bedside when he died. Nevertheless, there I was on a chilly Midwest fall evening almost 1,000 miles from the comfort and safety of my home, sitting in a hospital room as the man who had filled my childhood with terror was facing death.

I'd received a call the night before from a relative telling me that my father was dying. Truth be told, my first reaction was "Oh, well." The next morning, however, I found myself packing a suitcase and traveling from Colorado to St. Louis with no idea why.

When I arrived at the nursing facility, I was greeted by a woman who was both warm and curious since the staff was not aware that "Bill" had a daughter. After listening compassionately to a very brief sketch of my tragic family history, she assured me that even though I had traveled a long distance, I was in no way obligated to put myself through any further discomfort. In fact, she offered to put me up for the night and provide transportation back to the airport in the morning... guilt-free.

I deeply appreciated her empathy and consideration, but decided to push through with whatever it seemed I was there to do. Stepping into an elevator, this same thoughtful human being kept a reassuring arm around my shoulder. When the doors opened, I almost gagged at the smells of incontinence, talcum powder and disinfectant. As I approached my father's room, I admit to reconsidering the offer of a guilt-free escape.

I was stunned when I walked in. It had been more than thirty years since I'd seen him, and the form in front of me resembled nothing of what I remembered about my father's angry and menacing frame. Tightly curled into a fetal position, he was frail and small. His mouth was slightly open, his breath barely detectable. I stood motionless just inches from this man of my nightmares. I haven't a clue why it happened, but suddenly all of my fear washed away, and I knew why I was there.

I put my hand on his shoulder and said, "Once upon a time, there was a little boy named Billy. Billy was born with the birthright of all children — to be loved, to learn, to play, to grow in confidence and to experience all the wonder of living. There was a moment, however, probably very early on, when Billy got hurt — deeply hurt — and no one helped to heal that hurt. Perhaps the pain had no words — only tears that he may have had to shed when he was all alone. The hurt remained with Billy and grew with fierce intensity until it finally broke through and hurt everyone around him. But it's okay now for Billy to stop hurting. It's time for Billy to feel safe and loved. It's okay for him to finally go home."

For the next eleven hours, I sat there singing lullabies, telling stories, and sharing candidly all of the feelings I had dealt with over the years. It dawned on me that this man had never been loved by another human being. And he had been incapable of loving anyone else. I think he knew what he had done, and I sensed that he was terrified of leaving this life without someone "hearing" his story and without the possibility of "asking" to be forgiven. Several times during those quiet and profound hours, I told him that he was forgiven. He was "free" and so was I.

I knew almost nothing of my father's story, but I had heard that he was a sullen child, withdrawn and suspicious. I have seen only two photos of him as a child, and in both he appears sad and hurt, even as other children in the picture are smiling. How does a child get to that point? I don't believe that any child is born with a fiercely held shield against the world. What really happened, I'll never know. Everyone has a story, and everyone needs for that story to be told. The generic story I told that night did not excuse what he had done. It did, perhaps, explain it.

About 8:30 the following morning, exhausted after a long flight and sleepless night, I gave into both physical and emotional fatigue and rested my head on the bed. Immediately, I felt the slightest twitch of his hand against mine. When I looked up, I saw that my father's journey had ended. And a part of mine had just begun.

It's been more than twenty years since this event took place. Have I forgotten the traumas of my childhood? No. Nor should I. Our lives are the sum of our stories. I have come to understand that when things are happening to us, beyond our control, we may be the victims in those stories. But when we forgive, we become the storyteller, empowered and boldly wrapped with the authority to share the story in hope that forgiving doesn't happen in a vacuum.

I am free from the pain of my past. I hope with all my heart that my father is, as well.

— Dale Mary Grenfell —

# 35

# Daddy's Little Girl

> *Grudges are for those who insist that they are owed something; forgiveness, however, is for those who are substantial enough to move on.*
> ~Criss Jami, Salomé: In Every Inch In Every Mile

Ours wasn't your typical father/daughter relationship. The words "warm and fuzzy" simply didn't apply. I can't remember my dad saying, "I love you." There were no affectionate kisses. No hugs.

What I do remember is a lingering sense of impending doom as I wondered when the next verbal explosion might occur. Most of my memories of my father are of terse exchanges during the week or alcohol-induced outbursts on weekends, of being told on numerous occasions that I was not wanted, that I was an accident.

It's understandable, then, that as I grew up I struggled to find a way to make my father love me, or at the very least make him proud. That struggle happily resulted in high marks in school — so high, in fact, that I was valedictorian of my graduating class. At last, my dad had to be proud of me — he even said so, promising to stand and applaud when I received my award.

Graduation day dawned bright and sunny, made brighter by the knowledge that my dad had not had a single drink in nearly three months. As the biggest moment of my young life approached, my heart sank. My dad had left the house early that morning to run errands. As the minutes ticked by, I realized that the length of his absence likely would be directly related to his degree of drunkenness when he returned. As anyone who has lived with an alcoholic can tell you, we can often tell by that person's facial features whether or not they have succumbed to the "demon drink." As I saw my father pull into the driveway, I knew instantly that he had not only succumbed to the demon, he had completely surrendered. He was falling-down drunk.

The next few hours were a haze of anxiety, disappointment, and fear as I wondered if my big day would end in humiliation if my father decided to become vocal at the graduation ceremony. He didn't.

And that should have been the proverbial happy ending. But when he walked me down the aisle at my wedding a few months later — drunk once again — I couldn't find it in my heart to forgive him. He had cast a horrible shadow over yet another momentous occasion in my life.

We maintained a cordial but "arm's length" relationship for several years.

Then just eight short years after that nerve-wracking graduation day, my dad was gone, dead of lung cancer at the age of fifty-six. I no longer had to dread his outbursts. I also no longer had the opportunity to try to repair an obviously damaged relationship.

Over the next two decades, my thoughts often drifted to my relationship — or lack thereof — with my dad. Surprisingly, even though I still felt saddened, and at times angry, about our dysfunctional relationship, I found myself wondering what had happened in his short life to make him so unhappy.

In 2000, I visited France and the Normandy American Cemetery at Omaha Beach, and I began to understand my father and the man he was — somewhat distant, extremely proud of his service to his country, and stubbornly patriotic. As I stood on that desolate windswept beach in France, I saw the 9,386 cold stone crosses commemorating the soldiers who died there in World War II. I felt closer to my father than I ever had.

At the tender age of seventeen, my father had enlisted in the U. S. Marine Corps by lying about his age. Just sixteen months later, he spent three weeks battling the enemy, up close and personal. Most recall the battle of Iwo Jima as the setting of the immortal "raising of the American flag," etched in our memories by the famous photograph: six war-weary young soldiers struggling to raise the flag of the country they had pledged to serve, honor and defend. I believe my father, however, remembered — though rarely spoke of — something entirely different. Being left on an island filled with the enemy. Hand-to-hand combat. The "kill or be killed" mentality drilled into him for his own safety. Buddies falling dead at his side. The only battle by the U.S. Marine Corps in which the overall American casualties exceeded those of the Japanese.

Some who returned from that fierce battle were able to block out the horror and live fairly normal lives. I don't think my father was one of those "lucky" ones. I now realize that his frequent drunken weekend-long discourses about being a marine and fighting in what was considered one of the bloodiest battles of World War II were an indication of how profoundly those experiences had affected him.

As I reflect on our relationship, I hold firm to the belief that life is about choices.

Perhaps my father made some poor choices while I was growing up — perhaps there was a reason. Will I choose to hold the effects of my father's service to his country against him? His drinking, the verbal abuse, his inability to show affection?

No.

I can choose resentment or I can choose to forgive and be proud of the honorable man that was my father; the man who had integrity, an incredible work ethic and was as generous as anyone I know. I choose the latter.

And now, more than twenty years after his death, I can also choose to be Daddy's little girl.

— Linda Bruno —

# Dragonflies

*The influence of a mother in the lives of*
*her children is beyond calculation.*
*~James E. Faust*

It was two hours past the time that I was supposed to be moved to jail from the city cells. I was sick of Hungry-Man dinners and toast, and tired of sleeping with one itchy blanket in a cold, dark cell. I made all the calls I could, asking friends and family for bail money. No one accepted. They all had their reasons.

After three days inside, I was truly scared. When the guard came and unlocked my cell, I thought it was time for the move, so I steeled myself for whatever was going to happen next. In silence, he led me upstairs. Not knowing what to expect, I trudged along behind him, anxiety coursing through my veins. When I finally looked up, there stood my mother, the last person I expected to see.

My parents split up when I was very young, and though children of divorce are often raised by a single mom, my dad raised my brother and me. I don't think I ever forgave my mother for leaving. Because of that, among other reasons, we never saw eye-to-eye, never got along, and never enjoyed a good mother/daughter relationship. So, seeing her there left me stunned, especially since she was one of the many who had declined to bail me out.

But now she had bailed me out, and we quietly drove to my dad's in her car. I had no clue what awaited me, but as soon as I opened the door to the house, I had a pretty good idea.

And so it began — an intervention just like the ones on TV. All the people who loved me most were gathered there, but they were dead serious. They told me that I needed to change and clean up my act. They loved me, but they were not willing to stand by and watch me destroy myself. It had already been agreed before I got there that I was to move to my mother and stepdad's farm. If I refused, they would "disown" me. My dad and my brother meant everything to me, and I couldn't imagine my life without them, so there was no decision to be made. Of course, I agreed.

Mom lived just outside a tiny town of about 800 people, forty kilometers away. I started out there going through withdrawal. I slept for most of the first two weeks. I was so sick that I wanted to die. I didn't think I could get by without the drugs, the partying, and the friends, let alone live in the sticks with the woman whom I felt had once abandoned me. Everything about the situation seemed impossible.

Then came the day I still recall clearly. Mom came into my room and told me I had to get up. I had to get some fresh air. I just wanted her to go away and leave me alone, but she persisted. Muttering under my breath, I got up and went outside with her.

The sun was blindingly bright, and the breeze smelled like pasture. Believe me, that is not as pleasant as it sounds. We talked, enjoyed her flowers and admired the gathering of dragonflies. It was an especially hot summer, and they were plentiful that year. I have never seen that many since. She raised her pointer finger in the air and told me to do the same. I rolled my eyes, but complied begrudgingly. Then I watched, mesmerized, as the dragonflies landed on our fingers.

At that precise moment, I realized that I was missing the small things in life. I had a sudden awareness that there was so much to appreciate and so many experiences that I had yet to live. I had my whole life ahead of me, a life more valuable than I had ever thought possible. I realized then that the parties, drugs, and fake friends weren't really living at all. They were just a way to pass the time, a way to bury my anger, hurt and feelings of abandonment that I refused to let go. More importantly, I realized that I did have a mother. She didn't abandon me, and she was here now when I needed her most. I was still her daughter, and she hadn't given up. On that day out on the prairie, in the afternoon sunshine, she became not only my mother but my friend.

That was more than twelve years ago. Since then, my mother and I have formed a relationship I had never dreamed possible. She has become a big part of my life and that of my two wonderful children. They think the world of their granny. She has held me when I've cried, consoled me when I was in pain, celebrated my successes, and carried me through my failures.

Most of all, I admire how she held my hand through recovery, teaching by example the true meaning of life and love. It took me far too long to forgive her for not being there when I was young. And as much as I regret that, I understand. Because of her, I was able to get clean and begin a relationship with her that would be unbreakable. My children are also blessed with her unconditional love. Because she taught me how to forgive, they enjoy an amazing granny who shares with them the simple things in life, like catching dragonflies. I am forever grateful that she saved me and has shown me the depth of a true mother's love.

— Celeste Bergeron Ewan —

# Chapter 5

# Be Open to Family

# Painted Nails

*True healing involves body, mind and Spirit.*
*~Alison Stormwolf*

Three days before my mother died, we had a talk. We were sitting in a small lounge outside her hospital room with the sun streaming in through the windows. I was curled up in a chair, and she was in her nightgown with her swollen legs propped up on a coffee table.

She looked beautiful, as usual. Even on the way to her deathbed, she had taken pains to curl her hair, put on make-up, and apply lipstick.

From the chest up, one would never guess that she was dying. People would assume she was just a fifty-three-year-old woman in the prime of her life.

"Now, Barbara," she said. "I don't want you to cry."

She meant when she died.

"Mom," I said. "Don't talk like that."

"Look at me, Barb," she said very matter-of-factly, gesturing to the tumors painfully stretching her abdomen. "I could be dead any minute here. The doctor says there's a blood clot in my leg that could go to my brain at any time."

She was right. The only reason she was here was to die. We both knew it. She'd had colon cancer for three years. We'd watched it spread to her ovaries, liver, and lungs. Two days ago, when she almost suffocated in her own bed, we decided it was time to go to palliative care.

"Well, Mom, of course I'm going to cry. You're my *mother*, for

God's sake."

"Okay," she sighed. "You can cry a little bit. But I don't want you to let it ruin your life."

We sat there in silence for a bit.

Finally, I whispered, "Are you scared?"

She thought for a minute.

"No," she finally said. "I used to worry about your father, but I taught him to do the laundry, and I took him to IGA and showed him how to grocery shop. So, I think he'll be okay."

That made me laugh. In the thirty-seven years they had been married, my father had never made himself a cup of tea, let alone done laundry.

"The only thing I worry about," she said, "is you and your sister. You don't get along. You should get along."

Oh, dear. This was true. We definitely did not get along. I don't know why, exactly. It had a lot to do with childhood sibling rivalry. My sister, two years older, was the "beautiful" one. I was the homely, "smart" one. We competed for our mother's love. I guess we were still competing for it.

"I don't know why you can't be like your cousins," she sighed.

Oh, yes, our cousins, sisters — Paulette, Donna, Cathy, Marcella, and Gail. The Clarkin girls. They always got along. They were best friends, Mom reminded me. They helped each other out, did the housework for their mother without complaint, and loved each other. Unlike my sister and me, apparently.

"Well, Mom," I said. "Where you're going, maybe you can help us out there. Send down some love vibes from heaven or something."

She laughed and nodded. "Maybe I will," she said.

The next day, a bed became available at the palliative care unit where Mom planned to die.

Before she was transferred there, she gave my sister a shopping list. They were things she needed, she said.

I was jealous that she had given my sister this task and not me. Did she not trust me to fill it for her? Why Lois? Was she thriftier than me? Did she have better taste in drugstore amenities? Typical.

The things on the list, when I saw it later, were so very mundane that I found them jarring.

Deodorant. Razor blades. Toothpaste. Panties.

Panties? Who would think to order up new panties for their deathbed? I realized, though, that she wasn't dead yet. And, as long as you are alive, you don't actually think things like, "Oh, I won't need these panties because I'll be dead shortly." When you need panties, you need panties.

Tucked on the bottom of the list was written "Nail Polish — Pink."

The day she died, she woke up and told the nurse, "I'm going to die today." The nurse told us she said it very matter-of-factly. The nurse helped her to the washroom, and when Mom got back into bed, she began to fade away.

They called the family, and we all arrived at about the same time. It was a big family, and Mom waited until the last person had arrived before she allowed herself to go into a coma. At about noon, she was gone but for the heartbeat.

So, we all milled around her room, unsure of what to do. There was me, my sister, three brothers, my mother's ninety-two-year-old mother, my mother's three sisters, her brother, and various relatives who could not resist a gripping deathbed scene, including one or two of the angelic Clarkin sisters.

Mom was very popular in life and, apparently, just as popular in death.

A priest came in and performed last rites. We all perked up at this and vigorously prayed along with him. When he was done, we stood around her bed, all seventeen to twenty of us, staring expectantly down at her, waiting for her to die on cue.

She did not.

Her heart kept beating.

Her sisters decided to sing to her. So, they rounded up the various relatives and hangers-on and arranged them choir-like about her bedside again. They took part in a joyful and heartfelt round of "Amazing Grace." Then, again, we awaited the last breath.

It did not come.

**Be Open to Family**

So, we all awkwardly stood around, taking turns feeling her arms and legs and even taking her pulse occasionally, like we were medics or something. We tried talking to her, telling her it was okay to let go, that we were good with it.

Still, she did not go.

"It's her heart," the nurse said. "It's only a fifty-three-year-old heart. It's still strong. It doesn't want to stop beating."

After about five hours of this, people started to feel somewhat dejected. They began to realize that death would come when it came, and we had no control over it.

Slowly, people began to fade away, going to pick up their loved ones at work or school, to check in at the office, wherever they had to go.

At around 5:00 P.M., only the immediate family was left. Dad decided it was time to take Gram down to the cafeteria to get something to eat.

"We'll stay here with her," my sister said. I agreed.

It was dark in the room, only a lamp on for light. My sister pulled up a chair on Mom's right, and I pulled one up on her left.

We sat there, examining her.

"Let's paint her nails," my sister said, lifting up one of Mom's hands.

"Oh, yes," I said. "Let's! She's got new nail polish."

We giggled as we riffled through her drawer, laughing about the various items on her list before we got to "Nail Polish - Pink."

Since Mom got cancer, she was able to have nice nails for the first time in her life. Too sick to work, she could grow her nails and have glamorous hands to match her glamorous face and body. She used to talk about it all the time.

But now, we realized, her nails were a little chipped and in need of a fresh coat.

"We'll paint them so she can have pretty nails in her coffin," my sister said.

So, we went to work, she on the right hand and I on the left, painting her nails for her coffin.

While we were doing it, we were laughing, sharing what we, and only we, knew about our mother's vanity, and giggling about how we were going to preserve it.

We were just finishing up when we both noticed it at the same time.

"She's stopped breathing," my sister said.

"Oh, my God, she has," I said.

We both stood up and leaned over, my sister on the right and I on the left.

"She's gone," we said.

She was. Her heart had finally stopped beating.

She had decided to die when my sister and I were alone with her, enjoying each other's company and painting her nails for her coffin.

"Love vibes from heaven," I whispered.

At her wake, many people noted how glamorous and elegant she looked in the clothes my sister and I had picked out, together, for her to wear.

And everyone commented on how beautiful her nails were.

— Barb McKenna —

# The Power to Heal

*Until you have a son of your own, you will never know what that means. You will never know the joy beyond joy, the love beyond feeling that resonates in the heart of a father as he looks upon his son.*
~Kent Nerburn

My wife and I were getting ready to board a plane at our local airport. The gate attendants had just begun the boarding process when my phone rang. It was one of my estranged sons.

I looked down at my phone in disbelief. Answering his unexpected call, I was met with only static. *Oh, well,* I thought. *It must have been a butt dial.* Nevertheless, I texted him from my seat in the plane. "You just called me. I suspect that it was an accidental call. I hope you are well."

Several years earlier, in a life-changing cycling accident, I sustained a traumatic brain injury. Like so many others, my personality changed. And when it did, my sons backed away from a dad they no longer knew. The loss of my children was the biggest casualty of my injury. Over the years, I still texted my sons regularly just to let them know they were never far from my heart. My texts went unanswered for years. I was accustomed to it by then.

I never expected what happened next. "Dad, I did call you. We need to talk." His reply to my text left me staring at my phone feeling bewildered.

By this time, the flight attendants had announced that phones needed to be in airplane mode. We had a very short layover a few hours later. Through most of that first flight, I vacillated between being excited that my son had finally reached out to me, to being afraid that I was setting myself up for even more loss. It was a very long three-hour flight.

"I'll call him back when we get to our gate," I shared with my wife when we landed in Minneapolis. Unknown to either of us, the Minneapolis airport is the size of a small city. We got to the gate mere minutes before they swung the cabin doors shut on our next flight.

I called my son and heard the first words he'd said to me in a very long time. "My daughter was born six weeks ago. I am now a father, and you are a grandfather." My heart stopped. Not only did my son reach out to me, but he came with news I had never even considered. "We need to get together and talk," he said, his voice full of emotion.

We were again told to put our phones in airplane mode. In this life-changing moment, I paid no attention to the flight attendants. By this time, the pictures started showing up on my phone as my son texted me photo after photo of my new granddaughter. I sat by the window on our next flight in tears, looking at the pictures of a newborn baby girl over and over again.

Later that same week, when we were back home in New Hampshire, we got together at the invitation of my son. For a couple of hours, on what was perhaps the best day of my entire life, I held my granddaughter, met my son's family, and talked. That precious day was more than two years ago.

Over the past couple of years, our lives have changed in unimaginable ways. For most of that time, I watched my granddaughter one day a week. I watched her grow from a newborn into a beautiful baby. I watched her learn to crawl. I was there when she took her first steps, and I have been blessed to simply be part of her life. She calls me "Papa" now and smiles when she sees me, which melts my heart.

My daughter-in-law has said on many occasions that my granddaughter has healed other strained relationships. This tiny, wondrous human being has been a miracle child to me, and to others as well.

Earlier this year, my son's family grew again with the birth of our new grandson. My son recently purchased a home in our town, and not a week goes by that I don't see my grandchildren. For some, it's a pretty straight line from being a parent to becoming a grandparent. But for many people like me, there are twists and turns in the road. Somehow, against seemingly insurmountable odds, we have found our way—and it started with the birth of one precious granddaughter.

—David A. Grant—

# The First "I Love You"

> *The heart of a mother is a deep abyss at the bottom of which you will always find forgiveness.*
> ~Honoré de Balzac

I could describe in detail almost all the times when I've told my mother that I hate her. I would run out of fingers to count on before I would run out of stories. "She's insane," I would tell my friends, moving through the halls of my middle school.

"She just doesn't understand me," I complained to my high-school classmates.

"I can't wait to move out," I spat to her as I searched for cheap apartments after graduation. Anything to get away from her.

"Don't expect me to visit," I said, as I lugged my last overstuffed duffle bag to my car.

Oh, yes, I could tell you dozens of stories about my mother: the wicked witch who wanted nothing more than to control me. I could tell you about the dozens of times I screamed that I hated her. Every time I said those words, I truly believed that I did. I can also tell you about when I realized that wasn't true.

The genes were strong in my family; all of us women could have been carbon copies of each other. My mother gave me thick brown hair, thicker eyebrows and an attitude even fiercer than hers.

I remember her face when I drove away to my first apartment. She was watching me wearily, and I watched her watching me in my rearview mirror. Her arms were wrapped around her torso, pulling her sweater close around her body as if to warm her, although it was in the middle of July. She had her head tilted just enough to let me know she was watching, and I knew her well enough to know she wanted to say something. But I also knew her well enough to know that whatever she wanted to say would remain unsaid. I pulled out of the driveway of the home I had lived in for eighteen years and drove to my new apartment.

"You'll regret this, you know," my mother snapped at me when I informed her of my upcoming move. "This is way too expensive. You don't make enough money, and you're not ready."

"I don't care." I rolled my eyes. "I'd rather go broke in an empty apartment than live under your roof one moment longer."

Of course, she was right. One night, when my stomach was grumbling so loud I couldn't concentrate, when I was running off the last of my laptop battery, trying hard to figure out my online taxes before my laptop died, I found myself reaching for my cell phone, my fingers automatically dialing my home phone number. Through burning eyes, I completed the call and placed the phone to my ear. I choked back tears until I heard my mother's sleepy voice over my hoarse sobs.

"Miranda?" I heard her clear her throat and click on the light next to her bed. "Is that you? What's wrong? It's almost 11:00."

"Oh, Mom, I'm so sorry to bother you, but…" I gasped through my tears. "My computer is about to die, and I can't figure out this stupid tax website, and I'm so stressed out and confused and…"

"I'll be right there," she interrupted.

She disconnected our phone call, and she was at my door within a half-hour, clutching a bag of McDonald's in one hand and a steaming cup of coffee in the other. "I know you don't normally like McDonald's," she started, "but that's all that was open."

I gathered her in my arms, my beautiful sleepy mother, her short hair rumpled, a pillow mark still on her cheek.

"Thank you, Mom," I heard myself whisper. "I love you." Her body stiffened in my embrace, but soon relaxed before she pulled away.

"Let's get these taxes under control," she said. My mother raised an eyebrow at my living room, devoid of furniture, and cleared her throat again.

    We sat cross-legged on my living-room floor for three hours that night, eating double cheeseburgers and drinking far too much coffee for the middle of the night. My taxes were done in twenty minutes, but she stayed for hours. Our faces became streaked with tears of laughter until she finally left to go home, promising to be back with an old couch for me.

    "Thanks again, Mom," I said at the door. "I love you."

    "I know." She smiled at me with the same smile she gave me — with lips just slightly too big and teeth too far apart — a smile I'm proud to have.

— Miranda Lamb —

# The Strength of Forgiveness

*Forgiveness does not change the past,
but it does enlarge the future.*
~Paul Boese

My father was killed by a drunk driver when I was nine weeks old. At nineteen, Mom was a newlywed, a new mother and a widow. After several months of being consumed by grief, my mother decided to enroll in the local university. That's where she met Stephen. By the time I was three, they were married.

Although my mother and I were very close, Stephen was extremely hard on me. I never felt loved or accepted by him. At the end of my junior year of high school, he informed us he was quitting his job and opening a small business in a town 250 miles away. I felt as though the rug had been pulled out from under me. I was just about to start my senior year, and I wanted to graduate with the friends I had gone to school with since kindergarten. The day we moved, he literally dragged me kicking and screaming out of the house. I vowed that day I would never forgive him.

For the next ten years, it seemed like our family dissolved into nothing. My mother and stepfather got divorced and halfheartedly dated other people. After many years of loneliness, they started dating each other again. They began to attend church together, and they dedicated their lives and their relationship to God. After a year, they remarried. I was thankful I was 2,000 miles away so I didn't have to pretend to be happy for them. Just because my mother could forgive him didn't mean I could.

My mother tried to explain why she had allowed my stepdad back into her life. She told me why forgiveness is so important. "I didn't just forgive him for *him*," she said to me one day. "I forgave him for *me* because the unforgiveness was too much to bear." She explained how important it is to let go of resentment and live in love and forgiveness instead. I didn't listen.

In 2011, my mother was diagnosed with an extremely rare brain disease called corticobasal degeneration. It started with her losing her balance and progressed to her being confined to a wheelchair and living in a nursing home.

Mom had been in the nursing home for six months when I went to visit her. I didn't want to stay with my stepdad during my visit, but I couldn't afford an extended stay in a hotel, so I decided to put my feelings aside and make the best of it for my mother's sake.

I had planned on staying only two weeks, but when I witnessed how gravely ill she was, I promised her I'd stay until the end. The first few months with my stepfather were extremely uncomfortable. My resentment kept the wall up between us.

Every day when I visited Mom, she would ask me how my stepdad and I were getting along. I didn't want to disappoint her, so I made it sound like we were getting along better than we were. Many times over the next several months, Mom would ask me to reconsider forgiving my stepdad, as she had, but I ignored her.

Then my mother became extremely ill with a virus and was moved to a local hospice facility. Family flew in from all over to say their goodbyes. During one of my visits, Mom reached out and took my hand. Her voice was weak, but she spoke with strength when she told me it was time to let go and open my heart to my stepfather. "I want to leave this world knowing that you still have a parent you love and can rely on," she said.

She told me stories that illustrated how he had changed. He built the wheelchair ramp in front of their house so Mom could stay home a little longer. He helped her dress, bathe and get to doctors' appointments. He cooked and cared for her. And after she was admitted to the nursing home, he never missed a daily visit.

She told me that he encouraged her when she wanted to give up, comforted her when she was in pain, and showed her, as well as told her, how much he loved her every day. "This is the man I forgave and fell in love with again," she said. "The man you hate doesn't exist anymore."

When I walked in the door that night, he was sitting in the living room reading the Bible with his cat on his lap. In that moment, I saw the man my mother saw, and I realized she had been right all along. I was flooded with love for a man I had despised all my life. He looked up and saw that I had been crying. With a fearful look, he said, "Is your mom okay?" I told him she was sleeping comfortably when I left, and then the words I had kept locked up for years tumbled out of me.

I thanked him for taking such good care of my mother throughout her illness. I thanked him for allowing me to stay with him indefinitely so I could be with her. I told him I was sorry for all the years of distance and animosity. His eyes filled with tears as he apologized for the times he was cruel to me when I was a child, for moving me away from our home and friends, and for never being the father I needed. And he told me how much he loved my mother, how much he had always loved her, and how sorry he was for his part in the failure of their first marriage.

My mother didn't die that day. She's still in the nursing home. Every day is a struggle, but my dad (no longer "stepdad" in my eyes) and I work as a team to care for her. Now, I consider him to be one of my closest friends. I'm so thankful my mother didn't just tell me how important forgiveness is—she showed me. I feel as if I've shed a ton of bricks and lightened my soul. Proof that Mom really does know best.

— Kim Carney—

# 41

# At First Sight

*Anger makes you smaller, while forgiveness forces you
to grow beyond what you were.*
~Cherie Carter-Scott

It was hate at first sight. My fiancé Jake and I stood in his mother's dim kitchen. The scent of old coffee filled the air as my future mother-in-law looked me over.

She turned to her son and announced, "It's her or me."

I stepped back in surprise and looked at Jake.

He squared his shoulders, and a muscle twitched in his jaw. His face reflected the same stubborn look his mother wore.

Jake grabbed my arm and steered me toward the door. As we walked out, he called over his shoulder, "It's her."

Months of mother/son separation ensued. Even though they lived in adjoining towns, Jake and his mom refused to visit or even phone each other.

I'd heard the term "stubborn as a Missouri mule." Well, the mules could take a lesson from those two.

"Mom, why don't you and Jake make up?" Jake's sister asked.

"No. He chose that woman over me."

Jake's sister tried again. "Why don't you like her?"

Mom thought for a while. "I don't know," she admitted. "She just rubs me the wrong way."

After Jake and I married, visiting my in-laws during the holidays felt like torture. Jake's mom veered between ignoring me to icy politeness, but she showed genuine love for Patty, our four-year-old daughter from my first marriage.

My sister-in-law's twin girls were the same age as Patty. Mom showered them all with gifts, cookies, and love.

Still, no matter what I did, my mother-in-law liked me as much as a hernia.

If I bought her a present, it was the wrong color.

If I brought food, it was cooked incorrectly.

In the Great Cucumber Debacle of 1989, she disassembled my vegetable platter to slice the veggies thinner.

My bitterness and anger grew, leaving Jake stuck between two warring camps.

In the movies, a life-changing event transpires, and two adversaries lay aside their differences.

For me, it wasn't an action flick or spy-drama occurrence.

My life changed completely when I turned it over to the Lord. I told my husband, "From now on, I'm thanking God for all the blessings in my life. Even your mother."

Jake raised one eyebrow. "You're thankful for my mother?"

I hesitated for a moment, slowed by newfound honesty. "Well, I'm grateful she gave me a wonderful husband. That's a start."

I focused on gratitude each time I thought of my mother-in-law. Her influence had produced my husband's compassion, kindness, and thoughtfulness. Plus, I felt grateful that she accepted Patty as a beloved granddaughter.

Although it wasn't a dramatic movie-scene turnaround, a softening had begun in Mom's heart and mine. As the years passed, our once-prickly relationship grew into love.

Visits didn't seem like torture anymore. Mom and I would snuggle side by side on her plush living-room sofa. I'd wrap myself in a blanket and breathe in the scent of baking cookies. She, always warm, would rub my terminally cold hands with hers.

"Don't you ever get cold?" I asked.

She shook her head and smiled. "I've always been too warm. I used to stand barefoot in the snow to cool off."

One day as we sat together on her sofa, she took my hand and sandwiched it between both of hers. I waited for her usual, "Your hand is so cold."

Instead, she said, "I'm so glad you married my son. He couldn't have found a better wife."

I wrapped my arms around her, my heart overflowing with gratitude at her sweet words.

Life took a drastic turn when Mom went into the hospital for a cardiac ablation to correct her abnormal heart rhythm.

Instead of a routine procedure, she wound up with a nicked liver and a punctured heart. The surgical team worked frantically to save her. She lived, but she had gone without oxygen for far too long.

Despite therapy, she was plagued by physical issues and memory problems. She'd ask the same questions repeatedly. She, who'd always been so hot, couldn't get warm.

As time went on, her health declined.

She'd still touch my hand and say, "Oh, your hands are so cold." She'd cup my chilly hands in her icy ones and try to warm them, saying, "There, that's better, isn't it?"

"Absolutely, Mom. So much better."

In odd moments, she'd turn to me and say, "I'm so glad you married my son."

The night before she passed away, Mom and I spent some time alone in her dim hospital room.

She tossed and turned, restless and in pain. The beeping monitors and antiseptic smells added to her discomfort.

I held her hand and prayed quietly over her, then whispered, "I love you. Thanks for raising such a great husband for me."

She stopped thrashing and looked at me in a brief moment of clarity.

I leaned close as she squeezed my hand and murmured the last words she spoke to me.

"I'm glad you married my son."

"Me, too, Mom," I whispered. "Me, too."

The moment ended, and she began her agitated rocking again.

The next morning, Mom was gone. I was grateful she wasn't suffering anymore. Grateful for the years we'd spent as friends. Grateful for the husband she'd given me. Grateful for her impact on my life.

Yes, it was hate at first sight, but I'm so grateful it was love at last sight.

—Jeanie Jacobson—

# Tasting Forgiveness

*You are the one that possesses the keys to your being.
You carry the passport to your own happiness.*
~Diane von Furstenberg

I first met my stepmother on a sandy beach in Martha's Vineyard when I was sixteen years old. Really, we'd already met — actually many times before — as she'd been my dad's new wife for a few months by then. I just hadn't faced it until I stood next to her, in her bright orange bathing suit and wide-brimmed hat. It was looking at her flat stomach and my adolescent tummy that made it real. This was the stomach my father had chosen over mine. So for the month of August, I ate small pieces of salmon next to tiny trees of broccoli, drank lots of iced tea, and ran on the beach, sweat dappling my brown curls — a poor substitute for buried tears.

Prior to that summer, I'd always loved the Vineyard, where for one month my parents, sister, brother, and I vacationed. We left the busy confusing life of the New York City suburbs, where my father spent his life on the commuter train, my mother at her keyboard, and my older sister and brother in their field hockey, lacrosse, aftershave and lip gloss worlds. I carried a red rubber ball, played kickball for hours, and wondered what it would be like to have one of those families where everyone wasn't so smart and there wasn't any yelling.

On the Vineyard, my family was more like the one I imagined. My father wore sloppy shoes and khakis with buttery stains from corn on the cob. We rented an old home with dusty books on the bookshelves and stacks of poker chips as bookends. I learned to play poker with pennies we found at the bottom of my mother's purse and in my father's sock drawer. My parents played — my mother laughing at my father's jokes, and I'd catch a wisp of love between them. We played family tennis and I was allowed to rotate in, only knowing how to bounce the ball in front of me to serve. No one seemed to care, as competition was left behind, hidden in the towering trees of the suburbs. I was never scared at night, believing bad things didn't happen to children on vacation. And I'd awake to the smell of toasting bagels. It was okay to have sandy feet all the time and I learned to catch ocean waves, the salty thrill of creating your own ride.

But then it all changed — my parents divorced at a time when having a mom's house and a dad's house wasn't what everyone did. My brother and sister were away at college, so my mother, golden retriever, and I watched my father pack his belongings in big brown leather suitcases. I wondered if there was a way to keep it all secret, so my friends would never know. My father rented an apartment in the city that smelled like boiled potatoes with sparse kitchen counters that made it look like no one lived there.

Soon my Dad started wearing new pressed khaki pants and yellow Lacoste shirts. He introduced me to his new friend who had three children of her own. Then we were all standing around her kidney-shaped swimming pool watching them get married. My father kissed another woman as lamb barbecued on a fancy grill. We all blended together like polite cousins. At first, my stepmother was a distant aunt who introduced me to Bloomingdale's and taught me how to make a piecrust — kneading the dough until it was soft. But it wasn't until that first trip to the Vineyard that I realized she was there to stay. I buried my adolescent grief with every spoonful of food I turned away. I tried to learn the back and forth dance from my mom's house to my dad's house, but I tripped a lot.

After visiting my dad, I'd walk into our quiet new home, for just my mom and me. Instead of feeling the pain, I would feel the cold iron of our heavy black scale, sitting in judgment. I would pull my sweater and shirt off together over my head, my underwear tucked in my pants on the floor. I would put my watch on the bathroom counter. Then I'd pee, flush the toilet, and gingerly step onto the black rubber, lining my feet up perfectly. The numbers would spin high and then settle low, matching my slowing heartbeat. One more time, I would step off and on again for good luck. I would breathe and relax, my ritual completed for that afternoon. The soft yellow blanket I carried as a little girl had been replaced by the sound of the scale's heavy metal — tricking me into believing safety and security were wrapped in my thinness.

As a college freshman, I spent my time running through snowdrifts, reading French novels, eating cottage cheese, and chatting with my friends. But one day, the tone of our conversation changed as I sat pushing lettuce around my plate. You know — it doesn't have to be this hard, comforted my friend. I knew she was right, and I made my way to the counseling office, where a woman with sparkly eyes said, "Here, take a seat, do you want to talk?"

I started crying and my healing began. There were so many feelings buried under my baggie sweatshirt. At first I was so ashamed that I needed help — afraid of people thinking I was crazy. But I slowly learned to change my humiliation into humility. My therapist helped me talk about my feelings instead of swallowing them. One day, I put my scale in a brown garbage bag and threw it away in a nearby Dumpster. I learned to find nurturance in my relationships, wrapped by the security of friendships instead of harsh numbers on a scale. I always thought I needed to forgive the grown-ups in my life who had turned my world upside down. But it wasn't them I needed to forgive. Instead, it was me — the young girl with a small, soft stomach, who believed if I really had been good enough, thin enough, strong enough, I could have kept my parents together. It's amazing the lies we tell ourselves. Someday I'll go back to that beach just to be reminded of the salty, yet beautiful taste of forgiveness.

— Priscilla Dann-Courtney —

# Three Christmas Miracles

*Where there is great love, there are always miracles.*
~Willa Cather

I gazed into David's eyes as he squeezed my hand and mouthed the words, "It will be okay. I love you."

How? How could it be okay? Nurses and doctors swirled around us as I attempted to understand how the events of the day could have brought us here. In the frantic scramble to save my husband, bags of blood and drugs pumped their life-sustaining fluids through what looked like miles of tubes connected to his still body. I gave him a gentle kiss on his forehead as they wheeled him away and watched him disappear through the double doors for emergency surgery.

The surgeon said that even if he survived the night, I should not expect him to walk again. In a daze, I stumbled into the hospital chapel and dropped to my knees to pray for a miracle.

Six months earlier, we had stood together in our little Mennonite church, surrounded by friends and family as we exchanged our marriage vows. Many told us we were too young to get married, but young love often overrules common sense. So, at nineteen and twenty-one, we promised to love one another in sickness and health, not having any idea of how soon that vow would be challenged.

December 23, 1977. With only two days left until Christmas, David had spent the day taking full advantage of his dad's woodshop to build frames filled with wedding pictures as our holiday gift to family. Money was tight, and those handcrafted reminders of our recent "happy day" would be all we could offer our loved ones on Christmas morning.

At home, I finished up chores and waited for David to come. My family had chosen to celebrate Christmas a few days early on my dad's birthday — a double celebration before my sister's family took off for the holidays. A big dinner followed by gifts was what I expected for the evening, but as the clock ticked away the minutes, I paced back and forth in our little rental house. I was excited to spend time with my family, but anxious that David was so late. Where was he?

Finally, I gave in and dialed the phone number for my in-laws' home. It rang and rang. *Dave must be in the shop and can't hear it,* I thought. A few minutes later, I dialed again. After a few rings, a strange man's voice answered.

"May I speak to David, please?" I asked, wondering who this man was.

"No!" was the reply. *Click.* He hung up.

My hands were shaking as I dialed the number for the third time. The unknown man answered again.

"I must speak to David. I am his wife." The words were strong, but inside I was weak and scared.

After what seemed like forever, the man's response made my heart stop. "You must go to the emergency room at once! There has been an accident."

I don't remember how I ended up in the car with my dad. I must have called him to come and get me. I must have told the emergency-room clerk my name. They must have led me to David's side. But what I remember was that gurney taking him away and the hard chapel floor as I kneeled to plead with God to spare his life.

As family and friends arrived at the hospital, the story emerged gradually. A younger brother with emotional, drug-fueled anger. An older brother trying to set an example of how to walk the straight road — or else. A loaded rifle. A hard metal bullet. A moment and a choice that ended with my husband on the shop floor, blood spilling out his side. A tearful final exchange between brothers that resulted in words of forgiveness. An ambulance with medics rushing to stabilize the lifeless man. Police taking notes and shaking their heads as they led the brother away. A mother lying in a hospital bed, sedated and oblivious to the events of the evening, having suffered an emotional breakdown earlier that week from the stress of dealing with a cherished child under the spell of drugs. A tearful father unable to process what had just happened — his hands wringing, his heart breaking. A dying man, lying on the cold, hard concrete, surrounded by blood and encircled in white light. A peaceful voice whispering, "It's not your time."

We waited six long, agonizing hours. We were so tired as we slumped in the stiff waiting-room chairs, but no one slept. We just sat with dazed faces and blank stares. The surgeon finally returned. The bullet had torn a path side-to-side through David's mid-section, hitting the spine and grazing the spinal cord, shattering a rib, and blowing out a kidney along the way. He had severe blood loss and paralysis in his lower extremities. But he was alive. *Thank you, God!* We would handle the rest later. He was alive! That's what mattered.

It was now Christmas Eve. Just as the wise men brought three gifts to honor the birth of the Christ child, so God blessed us with three Christmas miracles that year. First was the miracle of forgiveness between David and his brother. Immediate. Powerful. Unexplainable and unconditional. The second was the miracle of life that baffled even the surgeon as David not only survived, but walked out of the hospital ten days later despite the severity of his injuries. The last was the miracle of giving, as our little church family blessed us with a monetary gift on Christmas morning to help ease the burden of hospital expenses.

It has now been forty years, but every year at Christmas, as we decorate the tree and wrap the presents together, I reflect back to that moment when the best gift was not wrapped in paper and bows. It was wrapped in the miracle of forgiveness, the joy of life and the power of love.

— Connie Nice —

# Just Let Them...

# No Shame in My Game

*Be who you are and say what you feel,
because those who mind don't matter
and those who matter don't mind.*
~Dr. Seuss

I looked in the mirror and nodded my head in approval. It was going to be a great day!

I'd recently been invited to help decorate for an upcoming women's retreat at a local church. Sylvia was on the planning committee and when she invited me to do some shopping for the event I eagerly accepted. It would be nice to get out of the house and I looked forward to getting to know this lady better. I wanted to make a good impression on my new "church friend" so I took extra care in my appearance. She arrived and I confidently greeted her at the door.

We agreed we would stop for lunch first, because shopping for tablescapes is serious business and you need your strength. Sylvia suggested Golden Corral, an all-you-can-eat buffet. We arrived and I headed straight for my favorite section — the salad! I loaded my plate with lettuce, cauliflower, and cucumbers.

As I reached for the salad dressing a man bumped into me. "Oh, I'm sorry. Excuse me," I said pleasantly. I hadn't moved so I knew it was he who had bumped into me. He was an older man and I thought that perhaps he'd stumbled. I felt a little sorry for him. I didn't want him to feel bad so I apologized first.

"I guess you just couldn't wait to get to the food, could you?" he answered curtly.

I was rather surprised by his tone but I just smiled and began to ladle on the ranch dressing.

"I mean, look at you," he continued. "Look how *big* you are."

"Just more of me to love," I answered, managing a nervous laugh.

Was this guy for real? As he continued his verbal lashing I had a flashback to a recent Friday night when my husband and I sat on the couch watching an episode of *What Would You Do?* The ABC show, hosted by 20/20 veteran John Quinones, features actors playing out shocking scenes in public and captures the responses of unsuspecting bystanders. We enjoyed the show but some of the scenarios seemed rather far-fetched to me. One such episode featured an actress playing an overweight woman at an all-you-can-eat buffet. The idea was that they would have another actor berate and humiliate her to see how the other patrons would respond. "That would never really happen," I told my husband. "Nobody is that mean." And I believed that statement one hundred percent.

Now here I was. Overweight. At an all-you-can-eat buffet. And I was being berated by a stranger who as far as I could tell was *not* an actor.

*Okay, John Quinones, you and your camera crew can come out now. This really isn't funny. And by the way, I no longer feel sorry for the old guy.*

John Quinones didn't appear and I stood frozen at the salad bar unsure of what to do next. I had ladled so much dressing onto my salad while contemplating my escape from this crazy old coot that I now had ranch soup. I decided to do what any grown forty-year-old woman who is being fat-shamed by a total stranger in public would do — make a run for it. I turned and took several steps away but the old man cut me off, blocking my path. He continued his tirade, his voice loud enough for everyone around us to hear.

"Look at you! You're *fat*!" He practically yelled it as he looked me up and down in a show of disgust. "I'm eighty-four years old and I have never looked like you."

I didn't know what to do or say. I looked down at myself, taking in the body he was so maliciously criticizing. A million thoughts ran through my head. Should I try to shame him by telling him that I had gained weight while suffering from depression after my daughter passed away? Should I try to explain that much of the weight gain had been a side effect of the anti-depressant medications I had been treated with after my loss? Would sharing something so personal quiet his rant? Would it matter to him that I hadn't always looked like this... that I had once been thin? And then it hit me... Did it matter to me?

Sure I had gained some weight, but I had gained something else along the way. I'd become much more compassionate toward other hurting hearts. I had found a sense of peace after surrendering my circumstance to God. I gained perspective and insight into the people and things that are truly important in life. I felt wiser, and I'd venture to say I was a better person than I'd ever been.

I had liked what I saw when I looked in the mirror that morning — a woman on her life's journey. I was finally feeling better after years of grieving my loss, and it felt good to feel good again. I would not allow this man, a complete stranger, to steal my joy.

"You're *fat*!" The old man said it again... in case the kitchen staff hadn't heard him the first time.

I noticed a woman take a step toward us. I looked up and was horrified. It was Sylvia! How embarrassing! She stopped and her mouth dropped open. I looked back and forth from the old man to my new friend as Sylvia's eyes and mouth grew wider with each hateful word the old man spewed at me.

Sylvia took a deep breath and I could tell she was about to say something. She looked mad, too. Good! My new friend was about to come to my rescue and I could tell she was about to let this crazy old bird have it! I waited... And then it came.

"That's not very Christian of you!" she blurted out as she stared the old man down.

I'm not sure what I was expecting her to say but I can assure you it wasn't that. The old man looked at her stunned. He was quiet for the first time in what seemed an eternity. He turned away and quickly disappeared into a far corner of the restaurant.

"Maybe he's senile and he didn't know what he was doing," Sylvia offered sympathetically as I sipped my ranch soup back at our table.

"No, I think he was just a jerk," I responded.

That evening I played the old man's words over and over again in my head. I knew exactly what had caused my weight gain, but what unseen "thing" would cause a person to verbally assault a complete stranger about her physical appearance? For the second time that day, I felt sorry for the old man. He was no more than a bully whose words said more about him than they did about me.

I was not about to let someone else dictate my self-worth, and as simple as it sounds, I let his words go. They weren't really mine to hold on to in the first place.

In the words of the fictional character, Aibileen Clark, in *The Help*: "You is kind. You is smart. You is important." And may I add, "You is beautiful."

— Melissa H.B. Bender —

# 45

# Worth the Effort

*Prayer is less about changing the world than it is about changing ourselves.*
~David Wolpe

No matter what I did, I couldn't please my mother-in-law. For the first years of my marriage, I tried everything. Every time she flew across the country for her two-week annual visit, I felt judged. My dinner was not as good as hers, my floor wasn't as clean as hers, and my parenting skills weren't in line with hers. It was as if her disapproval threw a heavy blanket over my spirit.

Part of the problem was my husband, the fourth child after three sisters. They called him "The Prince." That should have been my first clue. I would never be able to meet her expectations. Still, I tried. I scrubbed the floor and she complained I cared too much about the house being clean. I shopped for her favorite foods, but she grumbled that I pushed myself too hard for perfection. I whipped up dinner with her recipes, but she turned up her nose as she ate them. I prayed for her as I sat next to her in church, but she criticized the sermon for being too long. I kept my mouth shut but inwardly simmered.

Finally, I stopped trying. I cheered when my husband drove her to the airport after her visits. I admitted to myself that I didn't like my mother-in-law.

I kept praying for her, though. And then I felt like God said, "I want you to call your mother-in-law and ask her if she wants you to

Just Let Them... | 147

pray with her every week on the phone." That was ridiculous. But the idea wouldn't go away. I followed my heart and called her one Sunday morning. I thought she would laugh when I suggested we pray together on the phone.

But she didn't laugh. She said she'd love me to call every Sunday and pray. So, I did. I didn't know what to say, so I prayed the 23rd Psalm and inserted her first name, making it a personal prayer.

Her health declined and she couldn't come to visit. I continued praying with her on the phone, and the years sailed by. One Sunday after our prayer, she said, "That was great! I love you so much!" I pulled my iPhone away from my ear and stared at it. My voice wouldn't work. I barely recovered and murmured, "Thank you! I love you, too," and hung up.

Soon after, she became bedridden and moved in with her daughter, who was a nurse. A year later, she required full-time nursing care. Through it all, I kept the Sunday prayer calls coming. Her daughter eventually told me, "Mumma looks forward to your weekly calls. It changes her whole countenance and makes her day so much better."

Two years later, my mother-in-law died. Psalm 23 was read at her funeral. I was eternally grateful that I had managed to swallow my anger and humble myself to call and pray with my mother-in-law years before. It changed both of us — for the better.

—Suzy Ryan—

# Changing More than Diapers

*Follow your heart, listen to your inner voice, stop caring about what others think.*
~Roy T. Bennett, The Light in the Heart

The obituary in the alumni newsletter caught my eye. I was surprised to see one of my long-ago college instructors, Professor B., had passed away. I had neither seen nor thought about him for more than ten years. His photo brought back memories, none of them good.

My friend Nancy and I were in Professor B.'s engineering materials lab class in college back in the early 1980s. We were the only two young women in a class full of young men. I recalled the day when Professor B. was describing and showing new types of materials. As we passed around a new material that was designed to be highly absorbent for use in a disposable diaper, Nancy treated it like a hot potato, teasing that she didn't want anything to do with diapers! Professor B. let her have it. "Better get used to it, young lady," he'd proclaimed. "In ten years, you won't be working as an engineer. You'll be home raising children and changing diapers, as you should be."

The room fell silent. We were all stunned. Nancy had earned the respect of everyone in the class for her abilities, and none of us thought she should be spoken to that way. We all knew she would make a fine engineer, and if she chose to be a mother, she would

Just Let Them... | 149

make a fine mother, too. Although those harsh words were directed at Nancy, I knew they were meant for me as well. The young men in the class spoke up for Nancy with heartwarming support. Along with our fellow students, Nancy and I finished the semester, completing Professor B.'s class.

Just over ten years later, Professor B. was dead. At that time, Nancy was an engineering manager at a regional power company. I was working on my Ph.D. in biomedical engineering at a different university. Neither Nancy nor I had children, and we both had promising engineering careers. Professor B. had been wrong! His obituary said that he had two daughters; I wondered what kind of opportunities they'd had in life with him around to discourage them.

Twenty more years went by. I learned that Nancy had followed her passion, earning her master's degree and becoming a green/sustainable-energy consultant. I became a mathematics and engineering professor at a women's college. My job involved teaching and demonstrating engineering concepts to future teachers. The engineering class was hands-on, designed to enable future teachers to experience and master engineering concepts so they could, in turn, teach them to children.

I was hired midyear and worked hard to learn the material just ahead of the students. It didn't take long for me to realize that this was a required course for education majors, and many of them were only there because they had to be. Many were intimidated by math and engineering concepts. Some students even told me that they chose to teach kindergarten so they wouldn't have to learn math! But part of the goal of the course was to get future teachers excited about math and engineering, so they in turn could pass this excitement on to their students.

My weekend class included many women in their thirties who were raising families. Some were already teaching informally and had gone back to school to earn a teaching degree. At the beginning of the semester, they arrived with their course materials and serious looks of doubt. Part of my job was to help change their attitudes.

As the semester progressed, I watched my students discover, piece by piece, that they could master engineering concepts. They had each purchased a set of pink tools for the course. They learned about and built circuits, magnets, mechanisms (including levers and linkages, gears, and pulleys), trusses, and plumbing systems. During each unit, the students worked in teams to put together the concepts they'd learned to design and build functional engineering projects. At an open house to show off their work, they taught what they had learned to their fellow students and visitors. This classroom full of women — mothers who had changed many a diaper — wowed each other and their audience by demonstrating their engineering knowledge. Even Professor B. would have been impressed by their final projects!

As I watched these women discover their own power, I saw them take what they'd learned and apply it in real life. One woman began using her pink tools to fix things around the house, something she'd never done before. She confided that she was proud of her pink tools — and glad her husband didn't borrow them! While I'd initially thought to myself that the pink tools were kind of silly, I now understood their appeal.

A woman in my math class, after learning about compound interest and how to use the mortgage calculator on a credit-union website, refinanced her house and used the money she saved to run for the state senate. That's empowering!

When I look back over the past thirty years, I'm proud of how far we've come since Professor B.'s class. Perhaps Professor B. was a product of his generation. As products of our generation, Nancy and I followed our dreams. In turn, I was excited to pass on my math and engineering knowledge to my students, who followed their dreams to become teachers of another new generation.

My students taught me something, too. When they researched women inventors, they discovered that a mother named Marion Donovan had invented the disposable diaper to reduce her laundry load! By necessity, she became the "mother" of several related inventions, and she held several patents. In an aha moment, I thought, *We should have known that disposable diapers were invented by a woman. The joke has been on Professor B. all along!*

—Jenny Pavlovic—

# 47

# Grab Bag

> *I firmly believe that respect is a lot more important, and a lot greater, than popularity.*
> ~Julius Erving

Standing at her bedside, the doctor asked my seventeen-year-old daughter, "Piper, do you like school?" His crossed arms revealed his agenda to discredit her physical complaints and discharge her from the hospital. It wasn't our first experience with this line of questioning.

I knew what he was implying, and as her mom I ached to jump into the conversation to protect her, but I needed Piper to answer for herself. After all, I wouldn't be able to safeguard her from such accusations all her life. I waited for her reply. *Don't raise your voice,* I thought, *or he'll accuse you of defiance. Don't falter, or you'll appear unsteady, anxious. Don't cry, or he'll label you depressed. And, most importantly, don't give him approval through silence.*

She made eye contact with the man in the lab coat looming over her, and she said, "Of course I like school. I take advanced placement classes at a private school to challenge myself, so I can get into a top university after I graduate."

*That's my girl,* I thought. *Nice defense.*

But the doctor refused to back down. "Do you find yourself missing a lot of classes?"

"Are you kidding?" she said. "In AP classes, missing one day is like missing a week. I've only missed two days this entire school year."

I hate to fall behind." She looked at me, and I smiled because she remained self-assured.

She could've told him how she darted from classes throughout the day to vomit in the restroom and then quietly returned to her desk as if nothing had happened. Or she could've mentioned that before the first bell, while her friends chatted about last evening's events, she marched to the nurse's office to give herself a heparin shot in the stomach. And that during lunch, she returned to the nurse to swallow one of the many handfuls of pills she had to choke down each day that enabled her to attend school in the first place. But she knew better than to provide him ammunition. The more facts she reported to the man in white, the increased likelihood of being labeled a malingerer, a faker. She had learned to say as little as possible.

"Maybe it's just your monthly visitor," he blurted.

Stunned, I looked Piper in the eyes and saw a flicker of temporary confusion turn to disbelief.

Obviously, he thought her weak, unable to handle pain.

If only he'd witnessed Piper's disappointment when she couldn't pass the ROTC physical. How bravery and courage fueled her desire to defend our nation, but migraines, seizures, joint pain, numbness and tingling in her arms and legs, blurred vision, dizziness, shortness of breath, chronic fatigue, memory loss, and vertigo dashed any hope of donning a military uniform. Denied a future as an Army warrior, she still possessed a warrior's spirit.

I stepped in to teach my daughter yet another lesson in handling misogyny.

"Do you really think she'd go to the ER for her period? You realize she was transported here by ambulance from another hospital, right? If it were her menstrual period, the other hospital would've laughed at her and sent her home. They thought her condition severe enough to admit her here."

I waited for our punishment. How dare I question a doctor? A male doctor at that.

"Well, they were wrong. She can go home."

I flinched. "Does she get the courtesy of a proper diagnosis?"

"I think it's a flu bug," he muttered.

"She's been vomiting for months. Does the flu last that long?"

I braced myself, knowing I'd crossed a bigger line by challenging his diagnosis. But what did we have to lose?

He shook his head.

"Could you at least palpate her abdomen to see where the pain is coming from? Like I said, this has been going on for months."

He glared at me. "That won't be necessary. She can get dressed and go home."

He handed her an eviction notice.

I turned toward Piper, who was on the verge of tears, and gave her the don't-give-him-the-satisfaction-of-crying look.

And home we went: a place devoid of judgment, sarcasm, eye rolling, and degradation.

Knowing that she had a chronic disease and would have more encounters with indifferent medical doctors in months to come, Piper and I developed a plan.

"Can we just get up and leave when they're so rude?" she asked.

That thought had never occurred to me, being raised by parents and grandparents who held doctors in high esteem. With this question, I realized she did not believe that doctors were almighty and all-knowing. Why not leave? As paying customers, weren't we entitled to respect? Why would I continue to allow healthcare professionals to belittle, chastise, or question my daughter's character? Or to infer she faked an illness when she suffered every day, all day?

We devised ground rules: We would no longer entertain their talk of a school phobia, hints of gender weakness, accusations of malingering or faking, or the labeling of a mental health diagnosis without sufficient cause. The most important rule: We wouldn't be rude or disrespectful in return. We would uphold our dignity.

"I'll follow your lead," I suggested. "It's your appointment, so I want you to call it when you feel the doctor crosses a line. Your line may be different from mine."

"Let the games begin," she said.

First up, a visit to a gastroenterologist for her continued nausea and vomiting.

"It could just be related to ovulation or, perhaps, anxiety." Wow. A double whammy.

I watched for a signal. Piper reached over, grabbed her school bag and stood.

The doctor's eyes widened.

"Thank you for your time," she said. "Mom, are you ready?"

I followed her lead and plucked my purse from the ground. "The only anxiety she has is when a doctor doesn't take her pain seriously. And I don't think she's been ovulating every day for months. But thank you."

As the doctor tried to process our boldness, we walked away with confidence in our decision. We no longer rewarded disrespect. We no longer paid for incompetence. We no longer argued against an archaic establishment that continued to blame the chronically ill who sought help in hopes of alleviating their pain and suffering.

Next up, an allergist. "So, you've had Lymes disease in the past?"

*Ouch*, I thought, and waited for Piper's decision. She grabbed her bag, signaling the end of the appointment. "It's Lyme disease. Not Lymes. If you don't know how to say it, I don't know that you can treat it. Besides, there's no cure, so I still have it."

The doctor straightened and looked at me for a second opinion, and I nodded. Piper and I high-fived all the way to the car.

We now treat the first doctor's visit as an interview, deciding if the physician's views and knowledge of Lyme disease are compatible with Piper's needs. Based on the interview, we either hire or we fire. Our treatment for curing a doctor's arrogance and rudeness? We grab our bags and take our dollars elsewhere.

— Cathi LaMarche —

# The Empty Room

*Even on the weakest days I get a little bit stronger.*
~Sara Evans

I peeked through the front window, saw his familiar face and wondered when he'd become a stranger. He continued up the walk, past the river birch trees, and knocked on the door.

"I'm here for the furniture," he said, with defeat in his soft brown eyes. I glanced toward the pickup truck in the driveway. His buddy Richard gave an awkward half wave.

"Yeah. Uh… hi." I stroked my half-combed hair and pushed it behind my ear. I wondered if he missed me.

He stepped inside our former dream house — a refuge we'd designed and built shortly after the birth of our youngest, now in kindergarten.

"I'd like to take this stuff… this room of stuff." He motioned straight ahead toward the living room. "I think it'll fit into my new place."

"Yeah… Okay." I looked around slowly. "All of it?"

"Well, I need something to sit on. I need stuff. I have to live too, you know."

"Yeah, of course. That's fine."

As always with him, it happened fast. Out went the leather couch, the two chairs and the unusual coffee table shaped like a painter's palette that I had picked out a few years ago. He took the lamps, the books, the plants and the art off the wall. The last piece to go was a small Shona sculpture with a family of figures carved out of serpentine. It had been a Mother's Day gift.

After a few trips, the room was bare, except for a large area rug that stretched from one end to the other.

"I guess that's it for now," he said, wiping sweat from his forehead. "We can figure out the rest later."

I nodded and shut the door behind him. The unexpected echo sounded like ten doors closing.

With the kids at Grandma's, the house was strangely quiet. I stared at the empty room for a long while, thinking I should vacuum and maybe move a few things from other rooms in there. I thought about the decorating magazines lined up neatly in rows at the store. It was only two o'clock. I could pick up a magazine and maybe stop at a furniture outlet on the way home. Instead, I walked upstairs and slipped into my bed, pulling the covers over my head.

The next morning, the sun streamed through the window and woke me. I still wore my yellow sweatshirt and ragged jeans with the hole in the knee.

I went downstairs and looked into the belly of my house. It was empty.

I needed to escape the emptiness for a while, so I started searching for distractions. First came the older guy, with the boyish grin, looking for a wife. At least that's what he implied on the way to the restaurant. By dessert, I learned his youngest would be heading to college soon, leaving an empty nest behind. Then came the busy investor, who dated to fill the space between days with his kids. And then the young divorcé, who still parked on the far left of his garage as if she'd be home soon.

I learned fairly quickly that dating wasn't going to do the trick. My focus shifted to other things, like my fledgling communications business.

One Saturday, I stumbled into the self-help aisle at Barnes & Noble; I would be a frequent visitor for the next six months. I dug out my old running shoes and took myself to the gym a few times a week. I started to hit tennis balls against my garage, began writing again and signed up for sailing lessons. Eventually, I learned how to go solo to the neighbors' cookouts.

One Sunday, my kids and I volunteered to serve dinner to the homeless across town. Later that spring, we planted a garden in front of a women's shelter.

During all this time, the empty room remained untouched.

One summer evening when my kids were with their dad, I turned on some music, thinking I would hear it in the kitchen. Instead, the song called to me from the empty room's built-in speakers.

I tiptoed in and sat on the edge of the rug. Soon, I drifted toward the middle of the room. I lay down, closed my eyes and spread my arms open. I surrendered to the song, "The Prayer" by Andrea Bocelli. He sang, *When we lose our way, Lead us to a place, Guide us with your grace, To a place where we'll be safe.*

The next day, I put my dinner on a wicker tray and met Bocelli in the empty room for a picnic.

The rug was surprisingly comfortable. I settled in and looked around. With everything stripped away, I was able to see the simple lines of the room, the high ceiling and tall windows. I glanced westward and noticed something in the far distance. I blinked and shook my head.

*Is that a view of the lake? How did I miss that?*

I couldn't help but giggle.

The sun inched toward the horizon, painting bright orange and pink streaks across the sky that seemed to dance across the top of the water. I felt myself drawn toward the sun like the day lilies in my garden.

There on the floor in the empty room, I ate and watched the stunning show of color. It was a brilliant celebration. Soon, the last speck of orange gave way to nightfall.

As the moon gently lit the room, I realized that sometimes emptiness is just a wide, open space. Space to breathe. And maybe a little space is exactly what I needed… to find myself.

About a year later, we moved from that house. I never did furnish the empty room. I had grown to appreciate it exactly as it was.

—Mindi Susman Ellis—

# Can't Is a Four-Letter Word

*Never give up on what you really want to do.
The person with big dreams is more powerful
than the one with all the facts.*
~H. Jackson Brown, Jr.

After twenty years of marriage, I suddenly found myself a divorced mother of two with a mortgage and a car payment. At the time, I was a waitress in a small, family-owned business. My husband had informed me that he'd never really wanted children, that they were my idea, and that he was leaving.

I had never dreamed that I would end up divorced. The biggest surprise after my divorce was the reaction of my church family. I had truly expected that the very people who had stood next to me singing, "I love you with the love of the Lord," would stand by me. Unfortunately, they did not. To them, divorce was an unpardonable sin. When I had stated that no one hated divorce more than I did, I was told that if I'd truly hated it, I wouldn't be getting divorced, as if I could somehow have stopped it. I'd never felt more alone in my life, but I forgave their ignorance.

I loved my children, and I did whatever it took to provide for them. I worked as many as three jobs, with little to no child support. One Easter week, I worked so many hours that I ended up in the hospital from exhaustion.

Not once did a bill go unpaid. Not once did my children go without anything they needed. The concept of failure was not in my vocabulary. To me, "can't" was a four-letter word.

A regular breakfast customer at my restaurant suggested that I apply for a job at the post office. They were hiring temporary help. What did I have to lose? I went to the human-resources department at our local post office and asked to apply. She told me they weren't hiring. When I told my friend the next day, he told me to go back, so I did. Again, I was told that they weren't hiring. A week later, I went back again. This time, she took my application.

I was hired for a temporary position as a "Casual," making $7.00 an hour and working an average of 59.5 hours a week. I was only allowed to work six months out of a calendar year in any given position. It seemed ridiculous to give up my waitress jobs for a temporary position, but I knew in my heart that it was the right thing to do. I worked harder than I'd ever worked in my life. I worked six months as a carrier in every kind of weather. Then I worked six months inside as a clerk. There was no promise of a career position, but I believed I would get one.

It was difficult managing work and the kids' sports schedules. I hated missing soccer and volleyball games. The hardest thing was when I missed my son's eighth-grade graduation. It was in the afternoon, and I couldn't get off work. Believe me, I tried.

After a couple of years, I began to ask how I could get a permanent position. I was told who to talk to at the main office, and I made an appointment. I sat in his office explaining why I was there, and he listened politely. When I was finished, he laughed and said, "I'm sorry, but Casuals don't get hired for career positions." Something happened to me at that point. I became more determined than ever to prove him wrong.

Shortly after my visit to the main office, it was announced in the local paper that tests were going to be given in our city for career positions at the post office. This was my chance to get a real job. I went to a bookstore and ordered the practice test manual for clerk/

carrier positions. For the next six weeks, I took timed practice tests every spare second I had. I even took a memorization class offered at a local venue. I wasn't about to give up.

The day finally came for the tests, and hundreds of people showed up to take them. It was now or never. After the tests, we had to wait for what felt like an eternity to learn our score. When mine came in the mail, I was afraid to open it. I'd gotten a 91.5... success.

After I'd gotten my uniforms and completed my ninety-day probationary period, the man who told me I'd never get a career position came into our office. When he saw me casing mail, he stopped and said, "Well, I'll be. You actually did it."

I just smiled and said, "'Can't' isn't in my vocabulary. Never tell a woman she can't do something."

Last year, I retired from the postal service after a twenty-two-year career as a letter carrier. My children are both married, and I have five beautiful grandsons. My children saw me refuse to give up and I believe it made them who they are today. And the friend who suggested I apply at the post office? We're married and enjoying retired life together. Nothing can stop us when we refuse to give up on ourselves.

— Brenda Beattie —

# 50

# The View from the Back Seat

*If you surrender completely to the moments as they pass, you live more richly those moments.*
*~Anne Morrow Lindbergh*

The back seat is not a place I ever sought out — literally or figuratively. I loved being behind the wheel, enjoying the adrenaline rush while navigating unpredictable traffic. I was a control junkie in all the other areas of my life, too — the take-charge person who could sort out a situation and make things happen.

But that all changed abruptly when the career I loved ended with no notice. My world turned upside down. No longer did I oversee any people or projects. I was shattered.

When two part-time jobs came my way some months later, I was ready to take them on. One required some travel, including two road trips with co-workers. Each time we spent as much time in the car as we did at the events. While preparing for the trips, we talked about who would drive. It turns out that all three of us preferred to drive. Being the newest to the team, I felt it was expected of me to step back.

This was a new experience for me. Sounding more confident than I felt, I said I would leave the driving to them and sit in the back seat. Surprisingly, I found contentment there, as well as a new direction.

Not driving reinforced the fact that I was not in control. I did not have to focus on directions, road conditions, traffic, or timing. I set up the entire back seat as my little kingdom (perhaps using that word "kingdom" means I still needed a bit of control). I had my thermal bag with my drinks, a book, my phone and charger, a blanket, sweater and assorted sundries.

Now I found myself in the position of a learner. I listened to the conversation in the front seat and picked up subtleties I might have missed if I had been driving. I wasn't idle in the back seat. Instead, I was asking questions, seeking clarification, and learning to use new tools and get to know my traveling companions. By the time of the second trip, I was looking forward to riding in the back.

As I journeyed, I found that these trips gave me a framework for the next phase of my life. Most of my years of work had focused on creating, developing and leading various aspects of ministry and teams. I enjoyed that and found it was a good fit for my gifts, passions, and that stage of life.

My other part-time job did not require travel, but it placed me in a subordinate role to my co-workers. All but one were significantly younger than me. Many were on track for future promotions and career growth. Not me. My responsibility was to copy, scan, index, confirm appointments, make transactions, and assemble mailings. But it was good. I learned I no longer wanted or needed to prove myself. I was content to do what I could to help my colleagues shine.

And changes were taking place in other areas besides in my employment. My marriage improved when I let go of the need to control or always be in charge. A weight came off my shoulders. I'm not saying I never try to step into the position of leader; long ingrained habits change slowly, but I'm working on them.

I learned that the view from the back seat is beautiful. I am more aware of others and situations around me. I am not anxious to change that any time soon. If someone had told me years ago that I would find joy and fulfillment by stepping back I would have scoffed. Now, after a few years as a supporting player, I find it refreshing.

—Joan M. Borton—

# The Curvy Sister

*To be beautiful means to be yourself. You don't need to be accepted by others. You need to accept yourself.*
~Thich Nhat Hanh

I was born the third of nine children, but growing up, people always assumed I was the oldest. I was taller than one older sister and more filled out than the other. It was a source of pride for me in some regards. I could hit a softball farther, run faster, and raid Mom's closet at an earlier age. My size threw our family pecking order out the window, as my older sisters viewed me as their equal instead of a pesky little sister. I felt more than just confident about the way I looked; I felt unique and special, and I never gave my size or shape much thought. I was just happy to be me.

That changed one fall afternoon when I was thirteen. I was hanging out with one of my best friends, a boy my age who had yet to hit his growth spurt. He was shorter than me, pencil thin, and really funny. We hung out whenever we could and talked about everything under the sun. Maybe that's why he thought it was okay to say something that changed how I saw myself for years to come.

We sat in my back yard, under the shade of a massive oak tree. It was one of those completely ordinary afternoons. I found a small stick in the grass and slowly peeled the bark away with my fingernail while we talked about things like school and homework. Then I glanced up to find him looking at me with a rather cryptic smile on his face. I knew this expression all too well — it usually meant he had something he really wanted to tell me. I expected he had a juicy bit of gossip to share, or maybe one of his funny stories, but I never expected what actually came out of his mouth.

"You won't believe what my mom said last night," he said, watching me out of the corner of his eye. I didn't find this strange at first. He was always fighting with his mom about something. But then he said, "Oh, no. Never mind. I can't tell you."

Something in his voice got my attention. I suddenly had the feeling that whatever his mom said was about me. I wasn't particularly worried though, because she and I had always liked each other. I sat up a little straighter and looked at him. "Oh, come on," I said. "You can't say something like that and then not tell me."

He squirmed uncomfortably and shook his head. "No, I can't tell you." A nervous shiver ran through me. I had the sense that maybe she said something not-so-nice about me. But there was no going back now. I had to know.

"Oh, come on." I punched his shoulder. "Just tell me."

"Okay. She said…" he paused for a dramatic, deep breath. "She said you have a chunky butt and chunky legs."

For a moment or two, I just sat there, staring stupidly at the nervous smile on his face. A thousand thoughts raced through my mind: *How could she say that? Did she, someone I had always trusted, really think that or was he making this up? Why would he say something like this to me? Did he think it was funny? Did he think it was true?* And worst of all: *Was she right? Was there something wrong with the way my body looked?*

I imagine my face went white, then red. My throat felt tight with tears, but I refused to cry in front of him. By the time I staggered to my feet and began speed walking to the back door, my friend knew he had made a terrible mistake. He hurried to catch up. "Wait! Where are you going?" he asked.

I shoved him away and said, "I'm going inside."

He jumped in front of me and said, "Are you mad?"

Was I mad? Obviously. "What is wrong with you?" I finally yelled. "Why would you say that to me?"

I ran into my house, slammed the door, and hurried to my room.

I barely made it there before the tears came. I no longer felt unique and special, or proud to be me. I felt ugly and broken.

Later that night, in a rare display of teenage wisdom, I opened up to my parents about what happened. When I got to the "chunky butt and chunky legs" part, I wanted to curl up and disappear. I could barely get the words past my lips. But I forced them out, unable to look at my parents as I finished recounting what happened. I stared at the brown living room carpet instead, holding my breath and waiting for one of two things. Either they would tell me she was right or they would become indignant and angry and tell me she was wrong.

But my dad did neither. He simply said, "What do you think? Do you think she's right?"

This surprised me, but I mulled it over. My jeans were a size 6. No matter how I felt about my body, I couldn't call a size 6 "fat." I said to Dad, "No. I don't think she's right."

Dad sat back. "Then that's all that matters."

I left the room not quite convinced that Dad was right about this. It seemed too simple a solution. For many years to come, that afternoon stuck with me. As much as I wanted to be happy with my body, I couldn't fully take Dad's advice. Instead, I tried to make peace through diets, exercise, and creative clothing choices.

It's taken me nearly thirty years to realize Dad knew what he was talking about after all.

I am now twice the size I was that day, but I'm happy to be me again. I see my curves as a sign that I'm healthy and strong, and I wouldn't want to be anyone else. And I've learned a valuable lesson along the way: In a world of impossible ideals and a thousand different definitions for what makes a person attractive, there is only one opinion that really matters. Mine.

And I think I am beautiful.

— Debra Mayhew —

# Chapter 7

# Accept that Parents Are Not Perfect

# The Ritual

*Forgiveness is the cleansing fire that burns
away old regrets and resentments.*
~Jonathan Lockwood Huie

The phone rang at 10 p.m. "Is this Diane Caldwell?" an unfamiliar voice asked. I knew this was it. My eyes focused on the weave of the tapestry hanging on the wall by the phone. Noticing for the very first time the way disparate threads of red and blue and black interwove to create the scene.

"Your mother died of liver failure at 9 p.m. She died peacefully."

A wail pierced the silence. What a sound, I thought, and then I realized the sound came from me.

My mother had ruled our home as the Ice Queen. She had only to raise one eyebrow and I froze in fear. There was never a kind word or a gesture of affection from her. In fact, the only words I heard from her some days were: "Be a good girl, Diane," spoken in a tight-lipped snarl.

While other children ran about laughing, I sat in silence, my hands folded in my lap, afraid to do anything. "Be a good girl" became like a mantra. No matter what I did or where I was, I heard it in my head.

"Would you like a cookie, Diane?" Aunt Anne would ask.

"No thank you," I would say, fearing that to accept might be "bad."

For my first fourteen years, I lived as a "good girl," fearing and hating my mother.

And then I rebelled.

I ran away from home at sixteen. Ran off to New York. Panhandled on the dirty, gray streets of New York's Greenwich Village. Hanging out with the weird and alternative. My every act subconsciously calculated in defiance of my mother.

On a rare visit to my mother in her Delray Beach home, she looked at me out of the corners of her eyes.

"I was watching an Oprah show the other day…" her voice trailed off.

I glanced up from the book I was reading.

Mother's eyes turned from mine and studied her long, perfectly manicured fingernails. "It was about something called emotional abuse…."

Again she stopped, ran her thumb over each of her nails in sequence, cleared her throat just slightly.

"Diane," she began in her nasal Philadelphia accent. "Diane… Diane, did I ever say 'I love you' to you?" The last words came out in a breathy explosion, almost a hiss.

Silence. The only sound in the room was the quiet hum of central air conditioning.

"No," I said, holding my breath, waiting for the words I'd never heard my entire life.

The garbage truck rumbled past the edge of the complex. Trash tumbled from containers by the road. Silence hung in the room. Gears engaged and the garbage truck pulled away.

My mother rose like a ghost and walked away.

\*\*\*

Now she was dead and it was too late for us. But not too late for me to try and do whatever was possible to heal the wounds that continued to fester and poison every act of my life.

I knew I had to do something. The "Ritual" was created as an act of healing.

I assembled three of my best friends. Three friends who had also lost their mothers.

I laid the table with salty, sweet, sour and bitter foods: a good cheddar cheese, fresh baked banana bread, sliced lemons, and sliced radishes. Photos of Mom ranging in time from her young adult years to her wedding photo to our family holiday pictures lay in an arrangement at the top of the table.

We munched on the cheese.

Once my parents had a Halloween party. My cousin Shirley won the contest for dressing as a pregnant bride. My mother was roaring with laughter, but I didn't understand what was funny about it at the time. Then my mother invited everyone down into the rec room and they played "pass the orange." People had to pass an orange from under their chin to the next person, and they were arranged man, woman, man, woman. I remember sitting on the stairs watching—amazed. I had never seen my mother act like that before."

We tasted the banana bread.

"At rare moments she could laugh like a little girl," I said. "Every now and then, when I was really young, she'd let me into the bed with her on a Sunday morning and we'd play this silly game called "skinny bones," and we'd tickle each other and she'd laugh like she was no older than me."

The lemons were passed around the table.

"Oh God," I said. "My poor mother. She was the unwanted child of immigrants—born nine years after what her parents thought was their last child. I once heard her talking to her sister about how she had been called 'the accident' and left in bedrooms with tossed overcoats while her parents played cards with neighbors."

"Once she told me that she'd stuck peas up her nose at the dinner table trying to get some attention, but then nobody could get them out. They had to take her to the hospital and her mother didn't speak to her for weeks after that."

Only the radishes remained. We picked up slices and chewed.

"She wore her next oldest sister's hand-me-downs. They were nine years out of style, and way too short. Her sister was really short and Mom was tall. And she wore glasses and used to be called out of class for having head lice. I think she lived in constant shame."

Tears flooded my eyes.

"She never knew love. How was she supposed to give it? She embraced her fancy dresses and material possessions as if they were life rafts saving her from waves of scorn. Each new outfit was a step up out of a childhood in which she suffered daily shame and humiliation. My poor mother," I shared.

When the "ritual" was over, my friends hugged and kissed me and walked out the front door. As soon as the door closed, I broke down and wept uncontrollably — each sob a letting go of the hurt and hatred I had carried all my life. Beneath the hate was pain. Beneath the pain was fear. I let it all go until I felt something shift inside. I was suddenly lighter.

My childhood wasn't so bad, I thought. Mother did her best. I never knew what it was to be looked down upon for my old tattered clothes. She worked hard to provide me with everything possible that a little girl could want.

"I forgive you," I whispered to my departed mother. "I love you," I said out loud, saying the words I had longed to hear my entire life and releasing myself from the hardness that had imprisoned my heart like a metal cage. It's too bad it took death for me to finally let go. But it did.

— Diane Caldwell —

# Thoughts on Love and Forgiveness

*Forgiveness is the key that can unshackle us
from a past that will not rest in the
grave of things over and done with.
~Lewis B. Smedes*

In May of 2001, I received one of those dreaded phone calls no one wants to receive. My brother, Mike, called to tell me our dad was seriously ill and not expected to live. I was quite surprised by my feelings, because my dad and I hadn't exactly had the ideal father-daughter relationship. In fact, we hadn't kept in touch for years for various reasons, mostly because he had divorced my mother when I was around ten years old. He moved to another state and didn't seem to have much time for my brother and me. He missed our graduations, forgot birthdays and broke promises.

One Christmas, when I was about twelve years old, I truly believed he was going to "come to his senses" and come home to us. I sat for hours in our living room, facing the front door, listening to Bing Crosby croon "I'll Be Home for Christmas." I played that record so many times, I almost wore it out. I just knew that he would burst through the door any minute, loaded down with gifts for all of us, and ask for forgiveness. It was a scene I played repeatedly in my wistful daydreams. I made sure the porch light was on, so Dad could find our house. Of course, it never happened.

Even after becoming an adult, I still held onto some deep-seated sadness. I guess the little girl's pain inside me would never go completely away. But, I realized divorce is never just one person's fault and I began to feel differently about my dad. I wanted to have him in my life again.

I'll never forget watching a movie on TV entitled, *Max Dugan Returns*. It was about a grown woman's father returning to her life after years of separation, bringing outrageously expensive gifts, trying to make up for everything. The film had a profound effect on me. I wrote to my dad shortly after seeing it and it was the beginning of a slow road back to getting to know each other. Our letters, phone calls, and occasional visits were few and far between and usually only initiated by me.

As the years went by, I told myself I had forgiven him for everything, but I came to realize I hadn't completely done so. That happened after the time I went to Iowa to see him while he was in the ICU.

As he lay in the hospital bed, I held his hand and marveled at the softness of his skin. His hand was not the firm, muscular one I remembered grasping as a young girl. I felt tears roll down my cheeks as the emotions welled up inside me. I began to feel a love for him I hadn't allowed myself to feel in many years. It was at that point I thought to myself that no matter what, he still was — and always would be — my dad. I began to pray for his recovery and I asked God to give us more time together. He was seventy-six years old and I barely knew him. I wasn't finished with him yet.

As he began to recover, I realized I could laugh at his know-it-all ways and excuse his flirting with the young nurses. He had been married four times, yet here he was, a lonely old man.

After he was released from the hospital, we talked on the phone and e-mailed fairly often. He told me things that amazed me about those years he was away. He truly didn't know the hurt he caused us. He was so consumed with his own wants and desires, he really didn't understand the heartbreaking effect of his selfishness. It was very hard for me to understand why he chose to live his life the way he did, but my new-found forgiveness let me know I didn't have to understand it. I simply accepted it. I decided I wouldn't let the past stop me from trying to be the daughter my dad wanted and needed now. I wished he didn't live so far away, because I wanted to help take care of him, but it just wasn't possible.

Dad died the following year, a few days after Thanksgiving. I was saddened by his death, but also extremely thankful we had found each other and had reconnected.

When he and my mother divorced, she was so hurt, angry, resentful and embarrassed, that she scattered her emotions over and through our lives until my brother and I were as miserable as she was. Mother died years before Dad did, so she never knew I had come to terms with everything. I even forgave her for her self-pity during those years and for her lack of desire to see joy in everyday life. I never told her any of those feelings though, because she really wouldn't have understood.

A very wise friend once told me she believes part of our journey here on earth is to forgive our parents, whether they were wonderful, horrifying or somewhere in-between. I believe I have accomplished that. Being the joyful person I have become, I think my children won't feel the need to forgive me for any damaging emotional wounds. That would certainly be one of my proudest achievements.

— Becky Povich —

# Better Late Than Never

*My mother... she is beautiful, softened at the
edges and tempered with a spine of steel.
I want to grow old and be like her.*
~Jodi Picoult

As a child, more often than not, I woke to the familiar burnt-aluminum smell of another kettle whistling itself to death on our electric range. It was the starting-gun odor of my mother's daily race from behind.

Mom was chronically late, always doing "one more thing." She'd pick up a ringing phone, or have to place dishes in the sink, or lose her car keys. And heaven help my sister or me if she sent us to wait for her in the car. Then, there'd be no one to remind her there wasn't time to dust the coffee table.

I remember standing outside the elementary school every Tuesday, assuring my Brownie troop leader that Mom hadn't forgotten me. Mrs. Williams would snort a response that let me know she had more important places to be.

I was late for school, doctors' appointments, band practice, sleepovers... you name it. Each incident made me more uncomfortable and less forgiving. How hard was it to get out the door on time? Thank goodness, Mom's boss was tolerant. She charmed him with her quirky sense of humor and strong work ethic once she arrived, but the

Accept that Parents Are Not Perfect | 175

shadow of disciplinary action always loomed over her employment. In her defense, I'm sure her role as a single, working parent didn't help, but I wasn't ready to entertain that as a valid excuse.

My wedding was the icing on the three-tiered cake. After a thirty-five-minute delay, the guests were fidgety. My side of the crowd collectively rolled their eyes when my mother rushed in and raced to her seat. I walked down the aisle, tense-lipped, a few minutes later.

In my late twenties, Mom became seriously ill. She had battled sarcoidosis since shortly after I was born. The disease builds scar tissue on major organs in the body. In her case, it had begun attacking her lungs. For years, she'd disguised its symptoms and powered through its debilitating exhaustion without complaint. None of us had known how hard it was on her.

My husband and I made the decision to move her into our home, and I began to comprehend tardiness. I juggled a new marriage, an ailing parent, and a job. I struggled to be on time for *anything*.

When my son was born two years later, it was even worse. Mom's chronic "one more thing" became *my* life. Every time I needed to be somewhere, Mom required my attention, or my son needed a diaper change, or the new puppy threw up the diaper I just changed because I left it on the floor. Then my husband would call from work to ask if I could please make him a doctor's appointment. Meanwhile, my own appointment scheduled for thirty minutes earlier was long lost.

I finally understood Mom's years of failed punctuality. The phone that rang on her way out the door was a friend who needed advice, or my sister forgetting her gym clothes. And Mom's never-ending search for lost car keys? Well, that was a daily occurrence for me now. I even understood the dust on the coffee table. Once noticed, it had to be dealt with because later she'd be too tired. Mom had been responsible for it all as a single parent while suffering a chronic disease. And she'd done it valiantly with smiles and jokes that vexed me to no end as a child.

I apologized to her once in the midst of scavenging my son's diaper bag for my darn keys. Near tears, I looked up to find her holding them out to me.

"Oh, Mom, I'm so sorry. I used to get so mad at you when I was a kid."

She squeezed my shoulders. "Honey, we're all judgmental jerks when we're young. I knew you'd outgrow it."

What could I do but laugh?

When Mom passed, our family arrived early for her memorial service. We were greeted by a funeral director with a slight sheen of sweat on his lip, although it was a chilly October day.

"I'm afraid I have some distressing news," he said. "There is a problem with your mother's ashes. They will not be available until tomorrow."

Mom had managed to be late for her own funeral! My sister and I burst into laughter. We laughed until we cried, and then we giggled some more. Mom was more with us in that moment than if her earthly remains had arrived. As mourners entered the church, the news spread that an empty urn sat next to my mother's picture. People suppressed grins and whispered, "Of course." Mom had made sure we smiled in the midst of our grief.

After the service, I found myself alone in the sanctuary. It hit me how much I had taken for granted that Mom would always be there… eventually. I desperately wanted a few more minutes to make sure she knew how much I admired, appreciated, and loved her. But I was too late. Somehow, though, I knew she understood.

And now, when my son is hurrying me out the door, or I've forgotten his lunch money, I remind myself it's okay to fall short sometimes. My mother taught me that perfection has nothing to do with being an amazing mom.

— Leigh Smith —

# Finding Our Beat

> We must develop and maintain the capacity to forgive.
> He who is devoid of the power to forgive is
> devoid of the power to love.
> ~Martin Luther King, Jr., A Gift of Love

My father-son experience was, shall we say, complicated. There were many good times but few pictures of us together.

My parents had divorced when I was thirteen years old. Up until that point, I can remember never wanting to stay home with Dad alone. It was not because he was physically abusive. He was, in the most respectful way I can put it, a broken man. Now, I know a lot of us would say, "Me, too," but my dad wasn't as self-aware, and his brokenness created a living space that was rocky to say the least. When my mom would go to her second job at night, I would go with her to the mall and do my homework in one of the dressing rooms so that I didn't have to face his fury. I understand now that his mood swings were out of his control and heavily rooted in untreated PTSD from his time in the Vietnam War.

I can remember being nervous when the day finally came that my dad would be taking me to a WCW event. I hadn't seen him much since the divorce, and the few times I had seen him, he only talked about how my mother had hurt him even after years of him hurting her.

Growing up, I loved professional wrestling. The drama, strength and acrobatics of these men and women had me hooked each week.

It was one of the few things my dad really knew about me. However, even though I probably complained to my mom that he was taking me to WCW and not WWE, I was still excited to see what the other side was doing. It was the one and only time I got to see Ric Flair wrestle. My dad and I were amazed that this man, THE MAN, Ric Flair, who was my dad's age, was still going for it. Boy, he was impressive. He was being thrown in the air, doing crazy flips, and putting his opponent into the figure-four leg lock. It was a special occasion I'll always remember.

On my dad's seventieth birthday, I went over to my brother's girlfriend's house for a small get-together. I showed up in sunglasses because my eyes were bothering me that day. My dad began to make fun of me for wearing the sunglasses. I just wanted to spend some time with family and not have any arguments, so I avoided his attacks. I asked my dad what he wanted for his big day, and he said there was no way I could get him what he really wanted. I said, "Try me," so he went on to say he wanted a pair of Beats headphones. I told him it wasn't a problem and asked when he would like to go get them. I'd never seen that man jump up so fast. He got his keys, and we headed to the closest store. We ended the night taking a picture together, both of us in our sunglasses.

I found out later from various people close to him that he loved those headphones. He took them on golf trips and to visit my brother in San Diego, and he would wear them around his place when he was in the mood for music. I was happy that I finally found something to give him that he really wanted.

Time passed, and I'd see him on Christmases. He might call or text on my birthdays, but we still weren't very close. In 2019, I found out that my dad was sick, and it didn't look good. I called as soon as I heard, but the line just kept ringing. I was traveling at the time with work and kept sending him texts and calling, but I could never get through.

I became angry. Why was this man avoiding me now? What had I done that he didn't want me there during his final moments? I knew we weren't the closest, but I had to mean something to him, didn't I? It went on like this until one of my brothers called and said my dad had been asking about me. I told my brother that I had been calling and sending text messages but never got a reply. If he didn't want to see me, why would I go down to his hospital room? Well, turns out, my dad had recently gotten a new cell number, and no one had told me. Apparently, my dad and brother shared a laugh over this. I was less than amused.

When I arrived home from my business trip, I planned on going to see him with my oldest nephew. We felt that going together would soften up my dad, his grandpa, so that it would be an easier conversation to have. It had worked in the past, but it didn't work out so well this time. My dad had recently gotten into an argument with some other family members, and my nephew and I had to hear all about it. Even though he was clearly very angry, I could tell he was sad, too. My dad's voice had become weak and raspy.

I didn't know it then, but I'd never hear his normal voice again. So, my nephew and I sat there and took all the yelling my dad was able to muster before he finally got tired and changed the subject. He told my nephew and me to come back individually next time so he could talk to us in private.

I went back the next week and sat with my dad again. This time, he was in a better mood, but he was starting to fade. Due to the chemo, his hair fell out, he was bedridden, and he started to lose his appetite. At first, he'd ask whoever was coming to bring him a Jamba Juice or Mexican sweet bread. After a few more weeks, he stopped eating, and we knew it was close to the end. I got a gig to go to Atlanta for Friday and Saturday and told my dad I'd come watch football with him that Sunday. He was a big 49ers fan, and we bet a dollar on who would win the game.

I can't remember who the 49ers played that day, but I do remember that Sunday being a turning point in what would be the end of our father-son relationship. He told me not to hold grudges like he had and not to ruin my relationships. He encouraged me to try and be the bigger person when an argument came up.

The last time I visited, I walked into his room and heard him banging on his tray. When I opened the curtain, he was gasping for air. He signaled that he needed help, so I went to get the nurse. They gave him a breathing treatment, and he seemed to calm down a little. He could barely talk at this point but tried his best to communicate with me. Mostly, we sat in silence as we had plenty of times throughout my life.

Later that night when I got home, I got a call from the hospital telling me it was close to his time, and I should gather whom I could to come to his room and be with him. By this time, my parents had miraculously made amends, and my mom came with me as well as two of my aunts and my middle brother. My dad couldn't talk anymore, but he signaled for me, pointed to the gold chain with a naval cross, and then pointed back to me. He was letting me know it was time for me to have it. We sat with him that night as his breathing slowed and his eyes went dim. Then, he was gone.

The hardest thing about my dad passing was that we had finally gotten to a point where we felt comfortable around each other and were enjoying each other's company. I spent my entire life wishing that it was easy to be around my dad, and I only got that for a few weeks.

After we said goodbye and had his funeral, I spent a lot of time reflecting on that. I wished we had started mending fences sooner and that he could have been the kind of man he had been at the end. But that wasn't meant to be. It did, however, teach me valuable life lessons that I'll never forget. A few weeks later, I went back to work. I cried by myself at the airport, after a show in my hotel, and right after I moved to Los Angeles. I mourned a relationship that should have been stronger.

Whose fault was it? It was both of ours, and time was the enemy. Unfortunately, my dad taught me a lot about what *not* to do in life. But one major thing he did teach me was that there is still time to make things right if you try and fight for peace in relationships. It may not be possible with every person in your life, but it may be with those whom you feel *should* be loved and love you back.

We bet a dollar on that 49ers game. I bet him they'd lose, but they won. I didn't get a chance to slip him a dollar before he died, but I did get to slip one to him while he lay in his casket. His funeral was a perfect sendoff — with a gun salute, a dollar bill and a mariachi band playing some of his favorite songs. I now listen to some of those songs on those Beats headphones, and I am grateful that I have a picture of us together being silly and wearing sunglasses.

— Nicholas R. —

# The Gift of Forgiveness

*Mothers and daughters are part of each other's consciousness, in different degrees and in a different way, but still with the mutual sense of something which has always been there.*
~Edith Wharton

The last group of guests bumped merrily out our front door and down the steps. I stood in the open doorway answering the final round of good wishes as our visitors, walking down our front sidewalk to their cars, turned back to wave. Their voices sounded crisp in the newly arrived frigid air of early December. A full moon climbed high in the dark slate sky. I eased the glass storm door shut, and it instantly frosted up as the warm air of our living room hit the icy cold surface. Now, all I could see outside were the hazy gleam of headlights flashing on as our friends started their cars, and the brightly hued blur of Christmas bulbs on the bush just outside our door.

I shut the heavy inside door and turned into our living room. My husband, Mike, bit the leg off a gingerbread man and grinned at me as he sank down onto the couch. "Well," I said as I plunked down beside him, "it's beginning to look a lot like Christmas." A decorated tree next to the fireplace shimmered with tiny white lights, and a row of candles glowed along the mantel. Gifts wrapped in gorgeous holiday paper and tied with red, green, cobalt blue, or fuchsia metallic ribbon were piled beneath the tree. On some packages, I'd attached a jingle bell or two. Candlelight flickered on the dining room table, glinting off shiny glass Christmas bulbs placed among crystal pedestal cake plates and silver platters that still displayed an abundance of holiday cookies. The scent of cinnamon and cloves from hot apple cider perfumed the air, and the coffee urn emitted its own pleasant and comforting fragrance. Since I am enthralled with all things Christmas, this was bliss. We sat close and relished the quiet.

"Hey, how about some fresh air before we start cleaning up?" asked Mike after a time, breaking the spell.

"Good idea," I responded, happy to put off the job of restoring order to our kitchen. He rose from the couch and offered me his hand. We pulled coats, hats, gloves, and scarves out of the front closet. "My mother would have liked our party tonight. You know how much she loved all the Christmas hoopla," I told Mike as we suited up in our warmest winter attire and headed out for a late-night walk. Mike nodded silently, waiting for my cue on the direction of our conversation. My mother died three years ago, in her nineties, and what grieving I did was not so much about losing her, as about never having had her. Burdened with a melancholy outlook for most of her life, she was difficult to please. In my childhood I worked relentlessly, but ineffectively, to satisfy her. Then I worked just as hard in my adulthood to distinguish myself from her and to diminish any similarities between us, in an effort to convince myself that her disapproval of me mattered little.

Only with her death has our reconciliation begun. A cynic would say that I have fashioned this truce to meet my own needs, a convenient and thoughtful gift from an optimistic mind. However, I know otherwise. I sense her hand in the peacemaking, as I have been inspired to ponder the events of her childhood, a time of which she rarely spoke. Those few memories she chose to share about her youth were never pleasant. My concern has slowly turned from the ways in which she broke me, to the ways in which she may herself have been broken in the decades before my life began.

As Mike and I hiked through one neighborhood and into another in the brisk air, I absentmindedly led us into the area where I grew up. Hand in hand we traversed the sidewalk bordering the golf course in my childhood neighborhood. We traded stories of earlier Yuletides. "Is there a reason you're so nuts about Christmas?" he asked.

I considered the source of the giddiness and sentimentality that overtake me every year as soon as the carcass of the Thanksgiving turkey hits the trash. "I don't know," I said. "I'll have to think about that one."

I glanced over at the golf course, which is one block from my childhood home. I described to Mike how, when I was in early grade school, I begged my older brother to take me sledding there on winter afternoons. And how at dusk on Christmas Eve in my youthful years, our parents would send him and me over to these hills with our sleds. On that night we generally had the snowy slopes all to ourselves. We'd make several runs down the double hill, facing a magical spectacle of brightly lit, snow-frosted evergreens in front yards all up and down the blocks bordering that corner of the golf course. My excitement reached a higher level with every speedy descent because I knew that while we were gone, Santa was at our home loading heaps of presents under our Christmas tree. The short trek back to our house after sledding never seemed longer than it did on Christmas Eve.

It didn't matter to us that many of those gifts were necessities masquerading in bright gift wrap as luxuries: new underwear, socks, wool gloves, and school supplies. We were all the more jubilant when one of the boxes contained a toy train or a doll.

As Mike and I reminisced on our stroll, I realized for the first time the origin of much that I treasure about Christmas. The singing: my mom. The candlelight: my mom. The gift wrapping: my mom. Those tiny white twinkle lights: my mom.

And so my mother and I continue our reconciliation. As the weather gets colder, I become warmer.

— Beverly A. Golberg —

# The Trouble with Dad

> *If the only prayer you say in your life*
> *is thank you, that would suffice.*
> ~Meister Eckhart

My sixteen-year-old brother had gone downstairs to work on a small motor. His glove caught in the flywheel, and when he emerged through the trap door that led from the cellar of our old farmhouse, his right hand was twisted at the wrist in an awkward angle. The shock on my mother's face told me something was terribly wrong. The urgency with which she hustled him off to the hospital fifteen miles away alarmed me, and I was left alone with Dad.

I was only four and I didn't know what to think. *Would they cut off my brother's broken arm? Would he die? Maybe you bled to death if you broke your arm. And what if Mom never came home again? Who would look after me?*

I so much wanted someone to reassure me, but I couldn't ask Dad. You didn't ask him stupid questions or he would get angry. And you didn't make noise when he was around either. And you never, ever let him hear you cry.

I didn't understand it at the time, but I had just encountered the first emotional roadblock in my relationship with Dad. He just sat in his rocking chair that day reading the newspaper as if nothing had happened, as if I wasn't even around. I huddled behind his chair, where I could be close, but not be seen as a bother. And I was still there, cold and cramped and hungry, when Mom came home.

I started school, and despite getting good grades and being an obedient daughter, Dad seldom seemed to notice. In a rare mood he would occasionally admire one of my achievements, then just as suddenly throw up another barricade when he sensed the gap between us closing.

My poor mother was caught between the husband she loved and the daughter who feared him. She started showing me things from his past, from his World War I service. This was how I would grow to understand his pain.

Hanging on a nail in the hallway of our house was a khaki bag with a red cross on it. In it was a picture of a young man in Army clothes that Mom claimed was Dad, although I didn't recognize him in his uniform. Also in the bag were a few bullets, a knife, and a fork with one tine missing. A black booklet had his regimental number and name in it, the creased pages officially stamped by Canada's Department of Defence. One tarnished shoulder badge he had earned for outstanding marksmanship was in the shape of two crossed rifles.

I fingered the items with curiosity, especially a small photo showing lines and lines of wounded soldiers lying in an open field in France. At one point my father may have laid among them when a piece of shrapnel severed two fingers of his left hand, but I never asked him about being wounded. You didn't ask Dad much of anything, and certainly not about the war. Oh, sometimes when a drink or two loosened his tongue, he and an old fellow soldier would start to reminisce about the rats in the trenches, the lice that drove them crazy, the scream of the cavalry horses among the din of battle, and Army rations so awful they either chose hunger or stripped the food supplies from the slain. "All except the butter," I remember him saying. "You couldn't stomach the butter from off a dead man."

I learned very early never to approach Dad quietly from behind. Only once did I forget, and the hammer he was using at his workbench came hurtling toward me. I ducked, and then fled back to the house in terror. "Shellshock," my mother explained. "Involuntary reaction to any unexpected noise or movement." Thereafter I tried not to approach him unless it was absolutely necessary. He seemed incapable of demonstrating any affection, of identifying with any of my emotions. Never once did I hug him or sit on his knee. I had a hunch such overtures, if not rejected, would certainly not be reciprocated.

Dad was law and order, Mom justice and mercy. As a teenager, I often wondered why, indeed, Dad was the way he was — not that I didn't give him my respect. He was, after all, my father, and my mother defended him to the last. Sometimes I begrudgingly saw her unfailing devotion as an admirable trait; at other times, I saw it as blind devotion to a man who was not at all like the one she married. She told me as much herself, years later. We were discussing what is now called post-traumatic stress disorder, and how severe trauma can forever change a person's outlook, personality, and even values.

"Just think of your dad," she said. "He was never the same after the war. The emotional pain he suffered was so great, that rather than risk losing the ones he loved, he built up a wall that nobody could penetrate. All I could do was try to understand."

Instead of understanding, I blamed him. I failed to see those emotional wounds he suffered, and the permanent scars he bore as a result. Forgiveness did not come quickly, but settled slowly into my soul as year after year on November 11th the haunting sound of a bugle played "Last Post" from the Canadian War Memorial in Ottawa. When the television showed jerky footage of soldiers in the trenches of World War I, I wondered if my father was among them. Watching those youthful faces contorted in misery, my resentment toward him was slowly replaced by deep gratitude for the sacrifice he had made, and for which I had never thanked him.

The only public recognition for military service he ever received was at his funeral, when a local lad in dress uniform marched up to his open coffin and smartly saluted the old soldier lying there. Beyond that, nothing was ever said. That's how he seemed to want it.

Last November, while hurrying out of the supermarket I saw a frail old World War II veteran selling poppies, his wrinkled hands blue with cold. He was a small man, about the size of my dad, with those same steely blue eyes. I stopped.

"It's a miserable day," I said, trying to make small talk as I rummaged around in my purse for some coins.

The old veteran didn't respond. I dropped some change into his box and pinned a red poppy to my lapel. And then, very deliberately, I took his withered, veined hand in mine. Looking him straight in the eye, I said, "Thank you for what you did for us in the war. Thank you."

He never said a word, but tears escaped those steel blue eyes and trickled down the creases of his face. Temporarily, the wall that a toughened old soldier had erected in defence of his emotions crumbled.

For him it may have felt like defeat. For me it was a bittersweet victory.

Having failed to recognize the symptoms of my father's post-traumatic stress disorder, neither had I understood his suffering, much less forgiven him. He was the one who went to war, but in extending gratitude, at long last I am the one who is at peace.

— Alma Barkman —

# No Fault

*Your pain is the breaking of the shell
that encloses your understanding.*
~Khalil Gibran

I crumpled into a ball of hysteria on the floor of the sporting-goods store. "No! No! No! No!" I kept repeating. My hand grasped my cell phone so tightly that my knuckles turned white.

How could this be happening again? Only six weeks earlier, my sixty-eight-year-old mom had called me and blurted out, "I just took a bunch of sleeping pills."

I had sprung to my feet, trying to sound calm but inwardly freaking out.

"A bunch? Like how many?" I asked.

Within minutes, she was mumbling incoherently.

I was able to get the paramedics to her, and she survived, for which I was grateful. But I was also confused and angry.

When I visited Mom in the hospital, I wanted to scream, "What were you thinking? How could you do something so stupid?"

But she looked like a frightened child, and her whole body shook like a panicked dog during a nasty thunderstorm.

"I'm sorry," Mom whispered, her mouth dry and lips chapped from the tubes that had been shoved down her throat to pump her stomach.

I was desperate to say the right thing and paranoid I'd say the wrong thing. Mostly, I said nothing. I just sat beside her on her tiny hospital bed and gently squeezed her trembling hand, trying to make

Accept that Parents Are Not Perfect

sense of the senseless.

"I love you, Mom," I said slowly, almost methodically. I wanted to be sure the message got through and that she never did this again.

The next several weeks were spent talking to my dad and various doctors about how best to help Mom. We locked up all her medications. We rid the house of guns and knives. Dad promised not to leave her side. After a while she seemed to be doing better so Dad went back to work.

Now I was at the store with my boys, shopping for new bike helmets when the phone rang. And Dad had just said, "She did it again. Only it's way worse this time."

"I'll come right now," I said. "I can be there by midnight."

"I don't think you'll make it in time," Dad said.

I collapsed, knowing that, for all intents and purposes, my mom was gone.

The next several hours were spent waiting for the dreaded phone call. In those hours, I worked myself into a lather of anger.

"How could she betray me like this?" I cried, my face hot with rage. "How could she choose to leave me?"

I spent the evening replaying all of the times in my life when Mom had rescued me. When I was twelve and had dropped to seventy-three pounds, she hospitalized me so I wouldn't succumb to anorexia. When I was thirty-three and going through a painful divorce, she invited me and my son to live with her and Dad until I got back on my feet. When I was thirty-nine and had to have carpal-tunnel surgery on both hands, Mom cared for my toddler. Time after time, she saved me. And now, when it was my turn to save her, I had failed miserably. Guilt and gut-wrenching pain ate away at me.

I had just drifted off to sleep when the shrill ring of my phone led me to my worst nightmare.

"She's gone," Dad said. With those two words, my world turned to gray.

The next week was spent planning Mom's funeral — picking out her clothes, coffin, flowers, and songs. I was furious at her for putting me in this position. For anyone who died of cancer, a car accident or a heart attack, their death was outside of their control. But Mom chose this! She thought about it, she did it, and she lived. Then apparently she thought about it some more, did it again, and died. How could she intentionally put her family through such torture?

From the inside out, every part of me hurt — my heart, my head, my whole being. One night I sat alone on my bed, seething. Through clenched teeth, I screeched at the top of my lungs, "Why did you do this to me? Why didn't you love me enough to stay? Why did you leave me? Why?"

My heart pounded hard and fast as I continued reeling, going through the house like a rabid animal, frantically ripping down every photo of my mom so I didn't have to see her selfish face staring back at me.

For several months, I remained steadfast in my righteous indignation as I constantly teetered on the precipice of a meltdown. Regularly, I broke down in the aisles of the grocery store, at the park while my son was swinging, and — my personal favorite — while balancing on a rubber exercise ball at the gym, sobbing like a madwoman between ab crunches.

Then one night I saw a news segment on suicide that caused me to re-evaluate Mom's actions. Up until this point, I'd been drowning so deep in my own grief that all I could see was how Mom's death affected me. I hadn't stopped to consider what she must have been feeling.

About this time, I began attending a support group where I was surrounded by others who had also lost loved ones to suicide. I gained some valuable insight there, too. After a while, it became clear to me that prior to her death, my mom was in agonizing emotional pain that never subsided. I wanted her to hold onto life, and I think she did for as long as she could… until she lost all strength.

Something clicked inside me, and suddenly I had a newfound perspective, and with it, a newfound mercy for Mom. Clinical depression was her cancer. It was her car accident. It was her heart attack. She didn't choose to become afflicted by a chemical imbalance that messed up her brain any more than a cancer patient signs on to have cancer cells ravage her body. So while my mom died by suicide, it was depression that killed her. It wasn't her fault. The power to forgive provided me with both strength and clarity that enabled me to move through the hurt so I could heal.

"I'll always be sorry I couldn't save you, Mom," I said one night as I lay in bed. "But I'm not mad at you anymore. You fought hard, and you stayed with us as long as you could. You needed rest, and now you have it."

Tears ran down my cheeks as I continued, "I'm more aware and educated now. I no longer blame you, Mom, because I know you didn't do this to me. I hope you'll forgive me for my anger because I certainly have forgiven you."

Forgiveness enabled me to release the "whys" and embrace the "wows." As in, "Wow, I was lucky to have such a wonderful mom for forty-six glorious years."

— Christy Heitger-Ewing —

# Fudge and Fathers

*What was silent in the father speaks in the son, and often I found in the son the unveiled secret of the father.*
~Friedrich Nietzsche

I always felt comfortable with my grandfather, something I couldn't say about my own father. My father was high-strung, demanding and critical, especially of me, the oldest son. His father, Gramps, was the polar opposite. Gramps was hardworking, quiet and patient. In all the years I knew him, I never heard him say a negative word about anyone. I escaped to his house when things got too intense at home. There was always peace at my grandfather's house — peace and fudge.

My grandmother died before I was born, and Gramps never remarried. He lived alone in a red brick bungalow about two miles from my parents' house. Out of necessity, he'd become a good cook. Dinner was always red meat, a starch and a vegetable, but for dessert we had the best fudge in the world.

The fudge Gramps made was heavy, rich and dense. It was studded with walnuts and always tasted to me like the best concoction on the planet. The recipe was a secret he refused to share with anyone. After dinner, I was allowed to take two pieces of fudge into the living room to eat while I watched television. I ate it slowly as *Starsky and Hutch* or *The Carol Burnett Show* played. Gramps joined me after he finished cleaning up the kitchen, and we spent many pleasant evenings together in front of our shows.

As I grew older and spent more time with friends instead of my grandfather, those evenings occurred less often. I still visited Gramps, but other things and people took precedence. By the time I was in my senior year of high school, dinners at my grandfather's house had dwindled down to every other month or so. I had homework, college applications and, the most time-consuming, a serious girlfriend.

"You should visit your grandfather more often." Surprisingly, the person talking was my father. It was a Saturday afternoon, and my dad and I were cleaning out the garage, a chore I was eager to finish since I had a date that night.

"I see Gramps." *More often than you do*, I thought but didn't dare say.

"Not like you used to. You used to spend more time at his house than you did here."

"I'm busier than I used to be."

"And your grandfather is older than he used to be. He's not going to be around forever."

"Then maybe you should visit him," I suggested.

My father shrugged. "He doesn't want me to visit him. He wants to see you. You two have always been like two peas in a pod."

I wasn't sure, but I thought I detected a note of envy in my father's voice. That was a first. Was it possible my dad wanted a better relationship with his dad?

"Well, let's go over there now," I suggested.

"What?"

"The garage can wait. Let's go see Gramps now."

My father paused for a few moments. "No, you go."

"I have a date tonight."

"So go now. He doesn't want to see me."

"How do you know that?" I asked.

"We never got along. Five minutes into the visit, and we'd be all over each other. You go. You're the one he enjoys the most."

I tossed down the broom I was holding. "Didn't you just tell me Gramps is getting older? Don't you want to start getting along with him before it's too late for you, too?"

My father shook his head slowly. "It's already too late for us."

**Accept that Parents Are Not Perfect**

"Only if you say it is," I challenged.

There was a long beat of silence before he responded, "It's always been too late."

"Geez, Dad, I never knew you were a quitter. Gramps told me once that you never gave up on anything."

Angrily, my father opened his mouth and then shut it. After a few moments, he said, "Let's go."

Twenty minutes later, we were walking into the kitchen at my grandfather's house. Gramps seemed surprised to see both of us, but didn't comment. Instead, he got out a plate and loaded it with his famous fudge. "There's a game on. Do you have time to watch?"

In the living room, my father sprawled on the sofa, I sat on the floor, and Gramps relaxed in his recliner. We watched a football game in relative silence as we slowly devoured the entire plate of fudge.

"I forgot how good your fudge is, Dad," my father said after the game was over.

I'd forgotten, too. I'd forgotten a lot of things, like how peaceful my grandfather's living room was and how much I liked being there. I glanced at the clock hanging on the wall over the television set. I needed to pick up my girlfriend soon. Inspiration hit me for the second time that day.

"Gramps, would you mind if I brought my girlfriend over later? She's a big fudge fan, too."

"Then I'd better make another batch. You two finished that one." Gramps got to his feet and headed for the kitchen. My father and I exchanged glances.

"You know something? You're smarter than you look," my father said.

I found myself grinning. Coming from my father, that was about as big a compliment as I'd ever gotten. I got to my feet. "I'm going to help Gramps with the fudge. Maybe he'll show me how he makes it."

It *was* a day of miracles, after all.

— Mark Musolf —

# Mary's Girl

*Man has two great spiritual needs. One is for forgiveness. The other is for goodness.*
~Billy Graham

I didn't know we were different at first. As a little kid, I was unaware of how circumstances set me apart in our 1960s middle-class, 10th Ward neighborhood in Rochester, New York.

Squalor isn't a word or concept you understand at age five. By age nine or ten, I understood that my life was out of sync with the rest of the community when people referred to me as "one of the Herne girls."

By age twelve I realized that some neighbors shunned us while others allowed me to play with their kids, in their yards, and even hang around for supper now and again. They encouraged me by befriending me.

But not much penetrated the darkness of our home, a long-neglected dwelling of fetid air, dirt-crusted windows, filth, and the smattering of bare-bulb lights that rarely worked. Around age eleven, I took charge of my one room upstairs and scrubbed it from top to bottom. There were no pretty blankets or soft coverlets, but the thin sheets I found to cover my stained mattress were clean, if shabby. The pillow had a cover. I washed the floor weekly, and dusted the broken dresser as if it mattered. And it did matter. It mattered to me.

Sometime after I was born, my mother's brilliance was dimmed by chronic alcoholism and depression. Entire seasons went by that

Accept that Parents Are Not Perfect

I never saw or heard her. She spent long months locked away in her small room with secret, silent demons. She attempted suicide at least twice that I remember, and she cried over her lack of success.

I must have glimpsed the real person within her as a small child, because during the dark years I waited for that woman's reappearance. During those alcoholic stupors and fright-filled nights when my brother and I dumped her whiskey down a sink, trying to nudge her back to some form of normal, I believed there was another woman within the caricature I called "Mom."

There is nothing fun about a sordid existence, but I was blessed to attend a vibrant, busy Catholic school. My uniform allowed me to fit in. No one knew it was given to us at the Thanksgiving clothing drive. The plaid jumper was clean and tailored like everyone else's with no marks of identification. I was challenged and beloved by numerous teachers over the years, wonderful women who said I bore a true gift for writing. They made me feel special! As year piled upon year, I finally had to move out of my parents' house. I lived with my older sister, guilt-ridden because I left two younger brothers behind in the darkness and filth.

Then one day I came across my mother's poetry. As a teen she'd been instrumental in starting a high school magazine, a reasonably priced form of entertainment in the Depression-era 1930s. I didn't know that when I found her folder, all I knew was the sheer beauty of her words, cadence-strung emotion done with point and pride.

Instantly I saw where my talent came from. For the first time it was clear that whatever I'd seen as a small child, before whiskey dimmed the sparkle in her eyes and slurred her words, was real. I held tangible proof in my hands in the form of her teenage writings.

That book was my turnaround, my wake-up call to forgiveness. God had blessed me with a talent through my mother. While hers may have been scourged by time and circumstance, I realized that the woman I knew personally wasn't the real Mary Elizabeth Logan Herne, because "M.E. Logan" wrote with stunning grace and abandon.

I desperately longed to know that woman someday, but in the meantime I accepted God's grace, my time, and my life. A teenage girl's words on paper showed me what God wanted me to see, the lineage of hope. That day, for the first time, I thanked him for the grace of being Mary Elizabeth's daughter. And I decided then that someday I would use my God-given talent to make other women smile and grab hold of their faith and their lives, no matter what they'd endured. With God lay hope.

My mother quit drinking when I was thirty-three years old. Once in a while she'd lapse for a day or two, but she never fell into the pit of despair again. After three decades of waiting and loving, I finally got to know her. I sensed her old dreams and bitter disappointments, but what I saw and cherished was the bright light within her shining again, somewhat shadowed, but a glow that shone with God's love and humility.

My children never saw their grandmother drink. Their early visits to her were in the morning. Once she stopped drinking, this wasn't a problem, and to this day, the thought of their grandmother as the woman I'd known is alien to them. To my six children, she was the petite, gray-haired "Grandma" that loved to hear their stories and tell her own. Just as it should be.

When she realized she was dying of cancer, she gripped my hand, looked me in the eye and said, "I know you are serious about your writing. On that day when you become published, will you do me the honor of using my name? I want everyone in the world to know that you're mine."

I said yes.

My dream of publication came years after Mom's death, but her words helped me hone the talent she gave me. And when that first book came out, a novel of love, loss and second chances called *Winter's End*, it was dedicated to my mother, Mary Elizabeth Logan Herne, "from whence the talent came."

And the grace of God's fulfillment is in the name I use as I publish my books… Ruth Logan Herne — Mary's girl.

— Ruth Logan Herne —

# Move Forward after an Apology

# Losing Sophie

*Forgive, forget. Bear with the faults of others as you would have them bear with yours.*
~Phillips Brooks

My friend Sandy and I sat across from each other at our favorite Mexican restaurant, munching on chips and salsa while we talked and laughed. My cell phone rang. I didn't recognize the number, so I didn't answer. Less than a minute later, it rang again. Same number. Then a third time.

"Hello," I said.

"This is your neighbor, Dexter," the voice on the other end said. "I got your number off Sophie's collar."

Sophie was my eight-year-old, mixed-breed dog, part Boxer and part who-knows-what. Adults and children alike seemed to adore her. She didn't chase cats. She didn't turn over garbage cans. She didn't put her muddy paws on clean clothes.

Sophie had only one bad habit. She'd escaped my fenced-in yard so many times. She loved to chase the UPS truck. I couldn't quite figure out why. She didn't chase cars or motorcycles or bicycles. She was completely uninterested in the postal truck and the FedEx van. But something about that big brown UPS delivery truck lit a fire under her. The moment she heard its engine turn onto our street, she was after the truck like a shot. The surprising thing was that she loved Mike, the driver. As soon as he parked and descended the steps, Sophie wagged all over.

Move Forward after an Apology

Dexter was calling to tell me he'd been in his front yard when the UPS truck came tearing around the corner. "Sophie was in hot pursuit," Dexter said. "The driver took the turn too sharp and clipped her with his rear wheel."

Tears filled my eyes, and my hands starting shaking. "Is she…" I didn't dare say the word. "Is she hurt?" I stammered.

"It's hard to tell," Dexter said. "Her back legs are scraped and bloody, and she's breathing real shallow. But her eyes are open, and she thumps her tail when I talk to her."

I pulled a wad of cash from my wallet and tossed it on the table. "I'll be there in five minutes."

Sophie was just as Dexter had described. She raised her head when she heard my voice and licked my hand as I sank down beside her and cradled her head in my lap. I dialed my veterinarian's work number, hoping against hope that he might still be at the office on a Friday evening. No answer. Same with his home number.

There was nothing to do but call the emergency veterinary clinic in a nearby county. The on-call doctor promised to meet me there. Gently, Dexter placed Sophie into the back of Sandy's van, and we sped to the clinic. Sophie whimpered softly for the entire half-hour journey. Dr. Cunningham slid her carefully onto a stretcher and rolled her into the examining room. Sophie's big, brown eyes stared into mine.

I stroked her silky ears and put my face close to hers. "It's gonna be okay, sweet girl," I whispered.

"We'll need X-rays to assess internal damage," Dr. Cunningham said. "But I think the best thing to do now is get a catheter in and start an IV. That'll keep her comfortable overnight so we can take pictures in the morning. You go home and get some rest, and I'll call as soon as I know something."

Sandy and I drove away feeling good about Sophie's diagnosis. I even joked that I hoped this would teach her to never, ever chase the UPS truck again. My phone rang when we were about halfway home. I could hear the pain in Dr. Cunningham's voice. "Sophie coded while I was working on her," she said. "She passed away. I'm so, so sorry."

I sobbed. So did Sandy. I went down a long list of what-ifs. And then I let my grief turn quickly to anger. And hate. This was Mike's fault, no doubt about it. Everyone in the neighborhood knew he drove too fast. We worried he might hit a child on a bike, a young mother pushing a baby stroller, or an animal. Now he had. He'd hit and killed my beloved Sophie. And I was never going to forgive him for it.

I didn't call UPS management to report Mike, although I considered it. Instead, I seethed. I ignored his wave when I passed him on the street. I taped a PLEASE LEAVE PACKAGES ON PORCH note to my front door so I wouldn't have to answer his knock. For almost a year, I let my ill feelings toward Mike fester. Then one day, while walking out of the library, I came face-to-face with him. He set down the packages he was carrying and touched my arm.

"I've been wanting to talk to you," he said softly. "How's Sophie?"

Before I could choose my words, they came spilling out. "She's dead is how she is," I said. "And it's all your fault."

I wasn't prepared for Mike's reaction. Instead of defending himself, he burst into tears. "I'm sorry to hear that," he said. "So, so sorry. I knew I'd clipped her with my tire, but she got up and walked off, so I didn't stop. I figured you'd been keeping her fenced up since it happened."

I shook my head. "Her injuries were way worse than they looked."

Mike's hand was still on my arm. "I'm used to dogs chasing me," he said. "There's something about the whine of our truck engine that sets them off. But I want you to know I looked forward to being in your neighborhood because Sophie was always so glad to see me." My mind flashed back to Sophie's joy when Mike stepped down from the truck. I remembered how she walked with him to his customer's door and how he always bent down to scratch her ears after he'd handed over his packages.

Mike swiped at his eyes with the back of his hand. "I know I drive too fast sometimes," he said. "But you wouldn't believe how many packages I have to deliver every day. I hope you'll forgive me."

Right then and there, I did. I let go of the anger. I let go of the hate. I forgave Mike. And I told him so. Forgiving hasn't made me miss Sophie any less. The memory of her lying on the stretcher in the animal hospital will never go away. But, day by day, it's being replaced by happy memories. I wave at Mike now when I pass him on the street. I answer his knock when he brings packages to my door. I've even given him a print of my favorite picture of Sophie. Someone once said, "To forgive is to set a prisoner free and discover that the prisoner was you."

I'm no longer a prisoner. And for that I'm grateful.

—Jennie Ivey—

# The Polar Bears

*A sister is a gift to the heart, a friend to the spirit,
a golden thread to the meaning of life.*
~Isadora James

Diane was the youngest of the four of us. She was a bit of a rebel, but you couldn't help but love her. She was funny, strong, smart, talented, beautiful, and passionate.

One of her passions was protecting polar bears! She was in awe that such strong, dominant animals were seen as symbols of acceptance in some cultures. Fascinated with spiritual stories, she believed as they did, that in order to survive, the polar bear allowed spirits to whiten his coat to blend with the snow. "His acceptance," she confirmed, "is a sign of his strength." Diane would tuck photos of polar bears inside random cards that she would send when she knew someone needed words of support.

No one ever thought Diane would die of an accidental overdose, much less get hooked on drugs. A crippling accident in her twenties had introduced her to pain medications and she couldn't overcome her addiction.

My brother and I had said goodbye to our parents, our older brother, and many relatives and friends, but Diane's passing released too many emotions too quickly. For years we danced around our emotions. Holidays were the most difficult.

One particular Thanksgiving would be no different. It had been a long day visiting my younger brother and his family. Somehow, we couldn't stop talking about Diane, arguing about her, trying to resolve so many unanswered questions. We were angry with her and we hadn't been able to forgive her for the way she died.

I started my long drive home from my brother's house still haunted by thoughts of my sister's passing. "It will be a long night adding to the long day," I thought.

Halfway home, I realized I had forgotten to buy a birthday card for a dear friend who never forgot mine. I only knew of one grocery store close to home that would be open and fortunately, they sold cards. So, as midnight approached, I took the exit that detoured me to the "24/7" store.

The store was practically empty, just a few shoppers filling their baskets. I had the card aisle all to myself until I felt the presence of someone next to me. She was an old woman, dressed in a turquoise and gold sari. Her face was veiled, exposing only her dark, penetrating, yet gentle eyes. The deep, weathered wrinkles that encircled them revealed she was an old soul. "Here," she said in a soft Indian accent, "I believe these cards are for you!" She handed me two cards.

I thanked her, and looked down at the cards, which were the same. On the front was a photo of a polar bear with his giant paw across his eyes. When you opened the card there were only two visible words, "I'm sorry!"

I immediately knew what this was. It was a message from Diane — her way of letting us know she was sorry and that it was time for both of us to heal and to forgive. I turned to thank the old woman again, but she was gone. I raced through the store, up and down aisles asking the few shoppers and employees if anyone had seen her. No one remembered the old woman in the turquoise and gold sari.

I knew this was no coincidence. Diane was saying she was sorry. But there was more to it. Staring at the photos of the polar bears, I remembered her symbolic story of how they accepted a white coat of fur in order to survive in their snow-covered domain. I heard my sister's voice reminding me, "There is strength in acceptance!" I knew then, her real message for my brother and me, was about acceptance. It was the key component that was missing for our survival as well. In order to forgive and heal, we needed to accept not only Diane's way of life but also her death.

The next day, I mailed my brother his card with a lengthy note explaining how I received it. He understood and accepted the miracle that I had witnessed. Years have passed and we have healed, but my polar bear card from heaven remains on my fireplace mantle enclosed with my own personal note to my little sister: Apology accepted!

— Lainie Belcastro —

# A Wink from the Universe

*Coincidence is the language of the stars. For something to happen, so many forces have to be put into action.*
~Paulo Coelho

My relationship with my mother was strained, to put it diplomatically. After years of tolerating her guilt trips and ridicule, the last straw came when she issued me an ultimatum. It was either her way or the highway.

I chose the highway. As I left the house with everything I owned, she vowed to never speak to me again. *No problem*, I thought. *At last, we see eye-to-eye on something.*

But despite my bravado, for the first time in my life, I felt lost, alone, and confused. It was an emptiness I'd never felt before.

In an attempt to escape these new sensations, I agreed to take a road trip to Nova Scotia with my boyfriend.

Somehow, we scraped together just enough cash to do it, and in a cramped two-seater full of snacks, mix tapes, and youthful hope, we set off for the east.

When we arrived twenty-four hours later, I managed successfully to forget all the problems waiting for me back home. For one blissful week, we visited his family members, took in the beauty of the province, and indulged in all the east-coast food and drink we could handle. I loved every minute of it.

The day we were to leave, the weather was beautiful.

As I sat in the passenger seat and stared out the window, I couldn't stop thinking about all the great times I'd had over the past week. Dancing with my boyfriend's uncles at a down-east kitchen party. Devouring so much fresh seafood that our stomachs hurt. Stunning scenic hikes that took my breath away. I hadn't felt this happy in a long time.

But as night fell, the weather changed, and my mood with it.

A dense fog cloaked the road in a thick veil of gray. The headlights were of no use. Very quickly, the world felt dark and desolate.

Silence filled the car, the fog having smothered the conversation as surely as it had smothered the light.

Now, with no distractions, all I could think about was my situation back home. Did I make the right decision moving out? Would I ever speak to my mom again? Could I ever shake this feeling of emptiness and loneliness? Suddenly, I felt so sad.

BANG! I was startled out of my rumination.

"I can't control the car," my boyfriend yelled, desperately trying to steer.

"What's happening?" I screamed as the car swerved. The tires screeched. Rocks, dust and dirt swirled all around us.

"Brace yourself!" he yelled.

I thought I was going to die.

We came to an abrupt stop, a cloud of dust settling around us.

My boyfriend was slumped over the steering wheel.

"I'm pretty sure we blew a tire," he mumbled.

I breathed a sigh of relief, but it seemed our troubles weren't quite over yet.

"I don't have a spare. I just replaced these tires so I took the extra tire out to fit our bag."

"What are we going to do? We're in the middle of nowhere," I said, panicked and scared. I looked out the window, but the fog held no answers.

"I have no idea," he snapped, and then opened his door and walked to the front of the car.

I joined him. We sat on the hood in silence.

"Maybe once it gets light out, we can flag down a car to help."

He nodded. The silence remained unchallenged.

"Are you guys okay?" a voice asked suddenly from behind us.

Startled, we screamed and jumped off the hood, turning to confront our murderer.

"I'm so sorry! I didn't mean to scare you," the equally startled stranger explained.

"Oh, my god! Where did you come from?" I shrieked.

"Nowhere," he answered cryptically, "but I'm heading to the next town. Did you want me to call a tow truck for you?"

"Yes, that would be great," I said. Though I was starting to feel relieved, I still wasn't convinced this man wasn't going to pull out a machete or something. It was an odd mix of emotions.

"Don't worry. You're safe now." He smiled, and then turned and disappeared into the fog.

Baffled by his unexplained appearance (and disappearance), we did the only thing we could—stare at each other in silent disbelief.

Fifteen minutes later, two streams of light sliced through the fog and found us by the side of the road.

It didn't seem possible. The next exit was over forty minutes away by car. How did that peculiar stranger get there so quickly?

This night had gone from beautiful to scary to weird.

"Blew a tire, I heard," the tow-truck driver yelled as he walked toward us.

"Yes, we did."

"It was a pretty lucky coincidence, if you ask me," he remarked.

"Excuse me?" I replied, confused.

"You didn't hear about the pile-up?"

"What pile-up?"

"The fog is so thick past the next exit that it caused a massive car pile-up. If you hadn't blown your tire, you probably would have ended up in that crash."

I shuddered at the thought.

Before long, the tire had been fixed, and we were back on the road again.

Hundreds of miles later, I still couldn't stop thinking about what had just happened.

I had never really paid much attention to coincidences. Like most people, I'd dismissed them as chance or luck.

But this felt like so much more to me. I felt like I'd personally been given a wink from the universe, and I couldn't ignore it.

The fog lifted that day, and so did my feelings of confusion and loneliness. I'd been so upset, wondering if I would ever speak to my mom again, and without that tire blowing I might never have had the opportunity.

The fog and the tire, two seemingly unrelated coincidences, had come together and created a life-changing moment for me.

My relationship with my mom has never been easy, but I did make up with her once I returned from that trip.

And from that day forward, I paid much more attention to seemingly random, unexplained moments — a phone call from a long-lost friend I'd been thinking about, a financial windfall when I needed it most, an unexpected meeting at a social event that led to the perfect job opportunity. Together, these simple, amazing moments create something complex and beautiful, and guide me through this crazy life.

The way I look at it, the universe is always trying to guide us and speak to us. We have the choice if we want to listen.

I've got my ear pressed close to the ground.

— Heidi Allen —

# 64

# You're Forgiven

*Forgiveness is the key that unlocks the door of resentment and the handcuffs of hatred. It is a power that breaks the chains of bitterness.*
~Corrie ten Boom, Clippings from My Notebook

The ringing of the phone woke me from a deep sleep at 4:30 in the morning. I jumped out of bed and picked up the receiver.

"Hello, is this Mr. Pollock?"

I answered, "Yes, this is Mr. Pollock. What can I do for you?"

"This is the dispatcher for the Treasure County Sheriff's Department. There has been a series of burglaries in Hysham. It is possible that Hysham Hardware was one of the businesses burglarized. The sheriff would like you to come to your store. He would like you to park by your door and wait until the sheriff contacts you."

"Okay," I said. I sat down in a chair. My emotions went from surprise to anger like a racecar on a drag strip, zero to sixty in less than two seconds. I put on my clothes, told my wife what had happened, and headed out the door. It had snowed through the night, but I was so hot that the snow should have been melting wherever I stepped.

As I drove to town, I remembered that just a few days earlier I had felt like someone was watching as I closed for the night.

When I got to the store, I parked and sat there wondering where the sheriff was. The back door was wide open, and I was sure the furnace was running full blast. I felt violated.

Move Forward after an Apology

I sat there stewing. The sheriff knocked on the window and brought me back to reality. He confirmed we had suffered a burglary. Together, we entered the store and looked to see if anything was gone. They had pried open the front door. On the floor was a pile of tools the thief or thieves had used to try and open the safe. They used a half-inch drill with a hole saw, a reciprocating saw, a sledgehammer, and some chisels, which they had taken off the shelves of my store.

Papers from my desk covered the office floor like a tornado had hit the place, but as far as I could tell all the expensive merchandise was still there. The sheriff then asked me to return to my pickup and wait for them to check for fingerprints.

While I sat in my pickup, anger raged through my mind. I probably could have chewed on nails and spit out bullets. Soon, the sheriff and deputies left, and I began the process of cleaning up the mess and fixing the broken lock and door. My wife arrived, and together we worked. When she saw all the chaos, she also felt violated and filled with anger.

Later that day, we learned that law enforcement had caught the thieves. One of them had stolen a car, but the law had him in custody before he could get out of town. The other one had hitchhiked on a truck to Billings. When the truck driver dropped him off to call a cab, he flashed a wad of bills. The truck driver was suspicious, so he called the police. When this thief reached his home, the law was waiting for him.

When the trial came, I wanted these crooks prosecuted to the full extent of the law. They must pay, and pay they did. The jury found both guilty. With them both in prison, the fire in my heart began to cool, but I didn't realize just how much it had cooled until sometime later.

One morning about three years later, I was in the store by myself when a man I didn't know walked through the door. This was an odd circumstance as I knew everyone who lived in Treasure County.

He walked up to the counter and turned to me. "Are you the owner of this store?"

I smiled and replied, "Yes, I am."

"Have you owned it for a while?"

My eyes met his. "Yes, a little over twenty years."

**Move Forward after an Apology**

He looked away. "Then you owned it three years ago."

I started to say, "Well, duh," but for some reason, I didn't. Instead, I replied, "Yes."

Then he made a statement I will never forget. "I need to ask for your forgiveness."

I had no idea what he was referring to. "My forgiveness for what?"

Once more, he lowered his eyes. "I'm the one who broke into your store and made all the mess."

Without thinking, I said, "You're forgiven, brother." Somehow, all the pain, hurt and emotions were gone. This man had admitted his guilt and asked for forgiveness; I knew I must forgive him. I felt a weight lift from my heart.

He turned and walked out the door, and I never heard from him again.

I had always been one to hold onto a grudge, but I was able to forgive. Forgiving this man gave me a newfound freedom. My chains of anger dropped right to the floor.

—Lee E. Pollock—

# These Things Take Time

*In some families, please is described as the magic word. In our house, however, it was sorry.*
~Margaret Laurence

I came to motherhood late in life and all at once. One moment I was thirty-six and single, and the next I was married with three stepchildren, ages thirteen, seven, and five. For many reasons, this was destined to be a somewhat fractious situation because the kids lived predominantly with their mother 3,000 miles away. Except for two separate yearlong interludes, we saw them only during summers and the rare Christmas holiday. Even so, and despite my gross lack of experience as a parent, the kids and I managed to forge a mostly amicable relationship.

My stepson Anthony was an affectionate child who delighted in art, reading, and superheroes. We became particularly close, but this began to change as he grew from an endearing five-year-old into a truculent teenager. Hindsight, of course, is 20-20, but at the time neither my husband nor I realized the many issues that plagued him. All we knew was that our immensely likeable son had seemingly turned overnight into the Terminator — difficult to talk to, impossible to reach, and combative over the least little issue. Our relationship degenerated into a tense, battle-ridden landscape of sullen silence broken by argument and confrontation.

Everything came to a head one Christmas. Anthony was living with us at the time, but according to the terms of the parenting agreement, he flew to be with his mother for the holiday. No sooner did he get there than he called to say he wasn't coming back. We were stunned. My husband talked with him at length, but he was adamant. I also spoke with him, apologizing for my behavior and lack of patience, acknowledging my part in our difficulties and asking him to come home so we could work together to find a way back to where we'd been. He refused. At that point, I'm afraid I did one of the worst things a parent can do — I gave up on him. Although Anthony and his father stayed in guarded contact, he and I didn't speak again for six years.

Then one night my husband came to me and said, "Anthony's on the phone and wants to talk to you." Cautiously, I took the receiver and said hello. "I just want you to know I'm sending you a letter," was all he said before hanging up. I wondered what hate-filled message I was about to receive, but when it arrived, the opening words read: "First of all, I want to say I'm sorry." By the end of the letter, I was crying. When I got myself under control, I picked up the phone.

It took enormous courage and a willingness to risk rejection for Anthony to reach out to me after so long. It took immense trust in our past relationship and the belief that we could reconnect for the two of us to begin again. Slowly, we worked through our issues, coming to a clearer understanding of not only each other, but of ourselves.

Over the past ten years, our relationship has grown into something wondrous. Not only are we mother and son, but we're good friends as well — maybe even best friends — calling to share details of our day, a joke, or to offer support during difficult times. In a way, those years of silence worked to our advantage. But we would never have reached where we are today if it hadn't been for Anthony's bravery and desire to begin again and regain what we had lost.

— Melissa Crandall —

# Forgiveness Practice

> Courage doesn't always roar. Sometimes courage
> is the little voice at the end of the day that
> says I'll try again tomorrow.
> ~Mary Anne Radmacher

After a drunk driver killed my son Shawn on his high school prom night, my life fell apart. My vibrant charismatic nineteen-year-old had perished and in his place stood only broken dreams.

Searching for hope, I gathered memories seeking to keep them alive. I shared my feelings with friends and family on a daily basis. We reminisced about the sports Shawn played, the fish he caught, the hijinks with friends. I searched old photo albums, watching his progress from towheaded toddler asleep on Dad's chest to his senior picture in cap and gown. I reread sympathy cards detailing Shawn's impact on his friends' lives.

All those sweet memories faded when I saw his killer in the courtroom. For the first time in my grieving process, I was angry. The young man appeared stoic, devoid of emotion or remorse. Why was he alive and my son dead, his future gone? Shawn had a plan for life after high school — two years in community college and a part-time job with a carpet company.

Our son loved children and coached a youth flag football team where he patiently led small boys who idolized him. He wanted a future with a family and was fond of saying, "When I have kids, mine will be dressed in babyGap!" The world lost a good father. I lost an opportunity for grandchildren.

After several years of struggle, I began my journey up the steep hill of forgiveness. The theologians are correct: Progress cannot be accomplished if one is dragging the chains of anger and hatred.

The first step involved pondering a Sunday repetition of The Lord's Prayer: "Forgive us our trespasses as we forgive those who trespass against us." I had trouble saying the words.

During my daily walk, I wrestled with this dilemma. I shook my fist and told God I wasn't ready. Wisely, God didn't answer. Maybe I could forgive in increments, or practice forgiveness in percentiles. I began by saying, "God, I can forgive him ten percent." Daily I repeated this mantra. Shawn always defended the underdog, didn't he? The scabs on my soul began to soften.

Some days I managed to add another point or two, others another five. Two months later, I stalled before fifty percent. Why would I want to admit that I was halfway to total forgiveness? Not me, Lord!

Eventually I crawled across the fifty-yard line. Relieved at this milestone, I believed success was possible. Progress accelerated until I arrived at the ninety percent marker. Only ten points separated me from total forgiveness. The light at the end of the absolution tunnel beckoned, but my face turned away.

Spring passed, including what would have been my son's twenty-fourth birthday and the fifth anniversary of his death. I longed for completion of my task. What an accomplishment that would be — and an accomplishment I needed. Instead, I plodded into summer while still stuck at ninety percent. Depressed, I wondered if I'd make the final victory.

One morning in the fall, I awakened to the words, "Come into his heart Lord Jesus." Did I dream the phrase or did the voice speak to my innermost being? I believed the latter. The elusive 100 percent arrived, and with it relief and journey's end. At last, sounds were more musical, colors more vibrant, tastes sweeter.

The following May, a letter arrived from the drunk driver. The killer's note was composed two days before he was released from prison. At his sentencing hearing three years prior, the judge had directed him to write an apology to us. It began simply: "Undoubtedly, this represents the most difficult letter I have tried to compose... the content is derived solely from the inner-workings of my heart."

Why now? Why did this communication arrive after completion of my tortuous journey toward healing? The last line summed up my spiritual travels: "Be well in the meantime and may God give you guys the courage, strength, and wisdom to light your path."

The timing of the letter did not go unnoticed. May was the great equalizer—May 1st, the date Shawn died and the following week Mother's Day. Now perhaps I understood God's plan. Until I'd reached the 100 percent marker, I wouldn't have accepted the apology.

A scripture came to mind: "Thy word is a lamp unto my feet, and a light unto my path." Peace arrived in increments. I provided the math. God, through forgiveness practice, became the teacher.

— Rita Billbe —

# Learning My Lesson

*An apology is a lovely perfume; it can transform the clumsiest moment into a precious gift.*
~Margaret Lee Runbeck

I had just received my first long-term teaching assignment days earlier. It was November, and a teacher in an inner-city school had to take an early maternity leave. I was offered the position teaching Core French and Art to Grade Seven and Eight pupils, but I was warned it was a tough assignment. I knew it was in a "rough" part of town. But at twenty-one, I was fresh out of teachers college and full of enthusiasm. I accepted.

I had four classes with over a hundred students to deal with. Some were friendly, and some were quiet and observant, but it seemed that most of the students were loud and disrespectful. All my wonderful lesson plans seemed to go awry as discipline became my number-one priority. My head spun as I tried to identify the "class clowns" with their snickering, inappropriate language and rude body noises. I'm sure it became a challenge to some of them to bring the new teacher down. Needless to say, at one point, I felt they had succeeded, when I found myself weeping in the principal's office, telling her that I couldn't take it anymore.

The principal, a Sister, was very supportive and marched into the classroom, ready to issue suspensions. I was simply to tell her who the culprits were. The class settled down and she left, advising me to send her anyone who was being disrespectful.

I began reviewing French vocabulary and was asking simple questions relating to Christmas. "What will you give your mother for Christmas?" My eyes scanned the classroom. Several pupils (the ones who had never given me any trouble) had their hands up. Others had bored looks and were doodling in their notebooks. Others simply had their heads down. I decided to single out one of the pupils with his head down, Robert.

"Robert, qu'est-ce que tu vas donner à ta mère pour Noël?"

The pupils with their heads down looked up. The others stopped doodling and stared at me. *Progress,* I thought with satisfaction. I finally had their undivided attention. I turned to Robert.

Robert had looked up, but his face, unlike the others, had contorted into a mask of pain. "I hate you!" he cried, and ran from the room.

What had I done? Stunned, I met the sea of frozen, unbelieving faces in the room.

"His mother committed suicide, Miss," one of the girls near me said softly.

I wanted to cry. "I didn't know," I murmured in shock. "I didn't know."

Why, of all the pupils in the class, did I have to call on Robert? If I had known about his mother, I would never have used that question as an example. I felt heartbroken and battered, crushed and alone. *Poor Robert,* I wept inwardly. *How must he be feeling?*

The next few moments were a blur. Robert ran to the principal's office, and she came back to the classroom, allowing me to speak to him privately in her office. His body was slumped in sorrow. I did the only thing I could do: I spoke to him from my heart. I told him how sorry I was, that I hadn't known, and that I would never have wanted to hurt him or anybody in that way. I asked him for forgiveness.

Over the years, I have learned that when you speak from the heart, pupils listen. Robert believed me. I think he saw his pain reflected in my eyes. He sensed my sincerity and genuine sorrow. Robert taught me that you can't assume that everyone in your class has a mother and father; that you should find out as much as you can about the students you will have in your care; that pupils have histories that are filled with pain and loss; and that you have to remember that you are not teaching "subjects," but human beings with feelings and vulnerabilities.

As I struggled with the challenges and the shifting personalities of many students that first year, I realized that teaching was always going to be a learning and shifting experience, with successes and mistakes, triumphs and tribulations. Lessons to teach and lessons to learn.

Robert gave me my first gift as a teacher: the gift of forgiveness. And a lesson I'll never forget.

— Rosanna Micelotta Battigelli —

# The Pilgrim's Wife

*The land flourished because it was fed from so many sources — because it was nourished by so many cultures and traditions and peoples.*
~President Lyndon B. Johnson

It was only the third-grade Thanksgiving play but it was my first one and I was excited. I had my heart set on the main role — the pilgrim's wife.

The only drawback was that I had recently arrived in America from Czechoslovakia and my English was not that great. But since no one else appeared to be auditioning for the role, I was hopeful.

The day of the tryouts, I had butterflies in my stomach. I so wanted this! As others tried out for various roles and read the script in front of the room I mouthed the lines along with them.

Rudy was cast as the lead male pilgrim. When Mrs. Rosen asked who was interested in the role of the pilgrim's wife, my hand shot up. Two seconds later, Colleen Nelson raised hers. Had I known Colleen would audition I never would have bothered.

Colleen was a ginger-haired beauty with piercing green eyes and creamy skin, with just the right number of tiny freckles dotting her perfect nose. Even at the tender age of eight, she knew she had power.

I was taller than all the kids in class except for two boys who had been left behind. I had a massive head of dark-brown hair with a mind of its own. My skin was so pale, I thought I looked like a ghost.

Colleen read the lines from the script with ease. When she was done, she gave the class and the teacher a dazzling smile and sat down.

How could I compete with that? I walked nervously to the front of the room and stood next to Rudy. He read his lines, which gave me my cues. Then it was as if I were transformed. My nervousness disappeared. I BECAME the pilgrim's wife. I felt it. I knew I was good! I didn't need a script. I knew the part by heart.

But my accent was so severe. When I sat down, it was with a heavy heart. I wondered if my English was even understood.

The roles were announced the next day. Yolanda and Juan were cast as the Pilgrim couples' children. Jacob and Dorothy were to play the lead Native Americans. To my surprise, I was cast in the part I longed for — the pilgrim's wife. Everyone congratulated me, except for Colleen. I heard her voice from across the room: "How could SHE play a pilgrim? Didn't pilgrims come from England? She can hardly speak English. Besides, actresses are supposed to be beautiful. And she's not!"

I was noticeably hurt. Other kids tried to console me and voiced their objections but Colleen's anger had no end. "You're all sticking up for her because she's an IMMIGRANT!" She made the word sound so ugly.

I started crying and so did she. The teacher called the class to order.

Mrs. Rosen began: "This is America. That's what made this country great — immigrants. You may have been born here, or maybe your parents were, but take a look at yourselves. You are all a blend of many nationalities, religions and races."

We looked around and it was true. We noticed what had never crossed our minds before. There was as diverse a mixture of people in that room as could be. There were Vietnamese, Latinos, Africans, Irish, Italians, Asians and Poles. There were Christians and Jews and Muslims sitting side by side in a classroom and never giving their differences a thought. It was a regular United Nations — which we had taken for granted.

Mrs. Rosen addressed Colleen gently: "Where are you from, Colleen?"

"I was born right here in Queens, New York," she answered smugly.

"And your parents?" Mrs. Rosen continued.

Colleen wavered: "I think they're from Brooklyn."

"Well, before Brooklyn I know your parents came from Ireland. They were Irish immigrants."

"But... but," Colleen stammered.

Juan spoke up. "I'm from Mexico. But I am an American."

The teacher went on, "We are all Americans now. But most of our parents or grandparents or great-grandparents were immigrants. It's the diversity that made this country so unique, so exceptional. Why do you think America attracts people from all over the world? It's because America is a special place where all men are created equal."

The lunch bell rang and the class was dismissed. As Colleen headed for the door, Mrs. Rosen put a hand on her shoulder.

"May I have a word with you, Colleen?"

I left, disappearing into the girls' room to wipe my face and collect myself. Then I went to the lunchroom and sat away from the crowd, opening my lunch. But I was not very hungry.

A few minutes later, Colleen entered the room. I opened a book and pretended to read, not wanting to face her. But she headed in my direction.

"Can I sit here?" she began cautiously.

"Sure," I shrugged, still staring down at my book. She sat opposite me.

"Eva, I don't know where to start." She started tearing up. And so did I.

"I don't know why I said those hurtful things. I guess I was jealous because you did the part so well by heart and I had the script in front of me and I still messed up.

"And Mrs. Rosen's explanation about immigrants is so true. Most of us are immigrants or our ancestors were, unless we are Native Americans. And it was the immigrants who helped make America what it is today."

She continued, as both our tears started flowing freely: "And you ARE beautiful. I love your naturally curly hair and you have skin like porcelain. You don't have these stupid freckles like I have."

We both leaned over the table and hugged. The rest of the kids in the lunchroom were looking at us with wonder and amusement.

But we didn't care.

The Thanksgiving play took place in the school auditorium and all the classes and parents attended. I played the pilgrim's wife and the play was a big hit.

Colleen was an extra, playing a Native American girl. But what I loved the best was that at the end of the show, Colleen led the entire cast of twenty onto the stage, holding hands.

Then she stepped out of the line and, like an angel, sang, "God Bless America." It didn't matter that the song was written well after that original Thanksgiving took place. What mattered was that the spirit of America was within all our hearts that day.

Colleen and I — the child of immigrants and an immigrant — are still friends today. And America is still the greatest country in the world, made up of people of all religions, nationalities and races, from all over the globe.

— Eva Carter —

# Forgive Yourself

# The Support of a Family

*We all have regrets from past experiences.
You've got to learn to forgive yourself, to put
one foot in front of the other and go forward.*
~Rashida Rowe

I forgave the boy who permanently damaged my finger in elementary school with his discus-throwing dodge ball technique. I forgave Dad whenever he was too stubborn or opinionated. I even forgave my corporate nemesis who did his best to destroy my reputation. Whenever I forgave someone, my pent-up resentment lessened. But the hardest person to forgive was myself, for falling in love with a chameleon.

I was in my thirties when we met. One year older than I, he seemed perfect — fun-loving, bright, charming, and considerate. A nature lover like me, he introduced me to sailing and I introduced him to skiing. After seven years together, his hidden evil twin slowly emerged — the liar, the alcoholic, the adulterer, the skillful manipulator who knew just how to present himself to any audience for the desired effect. At first, I believed the man I fell in love with was the real one and this new creature was a temporary aberration. But as his behavior deteriorated over several years and he admitted that he had lied from the very beginning, I was forced to accept that the new him was the real one and I ended the relationship. Only then did my family tell me the rest.

It turned out that he had learned where my widowed mother hid her cash and had stolen thousands of dollars. Because she knew I loved him at the time, she kept the thefts secret and allowed this man to spend weekends with me at her home again and again until I cut him out of my life. Because of me, he shared two days at my cousin's house and stole from him too. For eight months, my cousin kept this secret, only revealing it after I told him about the theft at my mother's house. Even then, my cousin only said "something" disappeared. He never told me what.

I had allowed a conman to fool me. Because I brought this toxic person into our family, the hurt he caused was my fault. No matter that he fooled countless others—I should have known better. His affairs, the money he took from me, and the lies he told me paled in comparison to the anguish he caused my family. What he did to them could not be undone. The unknown "something" stolen from my cousin could not be replaced. When Mom told me about her missing money, I was too shocked to offer to repay her.

Later, she refused my repeated attempts to reimburse her.

"It isn't right, Mom," I said. "It's my fault."

"What he did is not your fault. The money is not important. What's important is for you to put this behind you and heal."

We hugged, I shed a few tears, and my cloud of guilt began to lift. Within two months, the cloud disappeared. Because Mom could forgive me, I could forgive me.

—Janet Hartman—

# The Fire Within

*Redemption is not perfection. The redeemed must realize their imperfections.*
~John Piper

White fluorescent lights flooded my squinting eyes as the *click, click, click* of cold, metal handcuffs shackled my wrists and ankles to a gurney in the trauma bay of the hospital.

Sharp pain in my knee. "You have the right to remain silent."

Dull pain in my shoulder. "Everything you say can and will be used against you in a court of law."

Stabbing pain in my tailbone. "You have the right to talk to a lawyer…"

I would learn later that I had blacked out, left my friends in my apartment near campus, got in my car, and drove over thirty miles before running a red light and colliding with an Uber driver and his three passengers at over eighty miles per hour. They were all injured.

Then I hit a median, flew over the top of two cars, and landed on my roof after flipping twice in midair. I would lose my driver's license, internship, and job, and serve time in prison while incurring tens of thousands of dollars of legal and medical expenses.

At that moment in the hospital, however, I knew none of that. All I knew was that everything hurt and I had double vision. For the first time in my twenty-two years of life, I was in handcuffs. I spent three nights in the hospital and one night in jail before my teary-eyed parents picked me up, thankful that their only son was alive. I had an eye patch, a limp, and enough guilt to make me wish I hadn't survived.

I quickly learned that no matter what happens in your life, the world keeps moving forward, with or without you. That weekend, four days after I was released from jail, I returned to campus and took my final exams for the fall semester. I passed them all but then put school out of my mind; I had a situation on my hands.

How did this happen? This was not me. I didn't drive drunk. I didn't even drink that often. I was a full-time accounting student, a part-time salesman at one of the major wireless carriers, and a competitive powerlifter. I had an internship and a fruitful career path at one of the Big Four accounting firms. My hobbies were going to the gym, reading books, starting to write (and abandoning) a novel, and working on my car. That's it.

By the time the next semester rolled around, my hobbies had become attending AA meetings, going to rehab, and trying not to break down every time thoughts of the people I had injured came to mind. No driving. No working out. No drinking with friends. In rehab, I was diagnosed with bipolar disorder and obsessive-compulsive disorder. Turns out, drinking while experiencing a manic episode is a recipe for catastrophe. While a part of me was relieved to have a diagnosis to help explain how I ended up in this situation, another part of me struggled to come to terms with the fact that I have a mental disorder, that I'm broken in some way.

At the time, it felt like the only part of my old life I still had was my mind, and therefore my ability to read. So, I read. A lot. This became my lifeline when the coronavirus pandemic sent my classes online.

Filling my mind with the wisdom of men and women greater than myself is what allowed me to keep my sanity through this living nightmare. I read fiction that taught me empathy, how to see the world from someone else's point of view. I read accounts of tragedy such as Viktor Frankl's *Man's Search for Meaning*, which taught me two things. First, people throughout history have gone through trials much more difficult than my own — trials they were forced into, not trials brought upon themselves by their own hand. Second, the only way I was going to make it through this was if I forged meaning amidst the calamity.

I knew what the meaning of my old life was. It was the epitome of the American status quo. Go to college. Pick a marketable major. Get a good job. Live a good life. That was the idea, at least. Not anymore. With two felony DUIs and prison time on my background check, I lost my internship and any chance at a future in accounting. I quit my sales job and took a semester off so I could go to prison, something that wasn't even in the realm of possibility for the old me.

What do you do when your plans are dashed, your future uncertain, and your faith in yourself is shaken? You stand up straight with your shoulders back. You do the next right thing. You lift your eyes to the mountain you must climb and you climb it, one rock at a time. What once seemed insurmountable will in time become manageable. On the other side of your mountain, you will find the path leading you where you need to go.

What remains when the external accomplishments that your identity is based upon disappear? The answer is *you*. The essence of your being. Sit down. Close your eyes. Breathe. Turn your gaze inward, look deep into your soul, and search for the crackle of flame burning within. That's you. The voice in your head and the tingling in your fingertips? That's life, coursing through your veins. Feel it. Cherish it. Do not take it for granted, for none of us knows the time nor the place when our flame will be extinguished.

What is the meaning of my debacle? Is there even meaning to be found in the aftermath of a drunken collision for me, the man responsible for it? Some would say no. I, however, believe that there is.

Coming so close to losing my life helped reveal to me what truly matters. Not money. Or status. Or material possessions. None of that matters when you look death in the eye. Don't look outside yourself for fulfillment, or you will never find it. Everything your soul needs can be found within. When disaster strikes, you'll learn who is really there for you. Treasure those people.

What is my meaning? To live my truth. The written word is my medium. I feel called to write, to share my story with the world. I finally fulfilled my dream of finishing a novel, with many more to come. This brings me more joy than any job or internship ever could. I hope that, in reading my story, you may learn from my mistakes and apply my experience to the struggles in your own life. Whatever you have to do, whatever challenges you must face, do it with the faith that no matter how impossible it may seem today, you will grow through it, and you are not alone.

—John Apel—

# A Story of Forgiveness

*To err is human; to forgive, divine.*
*~Alexander Pope*

In April 1993, at a young and irresponsible age, I found out I was pregnant. With much prodding, I reluctantly and regretfully terminated the pregnancy. I struggled with what I had done and went through several years of feeling unbearably guilty. As a Catholic, I went to confession, but after a brief, tearful session, I figured the priest must not have heard me through my sobs because God couldn't possibly forgive me with a couple of Hail Marys and Our Fathers.

After dealing with several years of depression, I found myself on a different path of self-destructive behavior. I was motivated enough to go to college, but not for all of the right reasons. I did okay at school and attended class regularly, but I partied extensively and dabbled in drugs. Once again, I found myself pregnant. This pregnancy was the motivation I needed to get my act together. I moved home and finished the one class I needed to get an associate's degree, and I picked up additional classes at the local technical college.

In July 1999, I had a baby boy who gave me a wonderful and healthy reason to live. I enjoyed every part of being a mom. Because of him, my life turned around entirely. Although I did not remain with his dad, I knew I was doing the right thing in raising my baby.

After graduating from college with a couple of two-year degrees and then a bachelor's degree, I felt like I had my act together. Still, two dates continued to haunt me: April 26th, the day I'd terminated the first pregnancy, and November 22nd, the day the baby was due.

In July 2005, I got married to a wonderful man who was willing to accept me, my son and all of my baggage. We were fortunate to become pregnant that August, with a due date of May 23rd. We were ecstatic, and two ultrasounds at the beginning of the pregnancy revealed a healthy, growing baby. It wasn't until our routine ultrasound in late December that we found out we were having twin boys. They pushed up my due date to the week of April 26th.

I didn't want to have the babies on that day. I had always vowed that I would think of my unborn baby daily, to somehow repent for what I'd taken away from that child. I felt like I needed to leave April 26th as a day of mourning. It was sacred in my mind.

At a routine checkup on the morning of April 26th, my doctor found that I was five centimeters dilated. It was time to have my babies. As much as I was ready to meet my boys, I choked back tears and confided in her about the irony of the date. She held my hand and offered me different options, but I decided that God had His hand in this, and I needed to do what was intended. Although I am ashamed to admit it, despite the fact that my faith in God is true, I couldn't get it out of the back of my mind that this was His opportunity to take something away from me as I had done thirteen years ago.

Eleven hours later, I pushed out the first baby — a four-pound, eleven-ounce miracle. We knew the second baby was breech, and the plan was to turn him around and deliver him normally. After the expert medical staff turned him around and all was going as planned, he stuck his arm out in one last attempt to enjoy some space to himself. In their efforts to push his arm back in to deliver his head first, the cord got pinched between his arm and his head. With no vital signs on the delivery room monitors, my mind raced with the penance I must be paying now. Surely, the Hail Marys and Our Fathers had been enough. Surely, the guilt I'd carried with me for thirteen years had signified my repentance.

My second baby was born via emergency C-section, all five pounds, fifteen ounces of healthy baby boy. After a very brief stay in the NICU, the babies were released to our care. For weeks after I had the twins, amidst the feelings of being overwhelmed and ecstatic, I could not help but question why God had not allowed me to keep that day to mourn and remember every year. I still feared that something was going to happen to one of the twins or that they would be taken away from me, but they remained healthy, growing boys.

Nearly five months later, I was attending a class in preparation for the boys' baptism. As we were the only family baptizing our children in November, my husband stayed home with the three boys and I was the only parent there. The instructor was a very kind woman who told me about her own family of girls and how she used to take in infants as foster children. The thought of having to raise these infants and then turn around and give them to someone else left me both touched and heartbroken. Feeling emotional from her stories and the thought of baptizing my boys, I struggled to remain composed. She noticed my tears and asked if there was anything she could do. I sobbed out my entire story.

When I had finished, this woman smiled at me compassionately. With the most soothing voice, she explained to me that the boys were not brought into this world on April 26th as a coincidence. They were given to me that day as a gift to our family and as a symbol of forgiveness that I could not ignore. I know this woman was in that room with me for more than just teaching me about baptizing my boys. I think she was there to re-baptize *me*. The sense of peace and forgiveness this woman offered me redefined my faith in God. I was more at peace that day than I had been in thirteen years.

— S.R. —

# The Angels on the Train

*Angels assist us in connecting with a powerful
yet gentle force, which encourages us
to live life to its fullest.*
~Denise Linn

I was completing the nineteenth day of a twenty-day jail sentence. I had been through one of life's storms, and I had temporarily lost custody of my three daughters as a result of my poor choices.

Fortunately, I had been granted work release during my sentencing. As I rode the train to work that morning, I felt a true sense of accomplishment. I had almost completed something that I thought I would never have to experience: jail. I felt alive for the first time in a long time, and I was mulling over what I could do to complete my community service and give back. I knew I had a long road in front of me to get my children back, but I had just taken the hardest first steps.

In jail, I had read a book about Rex, a military dog. As I thought about that book, I glanced up and noticed an old blind man two rows up from me. A light bulb went off. I could work with service animals! I had always been a dog lover.

At that moment, the train came to its next stop, but unlike every other stop, the recorded voice did not announce the stop we were at. I saw alarm on the old man's face.

Quickly, I stood and walked over to him. I told him the station we were at and asked which stop was his. He thanked me and told me of his stop. We had two more to go, and I told him not to worry because I would make sure he didn't miss it. He thanked me again, and I sat back down.

I took this moment to look at the people nearby. It wasn't particularly crowded at this time of day, and everyone I saw was looking at their phones. Nobody seemed to notice the exchange between the blind man and me. I did see a lady at the far end of the train with a baby stroller. We made eye contact, and she gave me the slightest smile. She had a knowing look in her eyes. It was a brief moment we shared, but I felt strangely moved by it. My thoughts lingered on her look for the next two stops, but we didn't make eye contact again.

We arrived at the blind man's stop, and I informed him that this was where he should get off. He thanked me as I helped him stand and make his way to the train doors. I asked if he needed additional help, but he said he was fine. This was his normal stop, he said, and he knew where to go. I smiled and sat back down as I watched him walk down the steps slowly with the help of his walking cane.

He turned right and began to make his way down the track beside the train. I looked around again at the passengers on the train. As I glanced back at the blind man, my heart froze as he made an abrupt right turn and was about to walk between the train cars. In a split second, I realized he needed help. If I exited the train, I would miss my arrival time at work. I would miss my phone call into the jail and face the consequences of being late, which would mean extending my sentence.

Even as I thought of spending more time in jail after being so close to being finished, I found myself moving between the train doors as they tried to close. In an instant, I was out of the train and grabbing the blind man before he fell between the train cars. He appeared very startled and thanked me again for my help. It didn't occur to me at the time that if this had been his normal stop, he should have known which way to turn upon exiting the train. In that moment, I made a decision to get the man safely to his final destination and gave no more thought to the consequences I would face for being late.

It may well have been the first truly selfless act I had done in my life.

I got lucky, though. The conductor had seen the events unfold, and he had stopped the train and come to help. He asked if the gentleman was okay. The man replied he was fine, and I informed the conductor I was going to help him reach his final destination. The conductor made one final inquiry of the blind man's wellbeing before heading back to get the train back on schedule.

I guided the man to the elevator and asked where we were going. As he began to answer, a hand touched me softly on the arm. I turned to see the lady with the baby stroller. She gave me the warmest smile and said, "I have him now. You have somewhere you need to be."

She turned to the old man and said, "Sir, I have nowhere to be today. Let me help you get home."

He thanked her, and she gave me one last look and wished me goodbye. I raced back to the train and miraculously got back on before it pulled away. As I headed to work, on time, I pondered what had just happened. I never saw the lady exit the train; she just appeared beside me at the elevator. How did she know I had a pressing need to be on time? And how did she know I was planning to stay with the blind man? What new mother with a baby stroller has nowhere to be and offers her help to a stranger? It wasn't until later when I sat in silence that I realized what had happened and wept.

That old blind man and that young mother were sent to test me at the end of a long struggle; they were there to offer me a chance to prove to myself that I had truly changed. I had a spiritual awakening that day, because I had put a stranger's needs above mine in a totally selfless act.

I thank God every day for those angels on the train. That day marked my walk back into the love and light that I know now. And I'm happy to report that "The Angels on the Train" bedtime story is often requested by my daughters.

— Ryan Freeman —

# A Walk with Thelma

> *The best reason for having dreams is that*
> *in dreams no reasons are necessary.*
> *~Ashleigh Brilliant*

"You look radiant," I squealed, locking my arm through Thelma's as we strolled down the cobblestone sidewalk. "Look at you. You don't seem ill at all—you positively glow!"

Like a couple of schoolgirls we giggled and caught up on the past few years. It felt incredible seeing Thelma again. Thelma was eighty-nine, decades ahead of me, but our age difference didn't matter. Our friendship had blossomed from the moment we set eyes on each other.

As we walked, I felt so relieved that Thelma appeared healthier than ever. "You know, Thelma," I said, "yesterday, I had the strongest feeling I should phone you."

Although the cozy little shops beckoned us, window-shopping could wait for another day. We were too enthralled, asking questions, and catching up with each other. The path that had seemed so long suddenly ended and we found ourselves standing alone before a green pasture.

"It's that time," Thelma announced.

After hugging, we clung to each other, our eyes full of tears. I wanted to hold her forever. "I know you know, that even though I don't call as often as I should, I love and miss you a lot," I said, embracing her once more.

Forgive Yourself

"I do know you love me," Thelma answered softly. "I love you too."

"We've got to do this more often," I cried. "I promise I'll come see you soon."

I'll never forget the love on Thelma's face. Her expression reminded me what I already knew in my heart, that there wasn't going to be another visit with her. Thelma's misty eyes gleamed as she grabbed my hand one last time and then gently let go as she faded away into the light.

And in that instant I woke up, brushing the tears from my face, knowing that I would never see Thelma again because I had received a call from her son, earlier that same morning, informing me that Thelma had passed away.

Upon hearing of Thelma's death, a feverish guilt consumed me all day. If only I'd followed through with visits or heeded my gut and called her the day before she died. "There's always tomorrow," I assured myself, but Thelma's tomorrows had run out and I hadn't even said goodbye. When I needed her most, Thelma's love reached me in my dream so that I could try and move past my guilt.

—Jill Burns—

# His Messenger

*If you can't feed a hundred people, then feed just one.*
*~Mother Teresa*

She came to me — a small, dark-eyed girl. She was God's messenger, but I wasn't perceptive enough to grasp it. Not then.

My story begins when I was an un-churched, forty-something woman from the suburbs. For most of my life, I had bowed to the god of goals, who demanded higher levels of achievement for my own glory. I bought into the intellectual formula for happiness: Earn good grades, so that you can attend a good college, so that you will land a good job with a large company, so that you can earn a good salary, live an affluent life, marry a successful man and live happily ever after. At no time did I consider the cost of that path or entertain the possibility of failure.

Single and childless, I achieved career success, but I did not find peace. I had affluence, but no gratitude. I traveled the world, restless. My pride drove people away. My self-centeredness led to loneliness. My remorse drew me to my knees. I dropped to the floor of my shower and wept. In the steam on the glass door, I wrote: "God help me."

Months after my "baptism" in the shower, I went to a local church and waited in the last row for the worship service to begin. A steady stream of unfamiliar people passed by, so I grabbed a bulletin and started to read. I hoped that I would remain unnoticed, but that was not to be.

God sat next to me and invisibly tapped my shoulder. I saw an invitation for a two-week mission trip to the Dominican Republic. I experienced a sudden desire to go to a place I had never visited, to serve people I had never met. Several months later, I was on the way to a divine encounter.

Everything about my first short-term mission was unfamiliar. I didn't know the people's culture or needs. I didn't know what to say or do. Most importantly, I didn't know God or His intentions. I had stopped attending church when I was nine years old. I read the words of the Bible as if they were poetry from dead saints — beautiful, but not relevant. Intense heat assailed my body and wilted my confidence as we traveled in a bus across the Caribbean island. I watched the view change from crowded city street to deserted highway to dirt road. Families lived in shelters made out of dried sugarcane stalks and banana leaves. Our guide pointed to children playing in muddy water.

"More children die every year from drinking bad water than will die from any other cause," he said. "Fresh water is a precious commodity."

I hugged my filtered water bottle like a security blanket.

We bunked with a Christian relief organization and gathered in the morning for a project overview.

"We're going to the village of Los Robles to help build an elementary school," the leader explained. "We provide one meal per day for every child who attends our school, and we give free meals to as many others as we can. We'll bring some gifts to give the children. We can't eliminate poverty, but we can show them love.

"One more thing: Don't give anything away if you don't have enough for the crowd. You could start a riot, and people could get hurt." He paused before adding, "Pay attention. God will meet you somewhere as you work."

Curious children ran through our project with more confidence every day. Young girls carried baby siblings with the poise of an adult. Dirt covered their naked bodies, but couldn't hide their natural beauty and gentle spirit. I was surprised to hear their constant laughter and see their joy.

On my third day in the village, a young girl approached and

smiled. Her braided hair was fastened with rainbow-colored ribbons. A too-large dress hung unevenly to the tops of bare feet. She pointed to the bottle of water tied to my waist. Her dark eyes sparkled with anticipation.

"*Agua?*" she asked.

I looked at her, and then at dozens of other children playing nearby. I remembered the instructions not to share anything with one child that I could not share with all. I remembered the warning about fresh water and feared for myself. I yielded to the loud voice in my head, not the soft whisper in my heart.

"No *agua*," I responded and kept working.

Her dark eyes lost the sparkle, but she did not give up. She stepped closer and asked again.

"Sandy. *Agua, por favor?*"

"No," I answered and turned away.

I started to cry. I was powerless to help all the people, but why had I declined the opportunity to help just one?

"Why am I here if I can't even provide a drink of clean water?" I shouted at God. In kindness, He remained silent.

In the morning, our pastor taught from the gospel of John. I heard the story of Jesus and the Samaritan woman at the well. Her story sounded like the events of my prior afternoon.

Jesus asked the Samaritan woman, "Will you give me a drink?"

Not yet aware of who was standing before her, the woman did not offer the stranger any water. She offered Him questions. He spoke about eternal life through faith. He already knew her checkered past, but still promised her the hope of God's forgiveness. The woman believed the stranger and went back to her village infused with joy.

After that teaching, we brought big jugs of fresh water for hundreds of children in the village. Within minutes, our supply was depleted, and the children returned to their homes. Ten days later, I returned to mine. I remained haunted by the look of disappointment in the little girl's eyes.

Months later, I remembered that my employer offered a line of well pumps in a different part of the company. I approached a senior manager and asked if he would help secure a donation for a tiny village. He agreed to assign help with the specification and installation process. When I learned the name of the project manager, I was amused and amazed: Jesus Rodriguez was assigned to help me. I exchanged regular e-mails with Jesus.

Less than a year later, fresh water flowed to thousands of villagers in a third world country. At last I had peace.

I discovered the truth of God's merciful love in a third world country. His young messenger asked me for a drink of water, and exposed my hard heart. Undaunted, God demonstrated the distance He was willing to go to help a child believe in forgiveness. I finally understood that I was the child God wanted to bless, so I too could become a messenger of grace.

—Sandra Wood—

# No Need for Goodbye

*More and more, when I single out the person who
inspired me most, I go back to my grandfather.*
~James Earl Jones

It had been a year since my grandfather passed away, and I was bothered by the fact that I never got to say goodbye to him. My parents had tried calling and texting me, but I was taking a nap, and my phone was in the other room. By the time I read my parents' messages and drove to the hospital, my grandfather had already passed away.

Although a year had passed since his death and I had a plethora of things to look forward to (senior prom, high-school graduation, the start of college, etc.), the fact that I never got to say goodbye to my role model weighed heavy on me.

I blamed myself for being asleep that day when I knew darn well that I should've gone with my parents to visit him. Of course, nobody knew that day was going to be his last. But if I had only gone with my parents to visit my grandfather, I would have been able to say goodbye.

One night before I went to bed, I was thinking about my grandfather and was overcome by sadness. I decided to close my eyes and pray to God. I asked God to allow me to dream of my grandfather; I just wanted to see him one more time. I didn't know if my prayer would be answered, but it was worth a shot. I cleared my thoughts and fell asleep.

Later that night, I felt a tap on my shoulder and jumped up. Darkness surrounded me, but that quickly ended when my lamp was turned on. The person who turned on the lamp in my room was a tall man, wearing pants and a shirt that were blindingly white. I tried to speak, but I couldn't; it felt as if my vocal cords had disappeared. The man in the white clothing softly took me by the hand and led me out of my bed. I was not hesitant at all, for his presence gave me a sense of comfort. The man walked me to the door of my room and slowly opened it.

On the other side of the door was an entirely white room. And there was my grandfather, sitting in his favorite chair. I stared at him motionless, not knowing what was going on. As I stood in shock, my grandfather began to sing his favorite song: "The Party's Over" by Willie Nelson. I ran toward him and hugged him while he sat singing in his chair. I cried on his shoulder. I didn't want to let go.

My grandfather then placed his hands on my shoulders and maneuvered me so we were face to face. He then said, "Everything is going to be alright. There was no need for you to say goodbye because I'm not going anywhere. I'll always be with you. I am so proud of the man you are becoming and look forward to watching you live your life. I love you."

I still couldn't speak, so I smiled and hugged him once more.

I arose to the sound of my neighbor mowing his lawn at eight in the morning. My eyes were still watery, but I couldn't help smiling, for I knew that everything was going to be all right.

— Arturo Guajardo IV —

# Empowering Humiliation

*Saying no can be the ultimate self-care.*
*~Claudia Black*

The phone was ringing again. It was my neighbor, Sandy. "Hey, can Angie come over and play with Mary?"

"Just a sec. I'll ask her."

My six-year-old daughter had a worried look on her angelic face. "I don't want to go, Mom."

I spoke into the phone. "Thanks for inviting her, but right now isn't a good time."

Sandy persisted. "Mary is bored. Why don't you just send her down so the girls can play, just for a little while?"

"Well, I don't think…"

Sandy interrupted me. "The girls can help me make cookies. Ask her again, pleeeeez?"

"Okay."

I put my hand over the receiver and whispered to my daughter with urgency in my voice this time. "Sandy said you and Mary can help make cookies. Please, why don't you just go down there for a little bit?"

My daughter got big tears in her eyes. "But I don't want to, Mama!"

"Alright, *fine!*" I growled.

I got back on the phone and said something like, "I'm really sorry, but she just doesn't feel well right now." That fib sounded a little nicer than "She really doesn't want to come to your house!"

Sandy was not happy. That was clear in her abrupt reply. "Well, alright then. Bye."

As I hung up the phone, I felt tormented inside. But why?

I nagged my little one again, my voice tight and harsh. "I don't know why you couldn't just go play with Mary!"

Angie looked up at me, and her huge eyes reflected her own stress. I looked into her sweet, worried face, and something suddenly broke inside me.

*What are you doing to your child? She's only six!* That voice of truth screamed from a very deep place within me. It jolted me to the core.

I held back my sobs long enough to say, "No, no, honey. I'm sorry. It's okay if you don't want to go over there. You don't have to."

I escaped to another room, and the dam broke. I'd known for a while that I had a serious people-pleasing problem. I had some sort of ridiculous fear of making anyone upset. It was so very difficult for me to say "no" to anyone. Yet in that moment of pressure, I'd put that same burden on my innocent child's shoulders.

I was overwhelmed with shame, confusion and despair.

It was one of the best, most life-changing moments of my life.

I remember another transformational time during that same year. My sister dropped by unannounced with her two young children. She asked if I could babysit them while she went to work that evening.

I said, "Umm, well, I really have a lot to do tonight." She said that she'd been called in to cover someone else's shift, and she really needed the money.

I could feel the conflict rising up inside me. I had two young children of my own. I gave in to short-notice babysitting for her on a regular basis. I was so very tired.

Reluctantly, I said, "Well, okay."

Sis stayed to visit for a while before leaving for work. I was trying to be pleasant, but I was wearing my resentment like a thick blanket around my shoulders.

My sister asked, "What's wrong?"

I hesitated, but then the truth blurted out. "You put me on the spot like this all the time! It sure would be nice if you'd ask me in advance."

She looked me in the eye. "This is your own fault. If you didn't want to do it, you should've said no. You can't agree to do something, and then blame me! Blame yourself!"

*Ouch!* I was furious at her for saying that, but it was the hard truth I had to hear. That happened many years ago, and I have reminded myself of it numerous times since then.

How could I have been so blind? Why did I almost always go into automatic "yes" and keep-the-peace-at-all-costs mode?

I had to find answers and get help to learn how to stop.

Yes, my empowerment had to start with my humiliation. What? Aren't humility and power opposites?

That's the ironic beauty of all this. I had to hit the floor, sobbing on my knees, to realize I needed help to change my life.

I bought a book and took a class about healthy boundaries. I sought out a good counselor and started going to therapy.

It's been a continuous eye-opening journey for the last twenty years.

There have been other books, mentors and counseling sessions since I started on my road to recovery. This long journey has empowered me in many ways. Mostly, I've learned how to have honest relationships with others and with myself.

My "yes" means yes, and my "no" means no—without inner turmoil, resentment or false guilt. Well, usually. But I'm still learning and open to receiving help. I know that's where my power and freedom are.

—Diana Bauder—

# Reservation for One

*Don't judge too harshly, for if your weaknesses were to be placed under your footsteps, most likely you would stumble and fall as well.*
*~Richelle E. Goodrich*

Drunk drivers are selfish, and mothers who drive drunk with their children in the car should be locked up forever with the other crazy, trashy, drug-addicted, prostitute, thieving women. There is no gray area… period. Even before I had children, I knew what kind of mother I would be: giving, loving, nurturing, safety-conscious — basically perfect.

I would never put my children in harm's way. I dreamt of being that soccer or baseball mom, you know, the kind that drives a minivan and volunteers at her kids' Christmas and Valentine's Day parties. I'd bake fresh oatmeal-raisin cookies (not chocolate-chip because oatmeal and raisins are healthy) and have them waiting, hot out of the oven with ice cold glasses of soy milk when the children got off the school bus. My babies would love me so much and draw pictures of them and me — with hearts for clouds; I'd hang their artwork on the refrigerator door. I'd be Supermom.

But, supermoms don't end up doing time and supermoms' mug shots don't end up on the front page of the local newspaper for driving under the influence with their children in their minivans.

On November 25, 2012 at 5:36 p.m., I was stopped outside the Walgreens on Madison Street in Clarksville, Tennessee.

"Ma'am, have you been drinking?"

"Um... oh... not much. Just a glass of wine or two this afternoon," I mumbled.

"I'm going to need you to step out of the van. Officer Mitchell will stay with the kids."

I obeyed. He asked me to walk in a straight line, heel to toe. I failed. He asked me to say the alphabet backwards. I really failed. My three youngest, ages five, seven, and nine, watched as I was handcuffed, with blue lights flashing behind the maroon Nissan Quest that carried them to and from school, baseball practice, and church on Sunday mornings. They watched as the police officer forced my head down into the patrol car. My children watched as I was driven away to jail, all but my eleven-year-old son who was at a friend's house.

I spent twenty-four hours in the holding tank. I was placed there completely alone. I sat on the cold, concrete floor and cried. Finally, around 5 a.m., I was able to make bail.

I never thought in all my years I would become an alcoholic. After all, I never had a problem with alcohol in college. I even worked at a winery and could take the wine or leave it. Something happened between college, marriage, first baby and fourth baby — something called life.

February 16th, the day I was to find out my fate, quickly came. I was oddly calm, thinking that surely the judge would be lenient. After all, I was a middle school English teacher and Sunday school leader and had never been in trouble in my entire life.

The court hearing whirled by me. It was fast and confusing. My lawyer came back with this proposal: Thirty days in jail — ten days for each child. I would get the child endangerment charges erased from my permanent file if I took the jail time. I decided that if I ever wanted a decent job again, I'd better take the plea, but how in the world would I be able to do jail time and with — those women? I shuddered at the idea.

I had two weeks or so to prepare before I turned myself into the Montgomery County Jail, two weeks to do my shopping for the list of items I could bring: three white shirts, socks, underwear, and three books. There would be no fashion shows in jail.

Those two weeks were just the amount of time I needed to organize my thoughts. I had to imagine that I was going on an unusual journey — a journey most women will never take, especially good, educated mothers. It was going to be a life journey — a time to gain raw experiences that would hopefully fill my personal storybook. I had an opportunity to see how those bad girls lived. Maybe I would pretend I was an undercover journalist or a missionary preparing to go into a war-torn country. Yes, that's what it would be. This would give me a chance to pull purpose out of this tragic situation. I would help those inmates any way I could.

March 1st quickly arrived. I had to turn myself in at 6 a.m. at the intake section with the big window that is just upstairs after you walk into the jail's main doors.

My mother had tears rolling down her cheeks.

"You'll be okay?"

"Yes, of course, Mom. This is going to be fun. Real fun. I am excited, actually. Really excited. Don't worry about me. It's great. It's going to be great. Great fun. Great excitement."

"I will write you and visit you," my mother affirmed.

"You don't have to, Mom. I mean, if it's too hard for you," I said.

"No, I will write every week, and I will visit."

I couldn't look back to tell her, "Okay" or "Goodbye." Knowing the pain she felt and the disappointment I had caused was overwhelming. It put too much of a damper on the pumped up enthusiasm about my upcoming venture, and without that enthusiasm, I think I would have lost it.

"Reservation for one," I said bravely, as I smiled at the shorthaired, hard-faced woman behind the smudged glass window.

"Huh?" she said.

"Oh, um, I'm here to turn myself in — Dana Clark."

"Sit on over there until I call you back," she demanded.

I sat on the cold bench and reminded myself to breathe, that everything was going to be okay, and that I would find hope in this journey by helping those women.

Finally a young male guard opened the heavy metal door that led to the processing area and then guided me to a fairly large room with windows to look out. I felt like I was in there for days before another young woman guard approached the locked door. I knew her from somewhere, but I couldn't put my finger on it. As soon as our eyes met, though, memories flooded me.

"Na'Tisha," I said.

"Uh, yeah," she replied.

For a moment I thought of leaving it at that. I didn't want her to know who I was. She had been one of my seventh-grade language arts students when I taught at Northeast Middle School.

"Aw! Mrs. Clark! I didn't recognize you. Oh, my God! What are you doing in here?"

"Uh... well... I kind of made a bad choice — totally not something I typically do, and um, yeah... that's it."

I lied. It was something I typically did. I had started out just drinking a few glasses of wine on the weekends to help deal with work and laundry and dinner and baths and homework and fighting siblings and baseball practices and soccer practices and dance recitals and on and on. Quickly, I was drinking every day — but not until after the kids were in bed. Soon after that, I was drinking after 4 p.m.; then it moved up to 2 p.m.; then coconut vodka in my morning coffee.

Alcohol was my pick-me-up. It didn't make me tired or lethargic. It eased my back pain. It eased my anxiety. It made me calm and happy and willing to let my girls help me make dinner. Before, I just wanted to do everything on my own. I didn't want the added messes and spills.

But when I drank, I felt like I was a better momma. I had the time and energy to sit on the floor and play Barbies or throw a baseball in the back yard. Alcohol convinced me I was okay to drive. Alcohol was like a really bad friend who gives you really bad advice. *It's no different than some crazy mom who is texting and driving,* I fooled myself. *At least I drive slowly and have my eyes on the road when I drink.*

Na'Tisha stuck her head out of the room, "Hey, you guys, this is Ms. Clark. Man, she was my favorite teacher. She taught me about linking verbs and shit."

My face turned fifty shades of pink. My stomach rolled over and over into a ball of sharp, pinching pain. I didn't think I was going to be able to do this. I remember telling my students to pay attention in school, so they wouldn't end up on the streets some day, or worse—jail—and here I was. The roles had reversed, and I was being checked into jail by my former seventh-grade language arts student.

"Ms. Clark," Na'Tisha shyly said, "I'm gonna need you to strip off all your clothes, and then squat and cough."

"Squat and what?" I said.

"Squat and cough," she repeated, "We gotta make sure you ain't hidin' nothin'... I'm sorry, Ms. Clark, AREN'T hiding anything... up your, uh, well, you know...."

"Like what in the world would I hide up there?" I asked.

"Man, you'd be surprised. Mainly drugs, but sometimes knives and candy and rubber bands."

"I promise you, I have nothing up there," I said as I gave a slight cough.

I couldn't believe this was happening. I stood there buck naked. I was so embarrassed... so ashamed.

After checking me for hidden contraband, Na'Tisha handcuffed my wrists and ankles and escorted me down to the P-Pod. With my one stained flat sheet; a rough blanket that was only the thickness of a sheet; and my thin mat under my arms, I followed her down the long hallway.

The P-Pod was dark and chilly. Ten or so cells were arranged in a circle around a hard cement floor they called the commons area. This is the place where you can walk around freely for one hour a day to shower, get your exercise, and socialize a bit.

"Okay, Ms. Clark, this is where you'll be for a few days until we move you to the M-Pod. It'll be all right. Don't worry."

I could tell she wasn't too convinced that everything would be all right, but her kind words helped a little bit.

As she walked me closer to my cell, a pretty, young black girl with a shaved head shouted through the tiny window of the door, "Hey, she gonna be my celly? Damn, she fine. Look y'all the newbie be wearin' real make-up. Ain't she pretty? She's all mine."

Guard Na'Tisha handed me my bag of clothes and books, and then opened the heavy metal door to my new sardine-box sized home.

"This is Samantha — but they call her 'King X.' She's not too bad," Na'Tisha explained.

Na'Tisha told me to go in and make my bed. She told me at around 7:00 pm., I could go out in the commons area for my one hour of quasi freedom. I asked her what time it was. It was only 7:00 a.m. I jumped when the cell door slammed shut.

"Don't be scared," smirked King X, "I ain't gonna bite you. You gay? I'm gay. You pretty. We gonna get along just fine. You cute for being kinda old. How old are you? I'm twenty-one."

I was overwhelmed with the quick questions spewed at me.

"I'm Dana. I'm not gay. I like men. I'm thirty-eight-years-old," I answered.

"What you in here for?" she asked.

I told her the truth and she said she understood. She had been arrested for a DUI before, too, but this time she was in for domestic violence. She had beaten up her girlfriend, she said. She beat her up because she was flirting with other women. She told me that she didn't know why she got so angry. She said she had a five-year-old daughter that she had with a police officer who used to frequent her neighborhood. She had only been sixteen years old when she got pregnant. She said no one knew it was the police officer's baby. She said that he was good to her at first, but then he ignored her. She didn't care, though, because she liked women better anyway.

She told me I could have the top bunk — that she didn't like being on top. I was wondering how this was going to work since there was no ladder, and I had a lot of lower back problems.

"Hey! For real? Let me show you how we make our beds up in here. That flat sheet ain't gonna stay put if you don't tie the ends up like this."

She took charge. I didn't know how to do this. I had never been in jail before. It seemed there were going to be many tricks I was going to learn along the way during my stay. She grabbed my sheet and began wrapping my mat like a Christmas present, tying each end together in the middle like a bow. I was impressed, and I thought it very kind of her to help a stranger like that.

She went on to show me many other things—like how to keep my whites white.

"Don't ever have these fools wash yo clothes for ya. They'll come back brown. See, now, watcha gotta do is take some of this cheap-ass toothpaste—just use a little bit—and you take some of the shampoo, too. You mix it up with water, and scrub your underwear with it. Turns out really white. See? I did mine last night."

She reached for a T-shirt, a pair of underwear, and a pair of socks and held them up like she was a *The Price Is Right* model. She told me I could borrow some of her toothpaste when I needed it because I wouldn't be getting any sanitary supplies for another week. "They had already come yesterday," she said.

She took out a bag of Skittles that she purchased from the once-a-week mobile commissary cart, picked out the purple and green ones, let them melt in her hand, and then applied the color to her eyelids.

"Now see? This is how we wear make-up. Give me that pencil over there on my bed."

I grabbed the golf-game sized pencil and handed it to her. She used the pencil as eye and lip liner and then filled in her lips with a red Skittle. She told me to remind her later, and she'd show me how to make a permanent tattoo from pencil lead, a staple, and lotion.

I thought it very sweet of her to take me under her wing like that. She knew me from nowhere, and she treated me already like a friend.

The day went by fairly quickly. King X and I talked well into the evening, interrupted only by our tasteless lunch being pushed through a thin slit in our locked door. I learned that she had been abandoned as a child, left in her baby carrier on the front steps of her grandmother's house. She said that her mother was hooked on drugs and couldn't take care of her.

She does remember seeing her mother from time to time at Thanksgiving and Christmas. She said she didn't know who her father was, and that her grandmother, while she provided well for her, wasn't very nurturing. She told me that her uncle had sexually abused her when she was just three. She told me how badly she wanted to be a good role model for her own daughter, but things weren't working out that way. Her grandmother had custody of her daughter. She prayed that God would keep her daughter safe from sexual predators. The topic of her daughter brought tears to her sad and weary eyes.

"I never wanted this to happen to my daughter — you know, not be raised by her own mother," she said, "I swear when I get outta here, I'm gonna do better."

I began to think about my own children — how I had abandoned them, too, over the last few months, not physically, but emotionally, because of my drinking. The thought of me putting them in grave danger took my breath away. In that moment, I realized we are all capable of the unthinkable, given the right set of life circumstances.

King X told me that she would introduce me to the other women when we got out at 7 p.m. for our one-hour rec time. I was a bit nervous to meet them, not sure what to expect, but I felt that with King X on my side, everything would be okay.

Seven o'clock came and the cell door popped open like a jack-in-the-box makes a sudden jump. The noise was sharp and startling.

"Come on. Let's do this," King X said.

I cautiously followed her out into the commons area. There I was introduced to about fifteen women, many of whom looked just like me or looked just like my younger sister.

"Hey, y'all, this Mrs. Clark. She's my new celly. She cool. She gonna teach us some Shakespeare."

I met little Lily, a delicate longhaired redhead with freckles. She had been caught manufacturing meth. She said that she never thought she'd get hooked on that stuff, but she started using it when she began college. She said it helped her study better, plus it helped her lose weight, and because she had always been made fun of as a child for her pudgy figure, it was hard to give up. I told her that I had a daughter named Lily — my youngest, in fact. I shared with her how I had made up songs for each of my children that I sang when I rocked them to sleep. I sang my Lily song: *Lily, Lily, I love you. Lily, Lily, yes, it's true. I love my Lily. Of her I'm very fond. She's my little lily pad just a floatin' 'round the pond.*

"Awww, Mrs. Clark. I love that song. Will you make me a song?"

"Yeah, Mrs. Clark," chimed in Eureka, a very thin black girl with long braids, "will you write me a baby song with my name in it?"

I was overwhelmed with tenderness for these two young ladies. Everything I had thought about women in jail was slowly being chipped away. They weren't mean; they weren't evil; they weren't selfish and trashy. They were simply broken women with broken pasts, just like my own.

Eventually, I was moved up to the M-Pod where we were given a few more hours of social time a day. We were able to go out in the commons area from 10 a.m. to 12 p.m.; 2 p.m. to 4 p.m.; and 6 p.m. to 8 p.m. During these hours I met Stacey, an older lady who was a former physician's assistant. She became addicted to pain pills and was caught writing false prescriptions. She was sentenced to one year in jail.

I met Lori, Tabitha, and Lydia, all heroin addicts and who sold their bodies to support their addictions. I met a precious Latino lady named Maria. She led Bible studies during the 2 p.m. to 4 p.m. rec time. She also drew beautiful greeting cards and traded them with the others for candy or shampoo. I met Muffin and Tee-Tee who often were in competition for their unique hair-braiding abilities and showed me how to give myself a pedicure with water, lotion, and the top of a deodorant bottle. I met Sara who was caught shoplifting diapers. Sara had the voice of an angel and would often serenade us to sleep.

At least 90% of the women with whom I was in jail were addicted to either drugs or alcohol. I resolved to seek treatment when I was released.

"You ain't gonna forget me? Are you?" King X said as I walked out the cell door for the last time.

"No, King X, I will never forget you," I cried, "You are a beautiful woman with a beautiful heart. Go be a Supermom to that baby girl of yours. She needs you."

From there, I spent nine months at The Bethany House II, a restoration home for women where I learned to implement the 12-Step

Program, learned to deal with depression and anxiety in a healthy way, and most importantly, I learned to love and forgive myself.

Those women changed my world. I had been living in bondage for years trying to be the perfect mom. I finally understood that just because we *make* mistakes does not mean we *are* mistakes. I learned to abandon my presumptuous judgments and began to see the beauty and potential of every woman no matter what her past. It was in these lessons that I found true liberty for the very first time.

— Dana D. Clark —

# Chapter 10

# Make an Ex-Spouse an Ex-Enemy

# Ex's and Oh's

*For the spirit of Christmas fulfils the
greatest hunger of mankind.
~Loring A. Schuler*

Love is a funny thing, isn't it? It comes in all shapes and sizes, and you just never know when or where you're going to find it. Sometimes you know exactly where to find it; sometimes it finds you, grabbing hold of your lapels and shaking some sense back into your ever-hardening heart. And then there are times when you find that love was right there where you left it — not lost, really — like your car keys or the husband you divorced nine years ago, a man you had one partial life and two beautiful children with.

It was Christmas Day 2008 when I unexpectedly found love again. Oh, it wasn't the romantic kind of love that can go from inferno to fizzle in sixty seconds; it was the old, familiar kind — the slow burn — that can only happen between two people who once shared a life, the kind of love that can only happen between those same two people who shared the experience of giving life to two beautiful children. That's the kind of love I'm talking about, and to be honest with you, I didn't even see it coming.

He was just walking me to my car — Billy, that is, my ex-husband of nine years. I had just dropped our two teenage boys, Billy Boy and Alec, off at his house on Christmas morning. It's been our tradition since the divorce. After powering down breakfast and rifling through stockings at my place, I pack up the car with my boys and a couple of armloads of Christmas booty and head over to their dad's house, never bothering to change out of our pajamas.

It's at his house that we exchange gifts and pleasantries and then — after a bundle of Christmas hugs and kisses from my kids — I head back home with empty arms to spend the rest of the day with my mother. Oh, I know; it's not idyllic, but it's as close as we can get, considering.

Over the past couple of years our little tradition has included the new woman in Billy's life, Lisa. And even though I like her and she is good to my boys, it's a little disturbing when you find yourself sharing your family with another woman — and on such a day as Christmas, too. But such is life when you're a broken family. You learn to deal with it. I suppose it was a little harder on me this year after having just lost my job; I guess you could say that I was already feeling a little emotional, seemingly alone and left out in the cold as it was.

"Natalie, you know that I love you, right?" Billy whispered from out of the blue as we ambled toward my Jeep. His eyes unexpectedly welled up with tears as he — the consummate tough guy from Long Island — stood barefoot on that cold sidewalk in December in his green flannel pajamas, wearing his heart on his sleeve. "I will always love you."

Apparently he was feeling a tad schmaltzy, too. I hadn't heard the words "I love you" fall from his lips in a long while and even though I was completely touched by them, it was the tears in those sentimental green eyes of his that caught me off guard, those familiar eyes that brought back so many wonderful Christmas memories.

"I know," I whispered, my heart catching in my throat, as I, too, stood outside in the early morning hours of that cold Christmas day in my red, snowman pajamas, tears welling up in my own green eyes. "I love you, too."

It's not quite the exchange one might come to expect between two ex-spouses with an ocean's worth of water under the bridge. But before I knew it, we were locked in a long embrace, both of us weeping uncontrollably. What is it about Christmas that brings people together, temporarily lowering their defenses, those protective walls we build around our hearts?

It was as if — for just a moment — we were all alone, the two of us, held together by the warmth of what was and what is now our family, either that or by the static cling from our flannel pajamas. Who could tell? In any case, we were encapsulated in a proverbial snow-globe moment and we were both a little shaken. Meanwhile, deep down inside — in places I don't like to talk about at parties — I knew that Lisa and the boys were waiting inside for him; she would be making breakfast and Christmas memories all her own with my family — my children. That's not always an easy pill to swallow, even though I know in my heart I wouldn't change a thing — even if I could.

"We have two great kids together, Nat, and I wouldn't have wanted to take this walk with anyone but you," Billy breathed, giving me that same sideways (deliberate) grin that both my boys give me when they really mean something.

"Ditto," I smiled back.

I reached up onto my tiptoes, my arms squeezing evermore tightly around his neck, hot tears streaming down my cool cheeks and into the thickness of his shoulder. His arms tightened around me, too. And with all the love and sentimentality that Christmas brings with it, as well as all of the love and sentimentality that balls up between two people over the course of eighteen years, Billy and I gave each other a warm peck on the lips and wished each other a happy Christmas.

And it was then — as he tucked me into my car, shutting the door behind me — that I realized that even though life has a way of breaking our hearts — and even breaking apart our families at times — love is never really lost. In fact it can be found in some of the simplest of places — many of them locked tight in those Christmas memories both old and new.

— Natalie June Reilly —

# Close Encounter of the Healing Kind

*Love is a thing that can never go wrong.*
*~Dorothy Parker*

When I answered the phone and said, "Hello," I heard nothing except for a slight intake of breath. My first instinct was to hang up, thinking I'd received a nuisance call. For some reason, I remained on the line and repeated, "Hello?" The response was one word, my name, uttered in a hesitant voice: "Jenny?"

I hadn't heard that voice for eighteen years, but I recognized it immediately. It belonged to my first husband, Michael.

I couldn't believe it. We hadn't parted on good terms. There had been neither an "other man" nor an "other woman." I had merely realized after almost five years of marriage, we weren't seeking the same things in life.

Sadly, that realization was mine alone, and Michael felt betrayed by my disaffection. During the first year we were divorced, he called from time to time, hoping, I believe, that I would "come to my senses" and return to him, although I did nothing to encourage his optimism.

I then met the man who would become my second husband — the man who I remained married to for almost twenty-five years. I relocated to another state to begin life afresh with my new partner.

It wasn't long after I moved that I began receiving letters from

Michael—letters filled with animosity. I was devastated. His words destroyed a belief about the nature of love that I had had up until then. I had always felt that individuals who have shared genuine love at one time would always remain connected on some level. How could people who have wholly revealed themselves to one another ever totally forget such intimacy? That was the reason I had been willing to continue a relationship of sorts with Michael, even though the marriage had ended.

However, after receiving his letters brimming with condemnation and reproach, I severed contact with him completely. I hadn't heard from him for eighteen years.

Until now.

"Why now?" I asked, too shocked to manage anything more.

Michael told me that he and his family, which now included a wife and three children, were going back to the country where he had been born.

"I need to see you before I go. It would mean a great deal to me. Please."

It was a convincing plea, and, although I hadn't forgotten the letters, I admit that both curiosity and a resurrected desire for closure made me say, "Yes."

The day finally came. Michael was traveling from another city. I arrived at our designated meeting place early. As I waited, I worried. What if this meeting turned into another episode of recrimination? Feeling eyes upon me, I looked up. Except for a thicker waist and thinner head of hair, Michael looked the same.

He recognized me instantly.

"You're thinner," he noted. I wasn't, but didn't argue. I didn't want to introduce even the slightest hint of aggression.

Directly after ordering drinks, Michael began to unload parcels from a bag he'd been carrying. He plunked the packages down in front of me. "For you," he said.

Among an assortment of trinkets was a cassette that included a song entitled, "Jenny." It wasn't in English, but I knew it. It was an apologetic love ballad. Even before I had a chance to say thank you, Michael said, "Let's talk about your family and mine. But first, I want to tell you that hardly a day has passed in eighteen years that I haven't thought about you."

I wasn't prepared for this sort of emotional bombshell and I was speechless.

"It's not what you're thinking. I'm very happy with my wife and my kids. It's just that I've thought about how much in love we once were. I've been sorry that with such a bright beginning, we finished up so miserably. I couldn't leave the country without at least trying to end the bitterness between us."

I took his hand and smiled while I wept cleansing, healing tears.

As if on cue, our drinks arrived, giving us a chance to toast both days gone by and those yet to come.

As Michael had predicted, we spent most of our meeting talking about our respective families. We parted as loving friends. That meeting took place ten years ago. We haven't exchanged a word since.

That reunion had a profound effect on me. It verified my deeply-held belief that love has a life of its own and can sometimes survive a relationship that has died. Until I'd seen Michael again, the memory of his caustic letters had prevented me from remembering some of the sweet moments we had shared. For me, our belated encounter cleared a path to recollection, giving me back a memory of a love I can now reflect upon without regret.

— Jenna Romano —

# Baking Away Bitterness

*Cooking is like love... It should be entered
into with abandon or not at all.*
~Harriet Van Horne

Today is the first anniversary of my ex-husband's death. My mind is flooded with memories of Harry; my heart is filled with a jumble of emotions.

We spent sixteen years together, building a number of small businesses with various degrees of success. He was in charge of sales and I took care of production. We made a dynamic team — but we were better in business than we were on a personal level. So we kept our focus on work.

We founded a company that turned into my dream venture. I loved everything about it. I went to work each day with eager anticipation. It was my pride and joy.

After the third year, my husband became bored with the company. But I did not want to leave the job I had grown so fond of. So we decided to split our directions. He would start something new, while I continued with the already established business. However, without each other's abilities, neither of us was able to succeed.

I soon realized that without a business venture we could share, there was nothing keeping us together. We began attacking each other — not physically — but as many people know, mental scars can be the hardest to heal.

By the time our divorce was finalized, my bitterness toward Harry was overwhelming. I never wanted to hear his voice, see his face, or even hear his name again.

I remarried, and my new husband and I enjoyed our life together with our baby daughter. After a long absence, happiness was finally a part of my life again. A few more years passed, and we added two more children to our happy family. The bitterness was finally melting away from my heart.

One year, we invited our neighbors to celebrate Thanksgiving with us. I decided to make a carrot cake for dessert, mainly because my son had requested it. I pulled out my old recipe, and the stained 3x5 card immediately brought back memories of my ex-husband. I had often made this particular dessert for Harry's birthday and on other special occasions. It was his favorite. After a moment of hesitation, I went ahead and started to make the carrot cake.

As I assembled the ingredients for the cake, the phone rang. It was my neighbor, Herb. He was calling from the hospital where he had taken his wife, Nancy, because of a complication from a broken arm. Apparently, Harry was also in the hospital. The doctors didn't expect him to get out. Cancer had taken over his body. Because Herb was a long-time friend of Harry's, he had called to tell me that Nancy, he, and Harry would be having Thanksgiving dinner together at the hospital.

As I hung up the phone and stared at the carrot cake ingredients sitting on the counter, I felt a strange urge to send my ex-husband a large piece of the cake. For me, it would symbolize forgiveness. I knew, deep in my soul, that God was telling me I needed to do this — for Harry and for myself.

As I made that carrot cake, memories of good times with Harry crossed the barriers I had built up in my mind. I hadn't allowed myself to think anything but negative thoughts about him for so long, it seemed strange to not be angry anymore. I still didn't want to talk to him. I simply didn't have the words. I hoped the cake would let him know that I no longer held any hard feelings for what had happened between us.

I asked Herb to pick up my ex's piece of cake on his way to the hospital on Thanksgiving morning. That afternoon, he called. "When Harry found out the cake was from you," he said, his voice cracking, "I saw tears come to his eyes. And he refused to share a single bite with anyone, even me."

Harry died the next day.

Now, a year later, I'm thankful I was able to express my forgiveness to Harry before it was too late. I hope he understood it for what it was. I believe God made sure he did.

— Linda Fitzjarrell —

# Define Normal

*Divorce: The past tense of marriage.*
*~Author Unknown*

The house is deathly quiet now, but I swear I can still hear my poor Jeep Grand Cherokee panting heavily out in the garage after toting seven-plus Reillys around town for the past seven-plus days. Ah, the out-of-town guests have left for home; they boarded a plane just this morning and I am finally free to sit down at my laptop in my skivvies with a tall Coke and a short line to the little girl's room.

For the past week I have been entertaining my out-of-town in-laws; I took them to and from the airport, hauled them around town, fed them my famous homemade fried potatoes and scrambled cheese eggs for breakfast, played board games and charades around the kitchen table with all of the kids for hours and employed every sleep-able piece of furniture I own. When the boys weren't at my ex-husbands house — taking full-advantage of the ultimate bachelor's pad — my cozy, little house was stuffed like a summer sausage.

My friends don't seem to understand this bizarre relationship I keep with my ex-husband's family, especially considering that I've been legally unbound from that particular contractual obligation for almost ten years now, the unspoken rule that states that I am to put up my in-laws whenever they're in town. I mean, it's not like I don't have the paperwork to prove it.

"It's just not normal," they observe.

Well, that may be true, but I like to think that I was granted joint custody of my quirky, well-meaning "out-laws" — as I like to call them — in the final decree of my divorce. My ex-husband doesn't seem to mind that I'm still close with them. In fact, I think he likes it; those are the ties that continue to bind us as a family, and I think it's been healthy for our boys to see that we can all still get along. And, besides that, whoever said that there was anything normal when it comes to family, anyway?

I happen to love my sister-in-law, a woman who was once married to my ex-husband's big brother. Over the years we've become sisters of sorts. I know it sounds kind of complicated, but she and her three children are very close to me and my two children. We all seem to get along great; it's as if, somehow, we belong together, in some crazy, not-entirely-dysfunctional way.

When I look at her two boys and her daughter — who are almost exactly the same ages as my boys — I see a strong family resemblance and I can't help but conclude that it is exactly as the old saying goes: Blood is, in fact, thicker than water.

All I know is that when I watch my kids hanging out with their cousins, laughing and enjoying one another in a way that only family can, I know that my decision to remain close with my out-laws is something I'm meant to do, if not supposed to do. The contented expressions on my boys' faces say it all, especially when we spend the day with friends and family — at the request of my ex-husband — consuming two lanes at the local bowling alley, scarfing down greasy food and making the Clampetts look more like the Kardashians.

The thing is my out-laws are good people — a little crazy sometimes — but then again, aren't we all?

And now that they've all packed up their bags and are headed for home, I realize more and more how desperately I miss seeing their faces. I realize how quickly time is getting away from us as our kids are growing up, graduating and grappling with their own futures.

Truth: Life is too short to be spent fighting with family — in-laws, out-laws and the like. This sweet time in our life should be spent wisely, say, playing board games around the kitchen table with a humongous dish of homemade chicken nuggets and French fries placed strategically within everyone's reach, while everyone is eating, laughing and clamoring all at once — pretending to be pseudo-normal, but really coming off as looking more like what a family is supposed to look like, and that is happy. At least happy is what my family looks like to me and that's what matters most.

— Natalie June Reilly —

# Chicago Peace

> *The weak can never forgive. Forgiveness*
> *is the attribute of the strong.*
> *~Mahatma Gandhi*

As I drove to my office, a feeling of complete forgiveness towards my ex-husband, Ron, came over me. I recall the moment as if it were yesterday. I was heading north on I-95 and as I crested over the Baymeadows overpass, I had such joy and forgiveness in my heart towards him. For the first time in over a decade, I was able to say, "I forgive you."

Ron and I had been married almost eleven years before we divorced. Our three small children and I felt abandoned and heartbroken. We stayed in Illinois for a while after the divorce but then the children and I moved back to Florida to be with my family. Ron stayed in Chicago.

It was wonderful to be in Florida, surrounded by my parents and siblings along with their families. They encouraged us and provided support. Ron visited us once. It was not a happy visit. He was on a layover to a Las Vegas gambling trip and visited us for a few days. At that time in our lives, Ron was several thousand dollars behind in child support. I was bitter he was spending money on a trip to Las Vegas. My children and I had sacrificed and struggled for many years. It just didn't seem fair to me that their father was taking a trip when we did without child support.

To finally be at peace with Ron was a miracle. At times I wanted to giggle out loud. I felt such a burden lifted from my shoulders to know I could finally forgive and move on with my life. Although I didn't share this with anyone, I'm sure others sensed I had a change of heart towards Ron.

Two weeks later, as I entered my office, the switchboard operator stopped me and said there had been an urgent call from someone named Al in Chicago. I was to call him immediately.

Al was married to Ron's sister and he had always been a wonderful friend to me, even as Ron and I were divorcing. We had lost contact over the years so I knew Al was not calling me to chitchat. I dialed Al's number and heard him say in a grave tone of voice, "Ronnie was found dead early this morning. I felt you and the kids needed to know." My heart stopped. I can still close my eyes and be back in that stuffy little conference room hearing words I did not want to hear. My first thought was for my children. They had just lost their father — a man they would never have the opportunity to know. They would never have the chance to know and love him like I once did. I left the conference room with leaden feet and made my way back to my office to locate my manager. I needed to leave immediately and tell my children the sad news.

We left early the next morning for Chicago. It was a somber group. My dad and sister were with us for the journey. My oldest was living in Missouri and would fly to Chicago for the funeral. The following days were a blur. Ron's funeral was held the day after Father's Day. It was the first Father's Day my children had spent with their father in many years. It was bittersweet.

Jason, our oldest, was stoic. During the funeral service, he played "Stairway to Heaven" on his guitar. Tears stung my eyes as the beautiful melody drifted from the church balcony. Jennifer, our only daughter, shed many tears when we left Chicago. In spite of the circumstances, she was happy to finally meet some of her dad's family. Joey, our youngest, asked if I thought his dad was in heaven. I said, "Of course your dad is in heaven. He's there with grandma and they are watching over us." However, I wasn't convinced. I was sure God opened the gates of heaven only for good dads!

We got home very late and the weary travelers went to bed. I awoke early the next morning and while my brood slept, I poured myself a cup of coffee and headed out to the backyard. My dad had purchased three rose bushes two weeks earlier and we spent a Sunday afternoon planting them. I wanted to ensure they had survived a severe storm that occurred during our absence.

I made soft footprints in the early morning dew. The day was just beginning. I was sad about Ron's early death but also relieved he would not suffer anymore. I wasn't convinced he had made it to heaven though! I am from Missouri — the show-me state.

The rose bushes stood intact. Not one of the three had been damaged during the storm. I leaned over to smell the sweet scent of roses and as I did a leftover white tag on one of the rose bushes caught my eye. I went inside for a pair of scissors, returned to the yard and snipped off the tag. When I glanced at it, time stood still. The name of the rose bush was Chicago Peace.

Then I knew. God had been preparing me for Ron's death two weeks earlier by putting forgiveness in my heart towards him for all the years of pain. I believe that my forgiveness released Ron and he made it through the heavenly gates.

— Teresa Curley Barczak —

# I'm Not Going to Hate You

*Darkness cannot drive out darkness; only light can do that. Hate cannot drive out hate; only love can do that.*
~Martin Luther King, Jr.

My wife sat on the edge of the couch, her head down and hands fidgeting in her lap. She played with her wedding ring, slowly spinning it around her finger.

"You're going to hate me," she said quietly. Her lips quivered, and her blue-grey eyes began to flood with tears. "You're going to hate me."

I was confused as to what this was about and why my wife was so shaken up.

"I'm not going to hate you," I said. "I could never hate you." She'd only come home moments before, sitting down quietly on the couch, so naturally my thought was that she wrecked the car. I asked if that's what it was, and she replied that it wasn't. This left me with a brief sense of relief.

"I can't do this anymore," she said. A lump caught in my throat. I swallowed, trying to release it.

"What can't you do? Can't sell the house? Can't move into a new home? We can back out of the sale. We can stay here, save money until we are more comfortable and ready."

"No, I can't do *this* anymore," she said with a sense of frustration at my not understanding. She looked up from her lap while throwing her hands into the air, indicating our life together.

I went into a sort of panic mode, asking if she'd cheated on me. "No," she reassured me while looking directly into my eyes for the first time. "I didn't cheat on you."

"Then what is it? Why can't you do this?"

She went back to fidgeting and then started to sob uncontrollably with her face in her hands. I watched her shake as she cried there alone on the couch, helpless and scared. I wanted to wrap my arms around her and pull her in close to reassure her nothing was wrong. But I wasn't even sure myself if that was the case, and I was strangely frozen where I stood from the shock. The sound of her struggling to breathe in between the tears was heartbreaking. I just wanted the moment to pass and not be real. I wanted everything to be okay.

"I think I like women," she said.

At that moment, my whole world fell to pieces and slipped away completely. I couldn't fix this. All I could do was let it happen while I sat and watched. My wife no longer loved me the way a wife should love her husband.

I went from having my whole life planned to not knowing where I was going to be in the next five minutes. I went from building a dream home to living in a hotel alone. I lost my best friend. But the worst part was the hate and anger that bubbled up inside me. It was an anger I never knew I was capable of feeling, especially toward someone I'd loved with all of my being.

I let it consume me as I became more bitter with each passing day. I felt sorry for myself for what I had just been put through, blaming it all on my wife's selfishness to have only what she wanted. I spent the first night on the floor of my empty apartment with my dog curled up next to me on the cold carpet. I stared at the ceiling through flooded eyes with a fire still raging inside me. I was there because of her, and I hated her for it.

Then one day while walking along a trail, I cleared my head of hate long enough to put myself in her shoes. I tried to imagine the struggle she had dealt with alone — the secret she had held onto for a year before telling me. I imagined how alone and confused she must have been, knowing this life with me wasn't what she wanted or needed. I thought about the fear she must have felt, not really wanting to leave me, but knowing that if she stayed and tried to make it work, she might never find and feel the deep unwavering love like I had for her.

I knew then that I couldn't rob her of that. She had taught me what true love was and the passion that came with it. I couldn't continue hating her for wanting to find what I felt for her. To me, there is nothing better in the world than to experience true love. And I wanted more than anything for her to have that — even if it meant giving it all up myself.

After getting home from the trail, I sat down and typed these words to her:

> *Words cannot express how deeply sorry I am for how I treated you at times the last few months. I was mean, hurtful, rude. I wish I could take it back and do it differently. It was hard to control my anger because of you ripping my life away from me. I hated you for it, and it felt like everything you were doing was to spite me and make me even madder. I am truly sorry for all of it. I've never wanted to hurt you, but I did, and I am sorry.*
>
> *Most importantly, I just want you happy. I don't want you struggling and having bad days. You've been through a lot, and you deserve nothing less than to be happy. I have loved you more than anyone could ever love another person. I probably always will, but it wasn't what you wanted or what you needed. I am so sorry for that. I am sorry you didn't know sooner. I know you couldn't control any of this, and I want you to know that I honestly and completely forgive you for it. For all of it. That's a huge burden you carried that I will never understand, and I will never understand the things you did to me. I can't do anything but forgive you. You were in a lot of pain and carried a lot of mental stress. I can't imagine what you went through, or what you are going through still. Just know I am always here for you. You don't need to do it alone anymore.*

Thanks to those few words of true forgiveness, the hatred lifted completely off my heart. We were both able to begin letting go of the last bit of guilt and start healing in order to live and love again.

— Dustin Urbach —

# Guess Who Came for Dinner?

*A loving heart is the truest wisdom.*
*~Charles Dickens*

I still couldn't believe I'd invited him for dinner and that he accepted, especially after all that had happened between us. We'd had a fiery divorce, so getting together for dinner at my house some twenty-seven years later was something I never thought would happen. But here I was preparing meatloaf, Bob's favorite meal, and he was due at my door shortly. While setting the table, I reflected again upon this spontaneous invitation to my former husband. It was completely unfiltered. It had just popped out of my mouth. Actually it caught us both off guard, and if the truth were known, he probably accepted due to pure shock.

Several weeks earlier, my former husband Bob and I had come face to face at the funeral of a mutual friend. It had been years since we'd had any contact, but I'd recently been informed of Bob's heart surgery and other complications. Although I knew he wasn't doing well, absolutely nothing prepared me for the decline I saw. This once vibrant, high-powered businessman was now painfully thin, stooped and frail. While it was true we'd both aged, at least I had my health. Perhaps that's what caused me to blurt out the "surprise" dinner invitation, maybe out of gratitude for my own good fortune.

Stuffing a few of my garden's blooms into a beautiful antique vase,

I gave the table a once-over. "Not bad," I mumbled, and adding my usual touch of sarcasm, "I hope he realizes what he walked away from and regrets it all." Oddly enough, a spirited conversation I'd had with my sister several years ago came to mind.

"Don't you think it's time you started forgiving, Sis?"

"Let me tell you, getting over hurts and betrayals is easier said than done," I snapped. "Besides, you're married to a great guy so what could you possibly know about hurt and betrayal?"

"You're right, but you still love him. Love never goes away. It just takes on a different form."

Angry now, I set her straight. "Really? Well believe me, you have no idea what you're talking about."

"Maybe, but I read a quote once that said, 'regardless of circumstances, love never dies, it just sleeps until forgiveness wakes it up.'"

"Drop it, will you?" was my reply, and she never mentioned it again. But somehow I never forgot it.

"Anybody home?" It was Bob. "I knocked but no answer, so thought maybe you changed your mind." Always a charmer, he continued, "Sure smells good in here. Of course, you always did make the world's best meatloaf. Did I ever tell you that?" Then laughing, he added, "Obviously if I did, it wasn't often enough. Right?"

We spent the next hour or so chatting over a bottle of Chablis. It had been decades since we'd sat together. It was nice and it felt good. In fact I was surprised at the ease we both seemed to feel. He filled me in on his declining health, but was quick to remind me that he'd had a great life. We laughed at old times and when he asked how I was doing, I felt he sincerely meant it. I even gave him a tour of my modest home, and he appeared impressed. "You've done well, kid," was all he said, but to me that was praise from Caesar.

By now it was time to eat, and we continued our pleasant conversation throughout dinner. It was comfortable. Actually, we lingered, and it was nice. Maybe it was the ease I felt, or maybe it was the two glasses of Chablis, but suddenly I decided to tell him how I felt.

"I know I've been more than angry with you over the years, but what happened between us was my fault too and I'm so sorry," I began, "and I want you to know, I love you, Bob, and always will. You taught me so much, and I will forever be grateful for the time we had together and for the time we had apart. Maybe it was all necessary. I forgive you and I just hope you can forgive me." By now I was crying but somehow it all seemed good. In the dim light of the little chandelier over the kitchen table I noticed tears coming down his cheeks too and there was a silence between us that on some level said it all.

It was getting late and our bittersweet evening had finally caught up with us. Strange, but I sensed that neither of us were quite ready for it to end. We kissed goodbye and I mentioned again that I loved him and hoped he could forgive me. He just smiled and simply said, "There's nothing to forgive. Tonight proved that." I watched him shuffle slowly down the front porch steps to his car while carrying a Macy's shopping bag filled with leftover meatloaf and apple cobbler. Even the streetlight swathed our evening in a soft reassuring glow. We waved goodbye and with tears streaming down my face, I watched him pull away. Every angry thought I'd ever had about him was gone. That was the last time we saw one another. He passed away eight months later.

Since then, I've thought a lot about Bob, our time together, myself, and my sister's quote. Maybe she was onto something. Maybe love does sleep until forgiveness wakes it up. In fact, I wonder if that's what happened to me that night. When I found myself forgiving, surprisingly, I found myself loving. And for the first time in years, the stone in my own heart was gone.

—Linda LaRocque—

# The Gift I Needed

*Forgiveness is the giving, and so the receiving, of life.*
~George MacDonald

I swallowed hard, willing away nausea. Did I misunderstand the words of this young man who now held my grocery bags hostage? Leaning forward, I listened for an explanation. He said it again. "Ma'am, there's a problem with your check. I suggest you speak to a manager at the service counter."

I had been shopping at this particular supermarket for more than five years and had never heard those words. My cheeks flushed with embarrassment as I imagined the eyes of the other customers watching me walk toward the manager.

Nervously, I bit my lip as he reviewed the register's printout pertaining to the check. "You need to contact your bank," he said, looking me in the eye. "There's a problem."

I hurried to the nearest exit and marched across the parking lot to where there happened to be a branch of my bank. After explaining the dilemma to the manager, she entered my account number and searched the computer file. Immediately, she spotted the problem. "Your account is overdrawn," she calmly stated.

"How could that be?" I argued. "My paycheck was transmitted by direct deposit this morning. Surely there is money in this account. There must be a mistake."

The branch manager searched further and identified the problem. "Take a look at this," she said, turning her computer monitor toward me. "Your employer deposited the paycheck, but apparently someone withdrew all but twelve dollars."

I worked hard to blink back tears. I knew who "the someone" was, and this time he had gone too far. How could he? My husband had taken my entire paycheck to support his drug habit.

I knew that I should have seen this coming. For the last few months, he had been abusing drugs and money had started to disappear. However, I never expected that he would go this far, would take the money that I needed to buy food for our children.

I rushed home, determined that he make it right. My husband needed to put the money back in the account. Secondly, he owed the children and me an apology. But I soon discovered that the money had already been spent and he felt no remorse for his actions.

Nothing was going to change, so I packed up our two young children and left our home behind. I was bitter for years after that. My joy was gone.

Ultimately, I sought the help of a therapist. I wanted to change and I was prepared to do just about anything to feel better. Dr. Wade looked at me and said, "You will never get beyond this unless you forgive your husband."

They must have heard me in the reception area when I shouted, "That's not possible!"

Dr. Wade, who apparently was accustomed to this type of response, sat still and waited for me to calm down.

I didn't. "Because of him, we lost our home, furnishings, bank accounts, and cars. I can barely face the children or myself. He's destroyed us."

I continued ranting; and when I was finally exhausted from shouting and crying, Dr. Wade spoke: "There is a gift you need."

I took a tissue from the box next to the sofa and dabbed my eyes as I absorbed what she had said. "The gift you need is not something that anyone can give you. It is a gift you must give yourself. It is the gift of forgiveness. The forgiveness of your husband's actions," Dr. Wade paused, "and forgiveness of yourself."

I buried my face in my hands — too absorbed in my own anger and grief. Days turned into weeks and weeks into months before I began to comprehend. Almost a year to the day of that session, I awoke one morning from a dream. In the dream, a large package was before me. It was wrapped in the most unique paper I had ever seen — like that of a rainbow. I marveled at its brightness and was grateful that it was mine. I began to untie the white satin bow around the box. I loved its feel against my fingers. This had to be a really good gift, I thought.

But when I pulled the top off the box, the phone rang, awakening me. As much as I wanted to see what was in that box, I couldn't. The dream was gone. I never saw the gift inside.

Rattled from the experience, I thought through all the unnecessary bitterness that I had harbored over the years. My children deserved better, and today was the day I would begin to offer it to them. Still in my pajamas, I reached for my journal and wrote. I didn't stop until five pages later, where I laid out my complete forgiveness to my husband. And when I saw him again a month later the words, "I forgive you," came right after my greeting. He followed up with a smile and shared his surprise that I had come to this point. Of course, he too profusely apologized for his actions — something he'd done many times before. We never got back together but for both of us this was a turning point.

But there was one more thing needed in my life. The gift remained incomplete. I needed to forgive myself. I had wasted so much time being angry. When I accepted what awaited me in that gift box, I realized that nothing is more liberating than when one decides to forgive. Had I understood this all-important gift, I would have acted sooner. From that day forward, I committed to never hold myself hostage in this way again. By God's grace, I have stuck to that promise.

Forgiveness. What a wonderful gift!

— Yvonne Curry Smallwood —

# Chapter 11

# Liberate Yourself by Letting It Go

# 86

# The Blueprints

*And in today already walks tomorrow.*
~Samuel Taylor Coleridge

"I don't know if I can do this!" I sobbed and dropped to my knees.

"Yes you can. Together we can do it," my cousin said and knelt down beside me. She placed her hand on my shoulder and added, "C'mon, the sooner we get started, the sooner it will be over."

"That's the point. It will be final. The last of what's left of him will be gone." I covered my face with my hands and struggled to stop the river of emotion spilling over me. My father's death, it seemed, was only the beginning of the heartache and unbearable abandonment that I was feeling.

My cousin stood and faced the open closet containing the articles of my father's life: old shoes, six long-sleeved shirts, some jeans, some slacks, a couple of worn sweaters and a faded suede jacket. The scent of old suede, the sight of the right side pocket worn where he used to hook his thumb, a faint hint of the cologne he used to wear, assaulted my spirit. I stared at his belongings and wanted to wail.

My cousin wasn't going to allow that to happen though. She encouraged me to continue, to accept the grief and then go further and find closure.

Coat hangers slid across the metal rod. That's when I saw them — three sets of old blueprints rolled tightly and leaning against the back corner of the closet. My father had saved them for some reason, maybe as a reminder of the important man he had once been. I knew they must be at least ten years old. The yellowed paper, frayed edges and smudged fingerprints told me so.

In his short life my father had accomplished great feats in his construction business, only to throw everything away when drinking became more important. His business failed and he made drinking his first priority. I always found him slumped in a chair, chin on his chest and shoulders sagging in despair. A bottle of cheap wine sat on the floor beside him.

I didn't understand his illness and his abandonment of my sisters and me. Later on, I would come to realize this was not my fault. There was nothing I could have done to change him. God knows we tried, with AA meetings, several stays at recovery centers and a two-week stint at a county facility.

Now I couldn't resist the strange pull the blueprints were having on me. There were two large sets and one smaller. The smaller, I assumed, was for a single-family residence.

I reached inside the closet and wrapped my fingers around the small set of plans. His hands had gone over the paper and the details written inside many times. Carefully, I unrolled the thin paper. A beautiful two-story English Tudor emerged. A high-pitched roof, brick siding, and defined arches and gables were all there. I searched for a name on the prints and couldn't find one. Not an architect or a homeowner for that matter, and the specs were missing. This, simply put, was a rough draft of someone's vision. But whose?

"Look at this."

"Wow... it's beautiful!" exclaimed my cousin. "I wonder who the plans belonged to?"

"I haven't a clue. Look at the floor plan, it's so spacious and open."

She sat beside me and I spread the plans open across our laps. She shook her head like a revelation had just come to her.

"Looks like he left you something after all."

My eyes filled with unshed tears. "You might be right." I glanced back down at the floor plan. Carefully, I rolled the plans and placed the rubber band back on. We let a few heartfelt moments pass by in memory of who my father had been before the drinking consumed his life.

After a few minutes, we returned to packing his personal belongings. We filled two large garbage bags with his old clothes, his wallet and handkerchiefs and his shoes, except for one dressy pair. I held the left shoe in my hand. He'd walked in this shoe, traveled to meetings and then to bars. He'd worn it home and to my sister's wedding. I pressed the worn leather against my chest and then placed it in the box and whispered, "Goodbye."

Several months later, a friend needed to sell a parcel of land. It just so happened the acre was in one of my favorite areas — Wildwood Canyon, untouched and newly developed, with sprawling oaks and meadows growing wild with saffron grass. I jumped at the chance.

The top shelf in my closet had been home for the blueprints since finding them. Each day when I went to get my clothes out, I looked at them and smiled. They contained a dream and my duty became clear on a cloudy morning on the anniversary of his death. Instead of my clothes, I pulled the blueprints down and placed a call to a local architect. Within a month, those simple blueprints were developed into a full set of plans with specs, and six months later, the pad was graded and the foundation poured.

The first time I went to inspect the framing on the second story the sun was setting, the sky pastel and the wind gentle as it blew through the open walls. The plywood subfloor was covered with wood shavings and powdery dust, the scent intoxicating and familiar. I thought of my father and his dreams. In his lifetime, he had built apartment complexes and houses, and he had developed a mud and paint factory. He had accomplished much and then let it all slip through his fingers. Sadness filled me, but only for a moment. His life's path had taken a dark turn and he wasn't able to find his way back. In one fleeting moment, I realized he had left me a legacy.

I wanted to weep, but something held me back. Tears welled in my eyes and yet they didn't spill over. I felt my father's presence, near and yet so far away.

I have long since moved away from the Tudor that was once my father's vision. Proudly I sold the place two years after completion. Now when I think of the house, I think of him, and vice-versa. The original blueprints have a home in my attic now, and every once in a while, I pull them out and remember he was just a man, and he was also my father, one I still love to this day with all my heart.

— Cindy Golchuk —

# Shredding Sadness

*To forgive is the highest, most beautiful form of love.*
*In return, you will receive untold peace and happiness.*
*~Robert Muller*

Lately, I've been shredding documents I accumulated with my ex-husband. These always put me in a dark place. I have happy memories of Steve, but sometimes they get overpowered by the negative ones — the money I lost, the birthdays he missed, how sick he got, and the way I felt that he no longer truly loved me by the end of the marriage.

In all the years since Steve and I divorced, I had never dreamed of him. I spent enough of my waking time feeling guilty about our failed marriage; I had no need to do overtime at night. But just a couple of months ago, I dreamt of Steve.

*He was off in the distance, walking across a field toward the building I appeared to be living in. I peered out my window and knew that it was him but couldn't figure out why he was there. Just as he got close, a noise in my real house woke me from the dream.*

I remember how frustrated I was that I didn't get to see him face to face, didn't get to talk to him, and didn't get to understand why he was appearing to me.

Later that week, I missed a rare phone call from his son who was about to go into the Coast Guard. I felt frustrated about not getting to the phone in time or being successful in calling back. It had been four years since I'd seen Junior at his dad's funeral and seven years since

I'd seen him prior to the divorce. All these years, I'd often lamented our break in communication. And now he would be unreachable for eight weeks of training—maybe even the whole time he would be in the Coast Guard. I thought back to the dream and began to worry. Did Steve know something I didn't?

Unexpectedly, though, two months after the dream and the missed phone call, Junior appeared at my door. He'd graduated from Coast Guard training and was on his way to report to duty. At first, it seemed he might stay for just an hour, but instead he ended up staying for two days.

The entire time he visited, we didn't talk about the difficult stuff of the past. Why fill what little time we had together with sadness? Instead, we laughed and hugged each other often, reestablished our connection, and vowed to keep it going.

After that, I had another dream of Steve.

*This time, he was up close and personal. He pulled up in his blue pickup truck, pulling a large boat made of weathered plywood painted barn red—a ridiculous-looking thing with a large, enclosed captain's wheelhouse. I chuckled when I saw it.*

*"You didn't actually drive this thing all the way across the country, did ya?"*

*"Heck, yeah!" he said, puffing out his chest like a superhero.*

*I couldn't help laughing. "Are you sure this thing floats?"*

*"Guess we'll find out," he said, with a grin.*

*An instant later, we were at a table in a house I appeared to be living in. Steve came over to me with a big white bakery box. He took a birthday cake with lots of white icing roses out of the box, set it down on the table and dropped his head right down into it, taking a big bite. Next, using his fingers, he grabbed a huge hunk of icing and cake and joyfully shoved it into his mouth. His eyes sparkled. He was eating, laughing and joking.*

*"Now, your turn," he said, pushing the cake toward me while swiftly turning around and heading back over toward the other things he'd brought.*

*I hesitated for a few seconds and then said to myself, "Aw, what the hell," and dug in. Steve came back, grinning at my icing-laced face and fingertips. He laid another boxed cake on the table, one with big blue sugar-cream roses* on it — just like the cake at our wedding some sixteen years earlier. He cut into that one, too, but with a fork instead of his fingers. I noticed there was a third cake on the counter in the distance, a white one with yellow roses around the edges.

He left the table again and came back this time with several documents. One was a blank check. Another was a proclamation honoring and memorializing my late father — with whom Steve had felt very connected. I looked up at Steve and, seeing his warm, gentle smile, I understood immediately all he was trying to say.

I would've liked to stay right there in that dream and enjoy what felt like a warm wave of healing, compliments of Steve. But like months earlier when I first dreamed of him, a sound in my real house interrupted my slumber. As soon as I opened my eyes, my pint-sized dog licked my face, saying "Good morning" in her own sweet way. Then my husband Mark rolled over to wish me a good morning, too. I must've seemed distracted because he did what he always does when he can tell I'm in deep thought. He asked in a lyrical, six-year-old-kid kinda way, "What'cha doin'?"

I laughed like I usually do when he reads me so well and answered with the same lyrical lilt, "Think'n." Then I proceeded to share with Mark the details of my dream. As has always been the case with Mark, he was touched by my story of emotional connection with my ex and was especially happy to see and feel my positive energy while I described the ridiculous boat, the cake-eating fest, and the loving kindness.

I spent the rest of the morning thinking about that dream and the many things that have been happening lately that feel like opportunities for healing. I thought about the symbolism of the dream, especially those cakes. The first one reminded me of a photo taken of Steve a week before he died. He was still in the hospital but felt good enough on Thanksgiving Day to ask for donuts, which he then ate with complete abandon, covering his face with white icing. The second cake reminded me of our wedding day. And the last cake, with yellow flowers, symbolized friendship.

Mostly, though, I remembered that I had loved Steve. And I remembered that he loved me, too — enough to drive a weird boat across the country to see me, and enough to bring me a blank check and three meaningful cakes. It was time for me to focus on the happy memories, to honor the love we had once shared.

And that's what I did today. I let go of any residual pain that came from loving Steve. I fed the last of my less-than-happy documents into the shredder, never to be seen again. With it, I shed the self-inflicted sadness that for so long kept me from fully living my life. I fully forgave Steve for all he'd done. But more importantly, I fully forgave myself for all I'd done, too.

— Susan Maddy Jones —

# Walking in Another Direction

> *For you, as well as I, can open fence doors and walk across America in your own special way. Then we can all discover who our neighbors are.*
> ~Robert Sweetgall, *Fitness Walking*

When I moved into my current home almost 30 years ago, my street was a quiet country road. Most of the houses sat on lots of at least three acres, and several homeowners had horses, cows, or chickens. I rarely saw my neighbors unless I invited them over for a party, or we happened to visit the clustered mailboxes at the same time. As an animal lover, though, I often stopped to talk to the horses and cows and rub their noses during my evening walks. I loved walking after dinner, both for the gentle exercise and the uplifting effect that the animals and nature had on my mood.

Sadly, within five years of my arrival, developers began buying up tracts of land in the area and building huge homes on quarter-acre parcels. The horses and cows disappeared as the small farms became housing developments. Soon, my country road was a dangerous thoroughfare with cars rushing by. Since I could no longer walk safely on the shoulder of my own street, I began taking a route through Crestwood, one of the new developments nearby. At least it had a sidewalk and fewer cars.

Liberate Yourself by Letting It Go

One day, during a seminar at a local wellness center, a woman sitting behind me tapped my shoulder. "You look familiar," she said. "Do you live in Crestwood?" I said that I didn't, but that I lived nearby. "That's where I know you from — I see you walking every day. I'm Claudette." She said if I ever wanted a walking partner to knock on her door.

The next time I passed her house and saw her in the yard, we waved hello. She invited me to join her neighborhood "Girls' Night Out," which took place once every other month and rotated between several homes in that community.

At the first Girls' Night that I attended, Claudette introduced me around. It turned out that many of the women there also recognized me from my walks. Apparently, I was a regular fixture in the evenings, even though I had no idea people were watching me. Eventually, these women became my friends.

The women of Crestwood weren't the only friendly ones. Often, I passed Dave as he was doing yard work or playing catch with his sons, and we eventually struck up a conversation. His positive energy brightened my day. I got to know Jeff, a retired schoolteacher, because we walked the same route daily. We chatted frequently and got to know each other well enough that we eventually exchanged phone numbers and e-mail addresses. He encouraged me to call if I ever needed anything that he or his wife could help with, and I did the same. I also became friendly with most of the dogs along my route — from Bruiser, a teacup Chihuahua, to Duke, a Yellow Lab/Akita mix.

A couple of years ago, I retired, and my work-related social activities tapered off. I was a bit concerned I might become one of those reclusive "cat ladies" who have little human interaction, but I needn't have feared — my neighborhood social circle continued to grow. I walked more during the day and got to know other Crestwood residents I hadn't met before: stay-at-home moms and people who worked from home who were outside during daytime hours.

I like having a personal connection with people nearby — ones I can talk to without an Internet or phone line. This came in handy especially during an ice storm last winter that knocked out my power for days, but not Crestwood's. One friend lent me her portable cell-phone charger, and another offered to keep all my frozen food in her huge freezer. When Duke's owner broke her leg shoveling snow, I walked Duke for her until she was well enough to resume that activity, and she fed my cats when I had to go out of town unexpectedly. Periodically, I share travel- and health-related information with Jeff, adding depth to our discussions. And when Claudette's son, Michael, broke his kneecap, I told her I'd drive him home from school every day so she or her husband wouldn't have to leave work early.

Now on my walks, I enjoy my new neighbors' holiday decorations as the seasons change. I see the progress of their landscaping and home-improvement projects, and I watch their children and pets grow. I attend most of Michael's band concerts and school plays, proudly noting how his confidence and maturity are increasing.

Almost two decades since it was built, the once-stark development is now lovely, with tall flowering trees and meticulously kept lawns. My new walking route is just as beautiful as my old one, only in a different way. And walking there every day keeps me in touch with my new friends.

I never thought anything good would come from the developments in my neighborhood, but thanks to walking, I discovered a whole community of supportive new friends. I realized it's not the land and surroundings that make a community, but the people who live there. To my surprise, although I began walking for my mental and physical health, it had the added benefit of widening my social circle. One might even say that when I was run out of my old neighborhood, I walked into a new one!

— Susan Yanguas —

# Let It Go

*Sometimes our grandmas and
grandpas are like grand-angels.*
~Lexie Saige

All the grandchildren loved the unique player piano that sat in my grandmother's living room. This piano was manufactured in the 1960s, and we could purchase paper rolls of our favorite songs. The music roll was relatively easy for a young Mozart like myself to hook up, but the very best part was *how* we got the roll to move to make the piano play. At the bottom center of the instrument were two pedals, and if we pumped the pedals at the speed at which we pedaled our bikes when racing with friends, we could make just about any song sound like a honkytonk melody. By the end of the song, we kids started to lose steam, and our honkytonk tune switched to the pace of a church hymn. The beauty of the piano was that it could also be played manually by those fortunate enough to have the skill.

Grandma loved to watch the grandkids enjoy her music maker. We had an old upright at home, but it wasn't nearly as awesome as Grandma's modern piano. Our ancient relic had belonged to my dad's aunt, who was a piano teacher in my small hometown. The top layer of the keys had been broken off over the years, which created the illusion of asphalt under our fingertips rather than the "tickle" of ivory. Nonetheless, I loved it and sat for hours at that old piano until I taught myself how to play a few songs. I couldn't read a note of music, but I had the ability to listen to a song and echo what I heard through my fingers.

Upon arrival at my grandma's house, I'd run to the piano to serenade her with my latest accomplishment. Mom would join us in the living room, and the two would engage in adult conversation. Sooner or later, I'd tire of playing or stop because I feared missing some important bit of information they were sharing. Grandma would always cease talking and ask me to keep playing. She may have truly enjoyed my juvenile concerts, but now that I'm a grandmother myself, I can't help wondering if that was her way of keeping me occupied while they discussed topics too mature for my little ears.

When I was twenty-five, Grandma passed away, ten days after my grandfather. All their belongings would be dispersed amongst family members or sold at an estate sale. Needless to say, I wanted the piano. I guess the better statement would be that I felt I was *entitled* to the piano. Wasn't I the one Grandma always asked to continue playing for her? I was her private pianist, and that was my fondest memory with her.

I immediately let my mom know how I felt about the piano and that I intended to claim ownership of it. She presented the idea to the family, but there was an issue. One of her six siblings wanted it, too, and they had seniority over a mere grandchild.

Daily, I harassed my mother about the piano. She needed to understand that I was counting on her to be my voice, my legal representation, whatever it took! An appraiser had placed a monetary value on some of the more expensive belongings of the estate, and a value of $350 had been placed on the piano. My husband and I didn't have an abundance of money at the time, but I'd been saving for a trip and was more than willing to sacrifice my vacation fund if it meant securing this treasure.

As the weeks went on and decisions were being made, I got more aggressive in reminding my mom that Grandma would want the piano to be mine. She would want my future children to enjoy it as much as I had, and Mom had to stand up for what should rightfully be mine. I knew she was growing weary of my demands, but I was relentless. At some point, my aggressiveness crossed the proverbial line from determination to obsession.

One night after again reminding my mom that her parental obligation was to diligently represent me, I went to bed and fell into a deep sleep. Sometime during my slumber, Grandma appeared to me in a dream. She had the same smile that made me gleam with pride when I'd play for her, but her message shocked me. It was simple and straight to the point: "Let go of the piano." I couldn't believe what she was saying! There had been no doubt in my mind that she wanted me to have it, and now she was telling me to let go of it. My first instinct was to argue with her, but as quickly as she appeared, she was gone, leaving no time for discussion.

I woke up still wanting to plead my case, but to whom? A dream? My mother, who had already grown weary from my badgering? What I had to do was crystal-clear. I had to let go of the piano. I called Mom that morning and told her I no longer wanted her to fight for the piano and to please let the other family member know I was surrendering. No doubt she was curious how I had arrived at this decision, but I never told her about the dream.

Several more weeks passed as the family continued to divide up the belongings. I attended the estate sale and picked up a few mementos to remember my grandparents by, but I never asked about the piano.

The final days of settling the estate were drawing near when I got a phone call from my mom. After a bit of small talk, she asked me if I was still interested in the piano. I couldn't believe what she was asking! Of course, I was still interested! The siblings had decided to allow each grandchild to pick one item from what hadn't already been taken, and, much to my surprise, the piano remained. The greatest news was, if I wanted it, I could have it for 10 percent of the appraised value. So, for a mere $35, Grandma's beloved piano became mine.

The piano sat proudly in my home for more than twenty years. My daughters played with it but never really expressed an interest in learning to play it. A few years ago, just as Grandma had delivered the message for me to let go, I knew it was time for me to physically let go of the piano I had emotionally fought for so long ago. We desperately needed more living space in our small home, and the renovations required utilizing the space where the piano sat. I joyfully passed Grandma's piano on to my cousin.

The lesson I learned through that last visit from my grandmother is one that will never be forgotten. I had been selfish, and my grandmother had given me so much in her lifetime that I didn't need an object to remind me of the things I loved about her. After she convinced me to let go, I was rewarded in a way I never "dreamed" possible.

— Tamara Bell —

# Take Center Stage

> We have to learn to be our own best friends
> because we fall too easily into the trap
> of being our own worst enemies.
> ~Roderick Thorp

I am a charter member of the "Clean Your Plate, Children in Europe are Starving Club." As a first generation American, I heard that phrase constantly from my mother who emigrated from Bulgaria. I was led to believe that if I ate all my food, my distant cousins might somehow miraculously benefit. I needed little encouragement with the delicious cuisine served in my mother's kitchen.

Looking back to those days in the fifties, our daily fare was what restaurants now claim to be gourmet selections: succulent Bulgarian entrees such as roasted lamb, stuffed cabbage, and stuffed peppers; phyllo pastry filled with cheese; and baklava dripping with honey and walnuts. My taste buds were awakened and refined at an early age.

In grade school my brown-paper-sack lunch was easy to find when they opened the lunch cupboard doors. It was the one with a large grease stain on it from the leftovers from the previous night's dinner. No American peanut butter and jelly sandwich for me. My lunch was more like a juicy kielbasa.

In addition to developing a sophisticated palate, I also inherited Bulgarian genes, which meant I was short and a little stocky. As a teen, I often carried 10 to 12 pounds more than I should have. Spread over a mere five feet, there was not a lot of longitude to disperse the extra poundage. My thighs and hips attracted the extra calories and were a constant source of frustration to me as I saw my pear shape reflection in the mirror.

I probably first became conscious of my weight and the direct correlation it had to my self-esteem at age fourteen, my freshman year of high school. I don't think anyone would have suspected that there was a lot of negative self-talk going on in my head, as I participated fully in every activity, had many friends and even made the cheerleading squad. Only I knew how much more enjoyable those activities were when my weight was lower.

I soon discovered I had a summer weight and a winter weight. As spring arrived, I could shed 5 to 10 pounds easily by browsing through the Sears catalog and visualizing myself wearing those cute pedal pushers. Living near Lake Michigan and going to the beach often, the thought of my thunder thighs in a bathing suit helped me say "no" to French fries or an extra helping of a delicious moussaka.

However, as the autumn days grew short and dark, I inevitably gained back the ten pounds. I'd be hiding them behind bulky sweaters all winter. My yo-yo dieting cycle was firmly established.

Through the years I tried every weight loss program: Weight Watchers, Nutri-System, Jenny Craig, Diet Center, Atkins, and Scarsdale. I was successful with each one, until I gained it all back.

Then, a few years ago, I had a revelation.

We were attending a Celebration of Life for a deceased family member and many of our old home movies were running. I saw my son's first birthday party and smiled again at the sight of a tow-headed little boy putting his entire hand in the icing. Then I saw myself on the screen, and I was shocked. I saw a somewhat attractive young mother, not the fat woman I thought I was.

In that moment, I grieved for all the occasions when I wasted negative energy because of 10 pounds. A mere 10 pounds often kept me from fully enjoying an experience because I thought I should have been thinner.

Today, at age seventy-five, I am still weight conscious, but more for health reasons than appearance. I am now the one preparing the delicious Bulgarian cuisine for my friends and family. I am twenty-five pounds more than my high school weight but active with tennis, pickle ball and golf. I often think of that home movie and vow to not let any negative self-judgment creep in as I participate fully in these activities.

The lesson I learned from that movie was that no one is judging me more harshly than I am. In fact, they are probably not even noticing my weight. Wasn't it Dr. Phil who said, "You wouldn't worry so much about what people think of you if you knew how little they do think of you. Most people are thinking of themselves."

I'm starting a new club. Not a "clean your plate" club, but a "clean your mind of negative self-image" club. I want to embrace myself as I am, so my daughters and granddaughters will follow my example, learning to love their bodies and not be led astray by the unrealistic expectations of society.

When my family looks back at the movies we are making today, I want them to see a woman enjoying life to the fullest, not one hiding in the background for fear the camera might capture her flabby arms.

What do you want your loved ones to see in the movies and memories they will watch in years to come? I hope it is you center stage, participating in life with a beautiful smile, laughter and joie de vivre.

—Violetta Armour—

# Forgiveness Is a Choice

*Holding on is believing that there's only a past;*
*letting go is knowing that there's a future.*
*~Daphne Rose Kingma*

In February, when my father passed away after a long illness, I felt called to give his eulogy. In the months that preceded his death, I sifted though my memories of him and pondered what I would write.

Dad had several qualities that were adorable, but none stood out like his ability to forgive people for being fallible. I was always amazed that no matter what a person did, he always found it in his heart to forgive. Part of my tribute to him had to be to point this out to the world. But, I was faced with a serious dilemma.

How could I tell people that he had taught me to forgive the seemingly unforgivable — while not having forgiveness in my own heart?

You see, my world was shattered when my marriage ended. My childhood best friend and my soon to be ex-husband moved in together, leaving me with two small children, a broken-down car, and no health insurance.

I was angry, blaming, and bitter.

Even simple procedures like exchanging the children drained me with hatred. Eventually, the boys stopped going to their dad's and I was relieved to not have to deal with it anymore.

It was a cold day in January when I called my ex-husband to tell him Daddy was dying. He promptly planned a visit with Dad to say his goodbyes and Dad graciously welcomed him.

Still, there was one more thing to do. I called my former childhood friend and asked her to meet me at the hospital. At first, she was concerned about the other members of my family and how they would react if they saw her there.

I asked for some time alone with Dad that night. As I sat with him, I was nervous. I began to realize that I wanted my friend's forgiveness as well. I hadn't exactly been an angel to her since the divorce.

Around eight o'clock, she showed up at the hospital. When Daddy woke up and found us both there, he looked surprised. For once, he was at a loss for words. We laughed when he opened his mouth and nothing came out. He finally managed to say, "Well, my lord...."

I regret I never asked him later what he was thinking, but knowing my dad, I'm sure he was proud and happy that I was able to put all the anger and bitterness behind me at last.

Daddy died a few weeks later and I gave his eulogy as my last gift to him. Yet, his last gift to me had been priceless.

Today, my friend and I have resumed talking and going to lunch or dinner occasionally. We have forgiven the hurt, and focus on old times and good times to come.

We are always accompanied by her little girl, who looks and acts remarkably like my oldest son. I enjoy being in her life and we have forged a special bond. In a way, I feel like I have a little girl of my own.

I have learned through all of this that forgiveness is a choice we can all make, if we are willing to set aside pride and hurt feelings. On the other side of forgiveness lies immeasurable peace.

— Katherine Van Hook —

# Return to Heart Mountain

*I will permit no man to narrow and degrade
my soul by making me hate him.*
~Booker T. Washington

Like a little kid who gets too excited waiting to ride a roller coaster, I feel like I might throw up. I have been looking forward to this and yet, my emotions alternate between complete euphoria and an overwhelming desire to turn the car around. I'm scared, but I can't turn back. There is too much riding on this venture and so I continue driving into the unknown at sixty-five miles per hour.

It feels like my husband, Mike, and I have been driving on this rural Wyoming highway for hours, when in reality barely twenty minutes have passed since we left our motel in Cody. The land before me is beautiful, but I am unable to appreciate it because I am so preoccupied with what is about to happen. My hands take on a life of their own, fidgeting with the seatbelt, the window, my sunglasses. My eyes search the road for any sign of our destination. In my hand I hold the directions given to me by my grandma. The frayed edges are becoming damp in my sweaty hands.

"Is that it?" Mike asks. I follow his gaze and almost miss seeing a small brown sign with faded white lettering on the side of the road.

This is Heart Mountain Relocation Camp. This is our destination and the reason for our trip. We have come to visit the site of the internment camp where my grandma spent three years of her life locked up like a prisoner during World War II simply because she was the "wrong" race.

"That's it!" I yell, but we have already missed our turn.

"Don't worry, I'm turning around," Mike says. He reaches over and pats my leg, both to reassure me and to make me sit back down in my seat.

"Here it is," Mike says as he exits onto a small dirt road. I stare at the land, devoid of any markers that would hint at its importance, as we slowly make our way towards the camp.

The humming sound of gravel under the tires of our car has a calming effect, but it can't drown the sound of my heartbeat in my ears or ease the tightness in my throat. I catch myself leaning forward, silently urging the car to go faster. The remnants of the camp come into view and I want to be there now. I need to be there.

We pull off onto what might have once been a dirt road, but is now nothing more than a path overgrown with weeds. There are no other cars around and even the birds that chirped non-stop since we arrived in Cody seem to have disappeared. As we park the car I sink back into my seat, unable to move.

Three buildings loom before me, the remains of my grandma's former prison, fenced in by a chain link fence. A thin line of barbed wire tops the fence and the sight of it sickens me.

They were fenced in like cattle, I think. And guarded like criminals in their own country.

The buildings are predictably worn down, but after years of staring at pictures of the camp in textbooks, I recognize them. I recognize the black tar paper that barely kept out the wind and snow. I recognize the tiny windows in the walls.

In the far distance, I can see a tower made of bricks. I know from my grandma's stories that it used to be a part of the internee hospital. It is infamous in my family because it is in that hospital that my grandma's first daughter died when she was less than a day old, a baby whose only day on earth was spent behind barbed wire fences.

I am no longer afraid. Instead, I feel the resentment my grandma has been holding onto for half a century collect in a lump in my throat. The reality of what happened to her so many years ago hits me harder as I stare at the same landscape my grandma stared at for three long years. I am angry. Big salty tears blur my vision and I lose sight of my surroundings.

"Are you ready?" Mike asks quietly when minutes after we have parked we are still sitting in the car.

I nod my head, but still don't move. Mike gets out of the car and I take little notice of him as he rummages through the trunk. My eyes are glued to the tower. Mike opens my car door and I jump at the sound.

"Come on," he urges as he pushes my camera into my hands. Suddenly, I am out of the car, brushing past Mike and running towards the buildings. I remember why I am here. This place, so desolate and run down, is a piece of my history. I am here to remember those who lost their lives and lost their years in this place. I am here to document what's left of their prison. I have brought years of resentment and anger with me and I intend to leave them here. I have come in my grandma's stead to make peace with the past that has held our family captive for too long. I have come for closure.

The land feels empty and eerie, but in a strange way it also feels welcoming, like it has been waiting for me. I move reverently among the buildings, snapping photographs and lightly tracing my fingers over the walls. I try to wrap my head around what I am feeling, but words escape me. I feel pain. I feel connected. I feel peace.

As I look through the lens of my camera I feel myself willing the buildings to give up their stories. For an hour I silently wander back and forth, taking pictures and taking it all in. As I walk, I can literally feel myself change. I unclench my fists and the anger that Grandma had felt, the anger that she had passed on to me, seems to drop to the ground like pebbles.

I close my eyes and take a breath.

"We forgive you," I whisper, and as my words are carried away with the breeze the roots of resentment that kept my family tied to Heart Mountain begin to untangle themselves from the ground. I bend down and pick up two small white rocks from the dirt. I am taking home a piece of this place: one rock for me and one for Grandma.

As we slowly drive away from the site, I turn around in my seat and stick my head out of the window desperate to watch it until it completely disappears. The wind whips my hair around my head in a frenzied dance. Years ago my grandma had lived here as a prisoner in her own country, forced to give up everything she owned. Today, I had walked the grounds offering forgiveness for the past and gaining closure in return. I did it for myself. I did it for my family. I did it for Grandma.

— Jessie Miyeko Santala —

# 93

# Recipes for Healing

*Comfort food is the food that makes us feel good — satisfied, calm, cared for and carefree... Finding comfort in food is a basic human experience.*
~Ellie Krieger

When my wife Jenn committed suicide in September 2018, it left a deep and profound hole in my life and that of my daughter. In the months following her death, I found myself in a dark place that felt devoid of hope or light.

Throughout more than twenty years together, Jenn and I had spent countless hours in the kitchen creating. I was sure that had ended until I came upon a simple black folder while cleaning my library. It contained over two dozen recipes for comfort foods written in my wife's handwriting. They spanned our years together and had everything from katsu chicken to chocolate-chip cookies. My wife had written comments in the margin about each dish. Some of the comments regarded the recipes; others were humorous observations made at the time about their creation.

When I began cooking, I discovered the light away from the darkness in which I had been living. While making my wife's "Finally Meatloaf" (thus named because, after years of tinkering, she had finally gotten it how she wanted), I found myself overwhelmed with feelings.

As I gathered and mixed ingredients per my wife's writing, a hundred memories of standing next to her in the kitchen flooded back. As the meal cooked and the aroma filled the house, I recalled dozens of warm memories from our past family meals.

Slowly but surely, with time and the help of that simple black folder, I have dug myself out of the dark, hopeless place I had fallen into. In the end, I learned that sometimes the longest lasting expressions of love and affection can be nothing more or less than a really good meatloaf recipe.

—Steve Coney—

# Relief Within My Heartache

*What a lovely surprise to finally discover
how unlonely being alone can be.*
~Ellen Burstyn

My mother, sisters, and best friend are here now, and I go sit in the bedroom, pretending I'm packing up. Instead, I sit on the bed, staring out the window, listening. I hear the bags and boxes being filled up by my best friend and then picked up and carried down the stairs and into the truck by my sisters and mother. Footsteps and grunts go down the stairs. I hear, "Turn, turn," and "Okay, I got it, I got it."

The bed of the truck makes loud sounds each time a bin is dropped into it. I can hear it all from outside the window, and what I hear is permanence.

In the heat of battle, I had packed up to leave three times before. One time I even stayed away for a month. I always returned though, and all my things went back into their accustomed places.

This time is different. I hear myself leaving with every noise from my helpers. With each trip they take to fill up the truck with my life, a piece of hope leaves, too. The relationship, the comfort, the memories, the future — are all now changed for good.

It's over.

I hide in the bedroom, crying, but I hear whispering in the kitchen.

There are a few things they are unsure of. I wipe my face when I hear, "Kiki, can you come out here for a second?" My mother, sisters, and best friend are by the cabinets where I had put some of my things. They look at me lovingly, and they're quiet. I try to look at their eyes in an effort to figure out what they want to know.

I can't tell if they're going to laugh or cry.

"So, um, what's the plan for the canned goods?" my oldest sister asks.

"Yeah, specifically, the black beans there." My other big sister points toward the cans.

"As well as the four opened containers of half-eaten almond butter," my best friend notes.

My mom looks at me, and her eyes say, "I didn't want to make you come out here to deal with this." She's ready to defend these cans if I need her to.

I look at their faces and then at the pile of pantry items that I, at some point, had apparently prioritized to make the big move with me to my sister's basement. I cry and say, "The almond butters can go to the trash, but the black beans are coming with me." They pause and exchange looks with each other.

I realized the absurdity at last, and I burst out laughing. We are all in hysterics now. "Black beans are a necessity; got it," someone jokes. We keep laughing, and they don't ask questions. Into the truck the special beans go.

It wasn't about the beans for me, though. It was about making choices that bring me joy and do not compromise my wants or needs. He hated beans, and we could never have them in the chili.

Relief comes in the most unexpected moments by the most unexpected things.

Today, relief within my heartache comes from a few cans of beans.

— Kellie Burley —

# Make Marriage Work

# Repairing Brokenness

*Blessed are the hearts that can bend;
they shall never be broken.*
~Albert Camus

In 2001, just a few months before 9/11, my future wife Lucy went to New York with her mom. They saw several Broadway shows and bought a snow globe filled with the city's top landmarks and signs from the more popular Broadway shows. She always enjoyed collecting snow globes from her travels.

Then five years ago, when we'd just gotten married and had moved to a new house, Lucy left the snow globe on the garage floor while searching for something in a trunk we had out there. She should have put it back where it belonged, but she didn't. I saw it there the next day. I was somewhat peeved that she'd left it there. I should've picked it up and put it back in its proper place, but I didn't. I was wrong for that.

That snow globe remained on the floor of the garage for several days. Each of us saw it and had multiple opportunities to pick it up and do the right thing, but both of us failed.

One night, I turned on the light in the garage, but the bulb blew. It didn't faze me. I continued to do whatever it was I was doing. Several seconds later, I accidentally kicked the snow globe over and it shattered into seemingly a million pieces.

My heart started racing. I knew she'd be upset. I picked everything up the best I could, discarded the glass, put the base in a box, and set it aside. It was something special, so I vowed to get it repaired one day. In my heart and soul, I knew it could be fixed.

Less than a year later, Lucy and I were divorced. We argued, fought, and even suffered a devastating miscarriage. We were broken. She took her stuff, and I took mine. I also took the broken snow globe. I knew it could be fixed.

We didn't see each other for a year and half, although we texted from time to time. Sometimes it was nice; other times, not so much.

Before her, I was alone yet never felt lonely. When I lost her, I was a mess. I served in the U.S. Army for many years, including three yearlong tours of duty in Iraq. My body hurt. My mind hurt. My soul hurt. My heart hurt. I was broken from head to toe.

There were times I turned to extreme amounts of alcohol to escape the hurt. I only hurt more. On one occasion, I went with three of my best friends to the Georgia Dome in Atlanta to see our beloved Auburn Tigers play the Louisville Cardinals. I watched the first series of the game and then disappeared. I sat on the floor in a corner away from everyone and never watched another snap. I was so alone. I hurt so much.

Finally, in early December, I stopped in at my local VA hospital to ask for some help. I could've walked in to the mental health clinic and seen a doctor right then, but it wasn't urgent. I wasn't going to do anything stupid. I knew I could be fixed. I just didn't know how.

The first available appointment was the last slot of the day on Christmas Eve. I thought that was quite special. What a gift! I saw a doctor for my physical pain and a counselor for my mental pain. I was well on my way to repairing my own personal brokenness.

I needed to cut Lucy loose. I had to. I needed to move on. "If you love something, set it free," they say, and I did.

Besides an occasional text, we didn't communicate at all for the better part of a year... until we did.

She was going through her own hard times, trying to deal with her own brokenness. One day, she felt that she'd hit rock bottom. Her mom, sister, and daughter told her to talk to me, because "Jody was the only guy who really ever loved her."

So, she called me. I was shocked. She's not someone who likes talking on the phone. We talked for a while. She said she was in the area, so I asked her to stop by if she wanted. The funny thing is that we lived in a small town, so she was always "in the area."

We spent the rest of that day just hanging out in my back yard. I had a bountiful garden, so we picked fresh vegetables and ate them raw. I think we cooked something later that night.

From that night on, we saw each other frequently. We were just friends enjoying each other's company; we were trying to get to know each other better than before.

Inevitably, we started talking about a possible future but knew we had to fix some things. When I saw the writing on the wall that we indeed could be fixed, I sent the broken snow globe to a shop in Colorado to be repaired.

I'd hoped to get it back by Valentine's Day. I had a speech and a romantic presentation laid out for her. I wanted to use the snow globe as a symbol for our failed marriage and how we both contributed to it but also as a symbol of how something so special could be repaired. Unfortunately, the repairs on the globe took longer than expected so I didn't have it in time for Valentine's Day.

It turned out that we didn't need the snow globe to symbolize our brokenness or our repairs. We made a decision to give our relationship another go while the repairs were still taking place.

When I finally surprised her with the repaired snow globe, she was blown away. It looked brand new — better than ever. She had no idea that I had sent it off and had no idea that it could be salvaged. I did. I knew it could be fixed.

Upon further review, it wasn't perfect. The Statue of Liberty's torch had broken off, but that was okay. It wasn't perfect, but it was close enough.

We've been back together for more than two years. We've truly never been happier. We live in my family home, which sits on fifty-eight acres of land in the country near a river just two miles down the road from my mother. Her mother lives a whopping nine miles away. It's quiet, and we love it. My late father was born in our house. It's special.

We're in a good place, figuratively and literally.

Speaking of babies, we have our own. Her name is Abigail. She was born seven and a half weeks early, in the back of an ambulance on Friday the 13th. Just your typical birth, I guess. She's perfect in every way.

When something is special and you know it, you don't throw it away. You keep it. You hold onto it the best you can, and when the timing is right, you fix it.

— Jody Fuller —

# 96

# What Dreams May Come

*Words could never tell the joy an uncle brings.
An uncle is a bond of faith that even time can't sever,
a gift to last all of our lives. An uncle is forever.*
~Irene Banks

Uncle Gary was one of my favorite people. He had a cowboy mentality and was a hard worker. He could fix anything and always had grease- or motor-oil-stained fingertips. He had a quiet strength about him.

He was like a second father to me, and to my husband he was like the father he always dreamed of.

My husband, Daniel, and I had a roller-coaster marriage. It was bumpy. Our hardest year was our fifteenth. We stopped talking. We fought constantly, and I was ready to call it quits. I had completely checked out of my marriage. My husband had, too. We knew that if we didn't fix what was broken, divorce was the next step.

Uncle Gary also passed away that year.

One night, I had a dream that Daniel and I were at Uncle Gary's house. The sounds and smells were so real that I felt like it wasn't a dream at all. My uncle said, "You two come outside with me and let me show you what I've been working on."

We followed Uncle Gary to his shop table where there were parts to something scattered all around. He picked up a few pieces and tried to *puzzle them together.* He handed a piece to Daniel and then a piece to me.

He looked straight at us and said, "If you don't have the right tool, you can't fix it. It can't be fixed without the right tools." He kept saying this to us until we assured him that we would find the right tool.

I had this dream four nights in a row — exactly the same dream every night.

Since my husband and I were barely talking to each other, I didn't tell him about the dream. On the fifth night, Daniel mentioned that he was really missing Uncle Gary. Having a wall up, I shrugged and said simply, "Me, too." After a few moments of silence, Daniel began to tell me about a dream he had about Uncle Gary every night for the previous four nights. Every detail, every word was the exact dream I had.

We both broke down and sobbed uncontrollably. Then, we did something we hadn't in years: We talked all night. We fixed what was broken, and the right tool was communication. My uncle knew we wanted to fix it. We just needed a little bit of help.

—Lindsay Shirley—

# 97

# Our First 5K

> *Unity is strength… When there is teamwork and collaboration, wonderful things can be achieved.*
> ~Mattie Stepanek

I warned my husband that something crazy was about to come out of my mouth. "I think we need to run a 5K."

I was not a runner. I was a stay-at-home mom still carrying double-digit baby weight from two pregnancies in the last three years. With my husband in graduate school, and a toddler and a baby in the house, exercise hadn't been a priority. Running was just about the last thing I ever thought I would do for fun.

But it was an idea I hadn't been able to shake for a couple of days. A friend had posted something on Facebook about a program that would take people from no exercise to running a 5K in nine weeks, and I was intrigued.

My husband, who had been to Army boot camp and served eight years in the Reserves, was all in from the start. He started researching running gear, jogging strollers and a 5K we could register for a few months later. Me? Even though it was technically my idea, I was hesitant. In high school, one of the physical-education requirements was to run a mile-and-a-half every year. I dreaded it and always came in near last. I remembered how slow I was. How I would sweat and feel like I was going to faint as my face turned deep shades of red. How I had to walk part of the way. I was literally in no shape to be running.

Sometimes, I joked that the only time I would ever run after high school was if I needed to save my life. In a sense, I did. Our marriage was only three years old at this point and had been dealt a serious blow. My husband had recently confessed to infidelity. While we were both committed to healing and keeping our marriage together, it was going to take work. We needed a lot of help to restore our relationship, and for some reason I thought running would be part of the solution.

I was desperate enough to think that training for a 5K would benefit our marriage. For one, we'd have to spend time together several days a week. We had registered for a 5K that was exactly nine weeks from when we started the training program, so we had to keep to a strict schedule. Quality time as a couple was something we lacked, what with two small kids and no family within 800 miles. During our training, we had a few offers from friends to watch the kids, but buying a jogging stroller was our guarantee that we wouldn't miss a workout.

Second, I needed to accomplish something difficult — to push myself beyond what was easy and comfortable. I wasn't sure if I could run a 5K or save my marriage, but I knew I couldn't do either if I didn't try. I hoped that training for my first-ever 5K would help me develop the kind of discipline and perseverance I would need to face difficult circumstances of all kinds.

Third, I wanted the physical act of striving toward a common goal to inspire us to do the same for our relationship. I wasn't sure which would be harder.

Nothing dramatic happened in those nine weeks. I didn't lose a bunch of weight. Our marriage didn't heal automatically. But, week by week, we stuck to the plan and gave it our best effort.

The morning of the race, I was up with the kids before dawn, as usual. Their grandparents came to town to watch them (and us) during the run. It was a cold November morning and I questioned our sanity. This idea had always been crazy to me, but now that the reality of it had arrived, I was even more sure that this unconventional plan was not something normal people did.

My body practically hummed with adrenaline and nervousness as we gathered with hundreds of runners at the start line. And then we were off — putting our training to the test on the actual race route.

It was an emotional 36 minutes. The first mile passed quickly. The second mile dragged. We saw our kids a couple of times on the route, and I blinked back the tears. As we neared the end, people we'd never met — fellow runners — shouted encouragement.

When the finish line came into view, my husband, who was slightly ahead of me, reached back toward me to take my hand. I couldn't hold back the tears any longer. That one gesture symbolized so much of what we had been through in the past months. After all that had happened, he was still reaching for me. We were still in it together.

We finished the race holding hands and sobbing. Running a 5K hadn't made our marriage perfect, but it had changed something in us, something I hoped would last.

That was eight years ago. We're still married. We've run a few 5Ks since then, and we've had more than a few challenges in that time. But the lessons from that 5K remain. We make time for each other. We push ourselves to do and say what is difficult because we know it will be good for us. And we keep our goals in front of us, working together as a team.

I can't say I love running yet, but I love how running makes me feel. Strong. Confident. Accomplished. All because I took a chance on a crazy-for-me idea.

—Lisa M. Bartelt—

# Mud Pie and Coffee

*There is no love without forgiveness, and
there is no forgiveness without love.*
~Bryant H. McGill

The University Inn restaurant was packed that night. A waitress set two plates of mud pie on our table, flipped through her ticket book, and hurried away. I looked at Steve across the table, tall and strong in his red flannel shirt, and thought how comfortable I felt sitting with him. But his silence worried me.

I pushed the piece of mud pie around on my plate, prying crust away with my fork. "I'm glad you took my call. I didn't think you would," I said, glancing at him.

He stirred his coffee, tapped the spoon on the rim, and folded his hands in front of his cup. "Well, you said you wanted to talk." He seemed guarded.

Looking back, I realize how much was depending on that little conversation in the University Inn twenty-seven years ago — three amazing kids, four Golden Retrievers, twelve cats, seven different house mortgages, two major career changes, and an unwavering partner for life.

Now, after two decades of marriage, I know Steve loves me despite my faults. It was in the vows we took one January afternoon before God, family, and friends. If they didn't go like this, they should have: "Thou shalt love your wifey when she feeds your prized trout to the cats; honor her when she wakes in the morning with dried saliva glued to her chin; and cherish her when she throws her Super Nintendo controller in the garbage after losing four *Monopoly* games in a row."

Over the past two decades, we've both had to apologize, both learned to forgive, and both committed the same transgressions days later. To err is human. To forgive is true love. To forget is humanly impossible.

But before we were married, there were no guarantees to love for better or worse. Forgiveness was still optional. On that night in the University Inn, when we were both in college, Steve had a choice to make — to forgive me or forget me. It was the first real test of his love.

On that night in the restaurant, I unfolded my napkin, feeling ashamed. "Steve, about that note. I didn't mean for it to sound the way it did," I began, wishing I'd never written it.

It wasn't a big deal, really. Lara and I were studying in the lounge with some girls from the hall when Steve walked through the door. Lara nudged me and wrote in the margin of my notebook, "Steve's here. You okay with that?" (Lara was a psychology minor.)

Embarrassed, I scribbled, "That's fine, as long as he doesn't talk to me." I put a smiley face in the margin because I knew Steve loved to talk — not about himself, but about everything else. At that time, he was a real Phil Donahue, searching for subjects to ponder and debate — from computers, to ancient Rome, to dream houses, to how the world will end.

I opened a packet of sugar and poured it into my mug, listening to the clinking dishes and muffled conversation around me. "I wrote that note because I had so much to read. I was happy to see you," I said, "but I knew if we started talking, I wouldn't get my paper done."

Steve propped his elbows on the restaurant's table. He wanted more.

My cheeks burned. "I'm sorry if I hurt you, Steve," I continued, smoothing the napkin over my knee. "I think you're a great guy, and I really do love talking with you."

I knew Steve had seen the note the second he sat down next to me in the lounge. He didn't talk to me for a week after that. My roommate told me he'd written me off.

Steve sighed, then dug into his mud pie and asked, "Marianne, why didn't you just tell me you were busy? I'm taking twenty-one credits this semester. I know how it gets."

I looked at his flannel shirt, thinking how soft it'd feel against my cheek. Steve knew about my checklist—the one I ran guys through to see where they rated on my man from Snowy River scale. When I saw *The Man from Snowy River*, I realized that's what I wanted—a quiet, rugged cowboy who'd ride through storms to my rescue on his mountain steed. Steve failed the test: He was a marketing major, played computer games, and had only ridden a horse twice in his life. Somehow, I didn't care.

I nudged the maraschino cherry off a mound of whipped cream, rolled it across my plate through fudge, and stabbed the cherry with my fork. "I didn't tell you because I was afraid I'd hurt your feelings," I answered finally.

Steve smiled. "It'd take a lot more than that to hurt my feelings. I'd rather you just be honest with me," he replied.

I picked a crumb from the table and dropped it on my plate. Good Lord, how could I be honest with him? If I showed him who I really was—showed him the mound of dirty clothes in my closet, told him my favorite lunch was a bowl of raw Top Ramen, and that my favorite album was *John Denver's Greatest Hits*—he'd run out of my life forever.

A couple laughed suddenly from their table two booths down. Steve poured more cream into his coffee. "Well, I'm just glad you called me. I appreciated that," he said.

Steve was my man from Snowy River in his own way. He came to my rescue when I needed it—not in the gallant flurry of galloping hooves, but in other ways. The week before our wedding, he stood outside in a blizzard pouring fuel additive into the gas tank of my truck when it wouldn't start. When I found my black Lab dead on the side of the road, Steve buried her. When I lost my contact lens in the parking lot at Garcia's, Steve picked it up from the pebbles. When I was in labor with our first baby, he made me a bologna sandwich (even though eating a bologna sandwich was the last thing on my mind). When I wanted to finish my last semester of college as a nearly thirty-year-old mom of three, he told me I could make it—even when no one else thought I could. And later, when I thought my world had ended after

Make Marriage Work

the kids had grown and left, and the house grew quiet, Steve showed me how our life together had really just begun. He's been my man from Snowy River when I needed him.

After two decades of marriage, Steve and I have a history. We've learned to forget and sometimes forget to remember. But that night at the University Inn, everything was still too new. There was nothing solid to hold onto — and I pleaded for someone to save me.

"I'm sorry. I didn't mean to hurt you," I said, on the verge of tears.

Steve stared at me for a bit, and then pushed aside his plate. "Well, Marianne," he said, leaning forward on his elbows, "you're forgiven. Don't worry about it," he said. And then my future husband squeezed my hand, flashed me a warm smile, and poured us another cup of coffee.

— Marianne L. Davis —

# Anything for a Buck

*It's so easy to fall in love but hard to find
someone who will catch you.
~Author Unknown*

If "Living without a Primary Source of Income" were a place, I would be the Queen of the Land. I don't accept this title willingly, but I have repeatedly been given the opportunity to learn how to manage our household on an irregular, minimal budget. In the ten short years that I've been married to my King, he has been out of work four times. Three times were for a period of almost a year. When he lost his job this time, the first words out of my mouth were "You'll get a new job immediately! You'll be back to work in a month!" I half-heartedly believed my words, uttered through a pasted-on smile, over a year ago.

This time we were victims of the economy, like so many others. My husband was replaced by a young chickadee taking home a paycheck half the size of his. However, knowing that fact didn't make it any easier to digest that all of our financial dreams were going to be put aside. We were going to slip out of thriving mode into surviving mode — again.

The next few days were a blur. Not just because I had difficulty seeing through my tears, but I was blinded with anger. I couldn't make eye contact with him, let alone body contact. I was physically unable to provide what my hurting man needed the most: an ego-building, estrogen-driven boost of confidence from his loving wife. How could he allow himself to be in a position that could jeopardize his loving family — again? Would he ever be a consistent provider? When would I have the security that I longed for? And the hardest question of all: Did I marry a loser?

I knew my most important wifely priority was to be my husband's number-one cheerleader in order to prevent him from becoming engulfed in both depression and our deep, comfy couch. Some couples quote their timelines by new babies or houses. Our timeline is based on "Oh, yeah, that was after you were laid off from the ice cream manufacturer but before you sold nuts and bolts." At least we had a freezer full of Ben and Jerry's to get us over that hump.

Terry has never simply been fired, or at least never fired simply. When I get into the details of his employment history, I begin to doubt the truth myself, and I was there. If another man's wife told me this dramatic tale, I know I wouldn't believe her. How can one man have such a long string of unfair treatment? I began to convince myself that not only had he deserved it, but he brought it on himself. But then I stepped back and took a look at the big picture. I realized that was logically impossible. If it wasn't Terry's fault, maybe it was God's. If even God wasn't going to help Terry with his career, who would be willing to hire a man who has never held a job for more than a few years? On top of my fear that I had possibly chosen the wrong man to marry, I had begun to develop a mistrust of employers. Any company that would hire him wouldn't be worth working for, and any job he was offered wouldn't be worth accepting.

Wow — some cheerleader I was turning out to be. But, I have to admit I was both surprised and proud at how Terry reacted to the situation. He got himself back into his job-hunting groups, signed up at the workforce center, and wasted no time in updating his résumé. He got a haircut, sent his suits to the cleaners, and registered for unemployment. He knew the drill, the steps that had to be followed, and he did them. He even skipped some of his usual self-deprecating detours like anti-depressants and getting sucked into watching infomercials in the wee hours of the morning. If he could deal with this like a mature adult, why couldn't I?

As word began to spread of Terry's new employment status, calls of condolence and curiosity began to come in from across the country. Most were kind and supportive. Some just dripped with pity. But one anger-driven, venomous call came from a relative who loves me dearly. She spewed indictments and grilled me with accusatory questions. How dare she label my husband as selfish, accusing him of not making his family the top priority? It was okay for me to think it, but for her to say it out loud? The nerve. In hindsight, I am grateful for her inappropriate behavior because it provoked me to fight back. It was in the act of defending my husband that I began to see the return of the respect I once had for him.

Each time a new call came in, it became easier to brag about the positive steps that Terry was taking to move forward. Each time I hung up the phone, I found it a little easier to feel the respect for him that he deserved. Eventually, I became the cheerleader that he longed for and requires for success. I support and encourage him in all his job-hunting efforts from application to interview. Participating every step of the way has made it "our" job search, "our" career goal.

If our past year were a game show, I imagine it would go something like this: "I'm Bob Womack, your host of *Anything For A Buck*! The game show that challenges your humility by asking 'Just what will YOU do for a buck?' Our first contestant is a happily-married father of two from Colorful Colorado! Welcome Terry!"

"Thanks Bob, glad to be here."

"As you know, Terry, our game is all about just how you are willing to humble yourself to earn money. So, contestant number one, just what will you do for a buck?"

"Anything, Bob. I am willing to do anything to care for my family. I will get up hours before the sun in the dead of winter and drive to the state line to set up cardboard cutouts of the Seinfeld cast on a college campus in order to put food on the table. I will carry two cases of beer, three dozen licorice ropes and a duffle bag filled with peanuts up and down the steep steps of a football arena, a baseball stadium, the rodeo show grounds, and two concert pavilions if it means I can pay the mortgage. I will do market research studies on consumer products and political opinions. I will mystery-shop hamburger chains and barbershops. Bob, I will even dress up as a six-foot gecko, ride around a racecar track in a golf cart and shoot T-shirts into the screaming crowd to keep the lights turned on. I will do anything for a buck!"

The real winner of this show is me. I won the grand prize: a husband I am proud of. One who is willing to do anything not just for a buck, but for our love and for our family. How could I not respect that?

— Karen O'Keeffe —

# Brown and White Butterflies

*True Love comes from God, and love
is demonstrated through character.*
~Philemon Laida

What do you do when the fire that once blazed with romance in your marriage dwindles to embers? Deep within the sweltering jungle of Costa Rica, my marriage hung by a thread. My husband and I served as missionaries in a small, isolated village on the Pacific coast. Time, responsibilities, kids, pregnancy, disappointment, and fatigue had taken their toll on our hearts and relationship.

As the host for short-term mission trips, I led the devotions for the teams that came down to help with our building project. We always tried to create an environment that would allow each person to see God in a new way.

One particular week, I decided to write a series of devotions called "Whispers of Love." Despite the ever-deepening hole in my marriage, I wanted this group to know how madly and perfectly God loved them. I led this group, which ended up being comprised of mostly men, on a journey into God's passionate pursuit of his beloved.

We talked about the love notes God sends us each and every day just as a reminder that he is deeply and totally crazy about us. So, we looked, and we listened. Some found him in the vastness of the cloudless sky. Others were blown away by the brilliance of a star-lit night. Still others were brought to their knees by the power of the surging sea. The circumstances could not have been more perfect for this study. I told them to look at the majesty of the sun as it disappears behind the sapphire sea. I encouraged them to sit on a mountain and watch the trees dance upon the melody of the wind. They were challenged to observe the intricate fabrication of a spider's delicate domain. For behind each of these wonders, someone is whispering words of undying faithfulness.

Each day, the group would expound on the majesty of nature and the unfathomable greatness of God's love. These tough men were truly being swept off their feet. I couldn't help but wonder if God had forgotten that women are the ones who like to be romanced. The time came for the God-walk, a chance for each person to go into the jungle alone with God. Almost everyone went away with grand hopes of a love letter in the form of a ferocious jaguar or a howling monkey.

I set out for my own time alone with the Creator of all this splendor and lover of my soul. I, however, didn't feel very loved. While everyone else had been swept off their feet, I felt that God was distant and unaware of my feeble existence. I prayed, "Lord, show me something big. Please, just take my breath away. I need to know that you care about me too." I sat down on a hilltop overlooking the turquoise ocean and began to wait. Nothing happened. After a few minutes, a small, brown and white butterfly floated down to a nearby piece of grass.

I have to admit that I was thoroughly disappointed. "Come on, God," I thought. "You can do better than this. I mean, this is the rainforest. Haven't you heard all the great things I've been telling these guys, and all I get is this ugly little moth? At least send something with some color." Meanwhile, this moth-like butterfly fluttered around me, pausing every so often, for what purpose I did not know. Then, suddenly, as if it was being called by someone, it lifted up and floated away. I was left with a gnawing emptiness in my heart that I had just missed something big. In my certainty that God was going to blow me away with the expression of his love, I had missed what he was trying to say.

I used this experience for another team later on to remind them that God's love letters may not come wrapped in exquisite envelopes. After this group's God-walk, one lady came running out of the jungle up to me. Breathless, she told me of her time with God, and how he had sent her a brown and white butterfly as well. Because of my story, she went over to it to take a closer look. When it paused on a branch, it stretched out its brown, boring wings. But what she saw then, I will never forget. For on those ugly brown wings lay the intricate design of two, perfectly shaped, white hearts. The message shouted to me that sometimes love doesn't show itself in the big things, but it's there even in the little, boring parts of everyday life.

I still often think about that butterfly. In my mind, it is the most beautiful of all the butterflies I saw while in Costa Rica. Even today, I think about it as a parallel to my marriage. I find myself sometimes complaining to my husband, asking him why he isn't romantic anymore. Why doesn't he sweep me off my feet like he used to? But what I find is that the deepest expression of love isn't found in long-stemmed roses, a candle-lit dinner, or elaborate surprises. It's in the strength of arms that hold me every night. It's in a hammock underneath the stars on a fall night. It's in a midnight trip to Taco Bell to satisfy a pregnant craving. It's in a heart that stays faithful to me even when I'm not exactly pleasant to be around. These are the brown and white butterflies, the fullest expression of the deepest love.

My marriage survived the jungle. It survived because I realized that it is more than romance, even though that is certainly important. It survived because I started looking IN the little things rather than FOR the big things. And guess what? Our love was indeed rekindled!

— Melissa Harding —

# Sleepless Nights

*Hearing is one of the body's five senses,
but listening is an art.*
~Frank Tyger

No question, when I look back on life with eyes tempered by advancing age and growing wisdom, I readily admit I got married too young. I was barely seventeen when that handsome young fellow (a man nine years my senior) walked into my life.

We met on a warm summer's eve. Our meeting was probably more of an observation event than it was an actual meeting. He and a friend were sitting at a drive-in café laughing at me and my friends trying to ditch a carload of guys we had no interest in meeting. A couple of days later, I met that laughing college boy and by summer's end, the smallest seed of a romance had begun to sprout. But then he returned to his university studies 500 miles away, and I returned to high school.

Time passed. We wrote letters back and forth. He finished up at the university and found a job while I trekked off in the opposite direction to business college in another state. On occasion, we arranged to meet up for a day or two but marriage never seriously entered into our conversations until nearly three years had passed. By then, we had to admit we were in love and perhaps were old enough to settle down. Oh, how little we knew!

I had barely turned twenty and he was twenty-nine when we married. We settled down in a small apartment hours away from either of our families. Perhaps that was a good thing since we had only each other to turn to during the tough times. Being young and in love made us oblivious to the practical things in life — such as living within our means. If social activities were happening around town, that's where we had to be, no matter the cost. Then came baby number one followed by baby number two. That's when the real struggling from paycheck to paycheck began. On top of the money stress, my fastidious nature kept me picking up behind him and the kids, doing laundry in the bathroom sink, wrestling with two busy toddlers, and cooking meals made from meager selections of groceries, while he, tired after a long day's work, simply flopped down in a chair and read the newspaper. Tired and irritated, I took to pouting over the smallest infractions, but he didn't notice — or pretended not to notice, I'm not sure which. A distinct chill factor settled over our apartment.

We decided to fix a bad situation. The solution seemed simple enough. We vowed to never again go to sleep angry at one another. If something bothered us, we would talk it out before going to sleep.

Sounds easy, right? Wrong! Here's why. When a bone-tired person is ready to slip into bed, the last thing that person wants is to get caught up in is a midnight heart-to-heart airing of grievances. Here's how it plays out. First come the tears, then the indignant denials, then more tears, followed by apologies and concessions. Finally, somewhere near dawn, comes remorse and forgiveness followed by the good stuff — cuddling together until sleep comes at 0-dark-thirty in the morning. Exhaustion has a way of making seemingly-huge disagreements seem trivial.

Truth is… the decision to never again go to sleep angry was a good one. We spent a lot of sleepless nights but we never again woke up angry at each other.

This year, we celebrate our forty-seventh year together and still agree that little resolution probably saved our marriage a dozen times over. Back then, it planted itself into our lives as a type of Golden Rule and remains there to this day. By choosing harmony, we allowed a new and deeper type of love to grow. We've seen other love stories fade and slip away because of hurt feelings and unresolved arguments, but we chose to protect our love, even at the cost of surrendering a good night's sleep. Or was it ten or twenty nights, or maybe more? I've lost count. But, no matter, the price was worth it then and it's still worth it today.

—Jean Davidson—

# Meet Our Contributors

**Heidi Allen** is the founder of the Positive People Army. What began as a blog has rapidly become a global movement with thousands of people from all over the world working together to make a positive difference.

**John Apel** is a survivor of mistakes he feared would haunt him forever. Whether writing about his life or writing fiction under his pen name, J.D. Neptune, he hopes his words may kindle his readers' belief in a better tomorrow. He lives with his girlfriend in Colorado.

**Violetta Armour** is a former English teacher and bookstore owner. Her debut novel *I'll Always Be with You* is a book club favorite. She lives in a retirement community in Sun Lakes, AZ where she is writing her Dangerous Pastimes Mysteries, including *A Mahjongg Mystery* and *A Pickleball Poison*.

**Teresa Curley Barczak** retired from AT&T in 2007 and devotes her time to writing, reading, cooking and spending time with family and friends. Teresa enjoys traveling, gardening, and volunteering for her church. She plans on completing a collection of short stories. Email her at tabarczak@bellsouth.net.

**Alma Barkman** is the author of nine books and her writing has also appeared in numerous publications, both secular and Christian. She is the mother of four boys and grandmother of eleven. Her interests include photography, quilting and gardening.

**Lisa M. Bartelt** lives in Lancaster, PA with her husband and two teenagers, and on any given day, she might be substitute teaching, writing, or working at her local bookstore. She publishes a Substack called "An Anxious Introvert's Adventures in Living" at lmbartelt.substack.com.

**Rosanna Micelotta Battigelli** has received four Ontario English Catholic Teachers' Association Best Practice Awards for her unique strategies in early literacy, promoting positive pupil interactions and self-esteem, and helping pupils who grieve. Her novel *La Brigantessa* will be published by Inanna Publications in 2018.

**Diana Bauder** is a young-at-heart mom of two and Amma of five grandchildren. She loves flower gardening and selling vintage collectibles and antiques. She previously worked as a caregiver for people with special needs and as a freelance author.

**Brenda Beattie** is a retired letter carrier, chaplain, and self-published author. Her books, *Finding Sacred Ground In The Daily Grind* and *The Case of the Missing Letter*, are available online. She feels blessed and is enjoying retirement life in sunny Florida with her husband.

**Lainie Belcastro** is an inspirational writer, poet, speaker and storyteller, and is blessed to have many of her true stories published in the *Chicken Soup for the Soul* series. She and her daughter, Nika, co-author children's books through their company, We Plant Dreams, LLC. Enjoy her creative journey at www.lainiebelcastro.com.

**Tamara Bell** fulfilled another dream in 2024-2025 by working in the reading department at Valley Grove Elementary School in Franklin, PA. Her students will serve as inspiration for many future stories. She and her husband, Paul, live in Cooperstown, PA, and their greatest joy is their grandchildren, Clara and Hayden.

Following a career in nuclear medicine, **Melissa H.B. Bender** is joyfully exploring her creative side. She recently moved to the Texas coast where she and her husband are renovating a thirty-five-year-old former Parade of Homes fixer-upper. She shares her home renovation and her stories at www.facebook.com/chicvintique.

**Jill Berni** is excited to be a contributor to the *Chicken Soup for the Soul* series for the fourth time. She is a history buff, animal lover and an avid reader. She lives in Mississauga, Ontario with her husband Fred. Learn more at www.jillberni.com.

**Rita Billbe** is a retired high school principal from Oklahoma City. She and her husband own a resort, Angels Retreat, on the White River in Arkansas. Two of her passions are fly fishing and singing in her church choir.

**Kathleen Birmingham** is a freelance writer and ghostwriter and is currently working on a number of children's books. She enjoyed her many years as the "reluctant volunteer" while her husband trained Sadie to be a wilderness search-and-rescue dog. When Sadie was not working, she enjoyed being a beloved member of Kathleen's family.

**Susan Boltz** is a retired medical lab technician and basic logic assistant. She is a member in good standing of St. Davids Christian Writers' Association. Writing devotionals and humor, biking, and baking cookies keep her busy.

**Joan M. Borton** is passionate about strengthening families affected by disability. She has been married to Jerry since 1995. When faced with a little downtime, you will find Joan reading in her hammock, swimming, or working on a jigsaw puzzle. Follow her blog at www.joanborton.com.

**Linda Bruno** is a speaker and writer. Her current project is a devotional (*All God's Creatures*) based on how our interactions with our pets mirror our relationship with God. She and her husband Guy have one grown daughter, five grandchildren, and two furkids. Linda can be reached via e-mail at lfbruno@cfl.rr.com.

**Kellie Burley** has recently revived her passion for writing and has found the process to be incredibly healing. Kellie lives in Massachusetts where she is Auntie Kiki to seven nieces and nephews, is an inside sales manager at a software company, and can be found practicing yoga or enjoying time with loved ones on Cape Cod.

**Jill Burns** enjoys living in the mountains with her loving family and their sweet fur baby, Lavie. She's a retired piano teacher and performer. She enjoys writing, music, gardening, nature, family, friends, and finding the magic in each day.

Twelve years ago, stifling sobs, **Diane Caldwell** boarded a plane to Greece. She hasn't lived in the U.S. since. She currently makes her home in Istanbul, where she dances with gypsies whenever possible and writes when the muse whispers. Her stories have appeared in eight different anthologies and on numerous websites.

**Kim Carney** is a freelance writer, lifelong music lover and passionate supporter of unsigned artists. Kim is a writer on staff for *Artistic Echoes*, a popular UK entertainment magazine. Currently, Kim is working on a book/merch series that will shine a light on independent artists from around the world.

**Eva Carter** is a frequent contributor to the *Chicken Soup for the Soul* series. Her background is in dancing, telecommunications and finance. She is originally from Czechoslovakia and now lives in Dallas, TX with her Canadian husband and their two (Texas) cats.

**Kathleen Chamberlin** is a retired educator living in Albany, NY. She began writing creatively during the quarantine period of Covid-19 and her poetry, essays, and short stories have appeared in both print and online journals and anthologies. She enjoys gardening, genealogy, and her grandchildren.

Radio and television guest **Kitty Chappell** is an international speaker and award-winning nonfiction author of articles, poetry and three books. As a Chandler Police Citizen's Academy graduate, she volunteers for them and is also a TSA canine decoy at the Phoenix Sky Harbor Airport. Kitty welcomes your comments at www.kittychappell.com.

**Dana D. Clark** received her B.A. in English (1996) and M.A. in education (1999) from Austin Peay State University, both with honors. She has four children (two boys/two girls). Currently, she works as a regional monitor for the State of Tennessee. Dana enjoys thrift-shopping, home decorating, and mentoring those afflicted with addiction.

**Steve Coney** is a freelance writer whose wide and varied publishing credits include *REPTILES* magazine as well as two previous *Chicken Soup for the Soul* books. A widowed single Dad, Steve lives in Endicott, NY with his daughter Maybellene.

**Melissa Crandall** is the author of *Elephant Speak: A Devoted Keeper's Life Among the Herd*, a biography of Roger Henneous, who for thirty years served the elephants at the Oregon Zoo with loyalty, kindness, and devotion.

**Melissa Cronin** is an author and journalist living in Vermont. A recipient of Notable Mention in The Best American Essays Series 2019, her work has appeared in *USA Today*, *The Washington Post*, *The Jerusalem Post*, *Narratively Magazine*, *Chicken Soup for the Soul: Recovering from Traumatic Brain Injuries*; and others. Learn more at melissacronin.com.

**Priscilla Dann-Courtney** is a writer and clinical psychologist and lives in Colorado where she and her husband raised their three children. Her columns have appeared in numerous national publications and her book, *Room to Grow* (Norlights Press, 2009), was her way to navigate the light, dark, and wonder of the world. Learn more at priscilladanncourtney.com.

**Jean Davidson** resides in Pocatello, Idaho. Her greatest writing interests are family stories and historical fiction stories about colorful individuals of the Old West. Her greatest joys are her family members, particularly her grandchildren and her cat Simba.

**Marianne L. Davis** received her B.A. in English from Boise State University and has twenty years of experience writing professionally in the tech industry. She's currently working full-time as a research writer at Our Daily Bread Ministries. Marianne married her college sweetheart, Steve, in 1991 and they have three children.

**Kathy Dickie** lives in Calgary, a western Canadian city nestled in the foothills of the majestic Rocky Mountains. She enjoys adventures with her remarkable granddaughters, traveling with her husband, family events, quilting, ancestry research and writing. Kathy is a recurrent contributor to the *Chicken Soup for the Soul* series.

**Shawnelle Eliasen** lives with her husband Lonny and the youngest of their five sons near the Iowa banks of the Mississippi River. They have a Labrador named Hazel.

**Mindi Susman Ellis** is a writer, artist, business owner, and now filmmaker since collaborating with her son, who adapted "The Empty Room" into a short film due to be released in 2026. Mindi adores her family, partner, dogs, pals, yoga, hiking, paddle boarding, and pickleball. Email her at mindicreates@gmail.com.

**Celeste Bergeron Ewan** works full-time as a supervisor in a pipe manufacturing plant. If that isn't busy enough, she is also a proud mother of two and a newly wed wife to her husband John. Celeste enjoys spending time with her family, camping, treasure hunting, and of course, writing. She plans to write an autobiography one day.

**Melissa Face** is the author of *I Love You More Than Coffee*, an essay collection for parents who love coffee a lot and their kids… a little more. Her essays and articles have appeared in *Richmond Family Magazine*, *Tidewater Family Magazine*, and twenty-one *Chicken Soup for the Soul* books. Read more at melissaface.com.

**Tracy Farquhar** is a professional psychic medium, teacher, and author. She has three published books: *Frank Talk, Channeled Messages from Deep Space* (co-authored with NY Times bestselling author Mike Dooley), and *Tarot for Today*. Learn more at TracyFarquhar.com.

**Linda Fitzjarrell** lives in Colorado. She enjoys times with family, scenic drives, photography, and finds writing about her experiences to be therapeutic. Linda credits her sister, Kathy Ide, for bringing this story to life. Kathy is a professional freelance author, editor, and speaker. Learn more at www.KathyIde.com.

**Ryan Freeman** is the father of three daughters, a tennis coach, business owner, and former schoolteacher. His experience that day on the train led to the creation of his non-profit, Zips4kids, and an after-school enrichment program, Ignite Their Spark. Learn more at Zips4kids.com and Ignitetheirspark.com.

**Denise R. Fuller** became a widow in 2012 at the age of forty-one. She has learned how to conquer grief and loneliness and how to forgive and live each day with purpose. She is an esthetician and her ferocious love for aesthetics prompted her to create the National Aesthetic Spa Network for salons and spas.

**Jody Fuller** is a father, writer, clean comedian with a Dry Bar Special, a Certified John Maxwell Leadership Speaker, and former Army officer with three tours of duty in Iraq. He is also a lifetime stutterer. *Alabama* magazine named Jody one of Alabama's top 40 men and women over 40.

**Lori Fuller** is a retired middle school and high school English teacher and has been a volunteer with animal rescue groups for more than a dozen years. She is a Lymphoma survivor and currently spends time fostering dogs and working part-time in Stadium Tours for the St. Louis Cardinals.

**Beverly Golberg**, of Minneapolis, MN began writing after retirement from paralegal work. Her essays have appeared in the literary journals *ARS Medica* and *Willard & Maple*, *Cottage Life* magazine, the *St. Paul Pioneer Press*, and various anthologies.

**Cindy Golchuk** lives near Las Vegas, NV, with her husband, her not-so-angelic grandson, Zack, and two dogs who rule the house with iron paws. In her spare time she enjoys reading, walking with friends, rewriting her three manuscripts geared toward a female readership and polishing her three-book series for tweens.

**David A. Grant** is a five-time contributor to the *Chicken Soup for the Soul* series and a staff writer for *WETA*. A freelance writer from southern New Hampshire, he is currently working on his next book. David enjoys cycling New England's back roads and being "Papa" to his grandchildren.

**Dale Mary Grenfell** is a retired educator, prolific freelance writer, storyteller and workshop facilitator. Loving life in the foothills of the Rocky Mountains, she also volunteers with the CSU International Friends program and with the Office of Restorative Justice. Email her at grenfell@q.com.

**Arturo Guajardo IV** graduated from Texas State University with a Bachelor's in English in 2019 and will be working toward obtaining his Master's in Secondary Education from Texas State University. He currently works as a server at Gristmill River Restaurant & Bar in New Braunfels and hopes to one day be a high school principal.

**Wendy J. Hairfield** has a B.A. in Journalism, with honors, from Temple University. After a rewarding career in public relations promoting environmental programs, she now enjoys writing, tennis, photography, and gardening. She has a daughter and stepson and lives in the Seattle area with her husband and two tortoises.

**Melissa Harding** lives in Colorado Springs, CO with her husband and three small children. She loves to travel and has lived in New Zealand and Costa Rica. When she's not changing diapers or breaking up fights, she enjoys hiking, boating, camping, and writing. She is currently working on an inspirational nonfiction book.

**Charles Earl Harrel** pastored for thirty years, serving churches in California, Nevada, and Oregon, before stepping aside to pursue writing. His articles, inspirational stories, and devotionals have appeared in various periodicals and in forty-one anthologies. He is a nine-time contributor to the *Chicken Soup for the Soul* series and has written five books.

**Janet Hartman** sailed away from New Jersey in 2000 to follow the sun along the East Coast for six years. While afloat, she left software consulting to pursue her never-forgotten dream of writing. Since then, her work has appeared in a variety of anthologies, magazines, newspapers, and e-zines.

**Judith Ann Hayes** loves to write! She is an avid reader. Her older daughter is a registered nurse, and her younger daughter is a make-up artist; both are happily married. Judith is a very proud grandmother. She loves to spend time with friends, but her greatest joy is having fun with her three grandchildren.

**Christy Heitger-Ewing** is an award-winning author who has published more than 2,500 magazine articles and contributed to twenty-eight anthologies. She's passionate about mental health and serves on the Indiana Chapter Board of the American Foundation for Suicide Prevention. Cats, running, and yoga soothe her soul. Learn more at christyheitger-ewing.com.

Born into poverty, **Ruth Logan Herne** believes in the power of faith, hope and love... and the greatest of these is love! A bestselling author, she's married to a wonderful man, has great kids and grandkids, and loves God, family, her country, chocolate, dogs and cappuccinos.

After retiring from a twenty-five-year teaching career, **Lillie Houchin** began her writing journey and has written a collection of memoir vignettes and narrative essays (*Shoebox Stories*), collection of poems (*Kaleidoscopic Verses*), and a novel (*Secrets at Dillehay Crossing*).

**Jennie Ivey** lives and writes in Tennessee and has contributed stories to dozens of books in the *Chicken Soup for the Soul* series. Visit her website at jennieivey.com or email her at jennieivey@gmail.com.

**Jeanie Jacobson's** writing shares hope, humor, and Godly encouragement. In addition to her book, *Fast Fixes for the Christian Pack-Rat*, she's been published in nineteen *Chicken Soup for the Soul* books, *Guideposts*, *The Upper Room*, *Focus on the Family* magazine, and various anthologies. Connect with Jeanie at www.jeaniejacobson.com.

During retirement, **D. Lincoln Jones** turned to writing to fulfill his creative needs. He's authored two books of historical fiction, with a third nearing completion. He also wrote a short story entitled "The Popsicle Kids" which appeared in *Chicken Soup for the Soul: Age Is Just a Number*.

**Susan Maddy Jones** is a former computer-science professional who gave up cubicles for creativity and the great outdoors. She helped design and build her own teardrop camping trailer, explores all manner of creative non-fiction writing, and handcrafts one-of-a-kind wire-woven jewelry. Learn more at SusanMaddyJ.com.

**Ruth Kephart** is a retired RN, lives in Pennsylvania and writes poetry in her spare time. She makes jewelry and crafts to support her mission trips to Haiti and has been to Haiti six times. She has had poetry published in several journals and anthologies including the *Chicken Soup for the Soul* series. Email her at hootowlrn@windstream.net.

**April Knight** is a frequent contributor to *Chicken Soup for the Soul* books. She is also the author of several books about Native Americans, including *Crying Wind* and *My Searching Heart* and others written under her tribal name, Crying Wind.

**Cathi LaMarche** is a novelist, essayist, and poet. Her work appears in over forty publications. In her spare time, she enjoys gardening, cooking, and traveling. She resides in Missouri with her husband and two rescued Collies.

**Miranda Lamb** is addicted to coffee, reading and using far too many commas in her writing. Her story definitely contains a spelling error. She is working on her second novel. Feel free to connect on Instagram @mirandadianalamb or via email at mirandadlamb@gmail.com.

**Linda L. LaRocque** is the author of several award-winning plays. Her numerous short stories have appeared in *Guideposts*, *Signs of the Times*, the *Chicken Soup for the Soul* series and various other anthologies. Her plays are published by Playscripts, Art Age Publishers, Smith and Kraus, Next Stage Press and Christian Publishers. She resides in Michigan.

**Mary Elizabeth Laufer** has a degree in English education from SUNY Albany. Her stories and poems have appeared in magazines, newspapers, and several anthologies. She received a Kirkus star and a Moonbeam Children's Book Award for her middle-grade novel, *Katelyn's Crow*, and is now working on a sequel, *Katelyn's Cat*.

**Kathryn Lay** is a full-time writer for children and adults in books, magazines, and anthologies. She enjoys speaking at schools and to writer's groups. She and her husband own Days Gone By Antiques/Vintage and can be found on Facebook and at Etsy at LaysDaysGoneBy. Email her at rlay15@aol.com.

**Jessica Loftus**, a seasoned psychologist and career counselor, provides individual psychotherapy at her private practice in Palos Heights, IL. She hosts a blog, "Pet Ways to Ease Stress," and will be launching a 4-part workshop, "Shed Your Bad Habits for Good," this summer. Learn more at easywaystoeasestress.com.

**Paul Lyons** graduated from Antioch University with a degree in creative writing. He is a professional comedian headlining on cruise ships and in comedy clubs. His latest book is called *Carpe Diem, Mañana: My Lifelong Struggle to Live Effortlessly*. He lives in Philadelphia.

**Debra Mayhew** is a pastor's wife, mom to seven (usually) wonderful children, part-time teacher, editor and writer. She loves small town living, time with family, good books and long walks. Learn more at debramayhew.com.

**Barb McKenna** has been a writer since she was six years old. She was a journalist for forty years in Canada before retiring to write her childhood memoir, *The San's Cellar*. Her personal essays have been published worldwide.

**Casey McMullin** is a poet and artist from Pennsylvania who believes in the transformative power of nature, love for the little things, and finding solace in absurdity. While they can be found daydreaming about their D&D characters, their work can be found in *Quiddity* ("Orphean Epilogue") or @casmcmullin on Instagram.

**Eugene Mead** served in the U.S. Navy Reserves for eight years. While in college he worked on the Apollo Moon Program and helped to put a man on the moon. He and his wife now live in New Braunfels, TX, and spend time visiting their four children and twelve grandchildren.

**Mark Musolf** lives in Minnesota with his wife. Mark enjoys football, house projects, and reading historical nonfiction.

**Connie Nice** is a wife, mother, and grandmother from Washington State. Writing for thirty-plus years, she loves creating children's stories, blog articles and has one adult novel "in the works." She shares her passion for history, nature, travel, family, and faith through the written word. Follow her at connienice.com.

**Jeannette Nott** is an actor, playwright, and stand-up comedian. She is a 2010 Colorado Voices competition winner and guest columnist for *The Denver Post*. Her story, "A Mother Never Forgets" appears in *Adoption Reunion in the Social Media Age: An Anthology* edited by Laura Dennis, 2014. Jeanne is the reigning Ms. Colorado Senior America.

Through **Karen O'Keeffe's** effort to glorify God, she strives to be the balanced, diverse woman that He created her to be — a wife, mother, sister, friend, writer, artist, homemaker, volunteer, teacher, and steward. She is a member of Words for the Journey Christian Writers' Guild. Email her at moneyhoney@q.com.

**Nancy Emmick Panko** is a retired pediatric nurse and frequent contributor to the *Chicken Soup for the Soul* series. She is author of award-winning books *Guiding Missal, Sheltering Angels*, and to date, five children's picture books. Nancy is a member of the NC Scribes writing group and the Military Writers Society of America.

**Jenny Pavlovic, Ph.D.** lives in Wisconsin with dogs Audrey, Brighty, and Maizy, cat Junipurr, and pony Keanna. She loves walking dogs and ponies, gardening, bicycling, swimming, and kayaking. Her books include *Pal the Pig's Best Day, 8 State Hurricane Kate*, and the *Not Without My Dog Resource & Record Book*.

**Lee E. Pollock** has been a salesman, a hardware store owner, and a pastor. He is now retired and spends his time writing and ministering to others. He has two adult children and six grandchildren. This fall he and his wife will celebrate their fiftieth anniversary.

This is **Becky Lewellen Povich's** eighth publication in the *Chicken Soup for the Soul* series. She has stories included in other anthologies, small-town newspapers and magazines. She published her memoir, *From Pigtails to Chin Hairs*, in 2013. Find her on Facebook under her name or e-mail her at Writergal53@gmail.com.

**Nicholas R.** lives in California where he uses his current home as the base for his work as a tour manager for artists and musicians. He is the youngest of three sons to his mother and late father. He enjoys music, traveling, adventures with friends and family, and attempting to better himself each day with good influence from his peers.

**S.R.** has an Associate of Arts and a Bachelor of Science degree. She is a working mom enjoying small-town living with her husband and three sons. She enjoys cooking, a rare quiet moment, opportunities for creativity and, most of all, spending time with her family.

**Natalie June Reilly** is a writer and book editor who has written more than a dozen stories for the *Chicken Soup for the Soul* series. She is a social influencer who founded the movement Nothing but Love Notes on the premise that a handwritten love note can save the day. Gratitude changes everything!

**Jenna Romano** (a pseudonym) is the author of a mystery novel, a memoir about raising her autistic daughter, and a children's book. Her short stories and articles have appeared in numerous publications. She lived, studied, and traveled extensively in Europe. She's been a singer/storyteller for twenty-five years.

**Suzy Ryan** is an author, an Ironman, and a teacher. She encourages struggling students to recognize that they are victors, not victims. Suzy lives in Carlsbad, CA, and enjoys spending time with her husband, their three adult children, and grandchildren. Check out her novel, *Saving Summer*, at Suzyryan.com.

**Jessie Santala's** love of the written word comes directly from her daddy. He was her favorite storyteller and the reason she wanted to become a writer. She has a master's degree in creative writing from the University of Denver but currently spends her days teaching and taking care of her three precious babies.

**Cathy Shavalier-Chernow** received her BA in Anthropology and her M.Ed. in Learning Disabilities. Retiring after thirty years of teaching, she now has the time to pursue her creative spirit in other avenues: painting and writing.

**Yvonne Curry Smallwood** has been writing and publishing inspirational stories for more than twenty years. But her absolute favorite pastime is traveling with her family and friends. When she is not writing, you can find Yvonne in a craft store purchasing yarn for the many crochet items that she donates to local charities.

**Leigh Smith** is a middle-age life voyager who currently resides in South Carolina with her enduring confidant and husband of twenty-three years, a wickedly intelligent and visionary teenage son who lights up their world, and two feline entertainers. She plans to keep dreaming and continue writing.

**Carly Sutherland** (IG: @poemsforpeoplelikeus) is a passionate advocate for mental health and the pursuit of well-being and identity in motherhood and grief. Her first collection of poems "all the wild women we are" is inspired by the loss of her mother. She lives in the Niagara

Region with her husband and two children.

**Dustin Urbach** received his bachelor's in mechanical engineering from Kettering University in 2012. Currently residing in Michigan, he works for Stellantis as a Prototype Build Engineering Manager and spends all his free time with his wife, Brittney, and newborn daughter, Everleigh. He enjoys being outdoors, camping, backpacking, and reading whenever he gets the chance.

**Katherine Van Hook** has been writing prose and poetry since childhood. She resides in Lexington, KY with her husband, Eric, and sons, Collin and Ryan. She and her sons are members of the "Lexington Poetry Meet Up" group in Lexington, KY.

**Sandra Wood** is a freelance author who writes stories about God's practical help and amazing hope in our daily lives. She enjoys capturing the beauty of sunrise, rainbows, and wildflowers with a pen, a lens or a song. Long walks with good friends are as delicious as chocolate.

**Susan Yanguas** is a repeat contributor to the *Chicken Soup for the Soul* series. Her short stories have appeared in regional magazines, and her novel *Bluff* was awarded a BRAG Medallion. She is also an editor and has taught writing classes when not walking around her neighborhood.

# Meet Amy Newmark

**Amy Newmark** is the bestselling author, editor-in-chief, and publisher of the *Chicken Soup for the Soul* book series. Since 2008, she has published more than 200 new books, most of them national bestsellers in the U.S. and Canada, more than doubling the number of *Chicken Soup for the Soul* titles in print today. She is also the author of *Simply Happy*, a crash course in Chicken Soup for the Soul advice and wisdom that is filled with easy-to-implement, practical tips for enjoying a better life.

Amy is credited with revitalizing the Chicken Soup for the Soul brand, which has been a publishing industry phenomenon since the first book came out in 1993. By compiling inspirational and aspirational true stories curated from ordinary people who have had extraordinary experiences, Amy has kept the thirty-two-year-old Chicken Soup for the Soul brand fresh and relevant.

Amy graduated *magna cum laude* from Harvard University where she majored in Portuguese and minored in French. She then embarked on a three-decade career as a Wall Street analyst, a hedge fund manager, and a corporate executive in the technology field.

Her return to literary pursuits was inevitable, as her honors thesis in college involved traveling throughout Brazil's impoverished northeast region, collecting stories from regular people. She is delighted to have come full circle in her writing career — from collecting stories "from the people" in Brazil as a twenty-year-old to, three decades later, collecting stories "from the people" for Chicken Soup for the Soul.

When Amy and her husband Bill, the CEO of Chicken Soup for the Soul, are not working, they are visiting their four grown children and their spouses, and their six grandchildren.

Follow Amy on X and Instagram @amynewmark. Listen to her free podcast — Chicken Soup for the Soul with Amy Newmark — on Apple, Google, or by using your favorite podcast app on your phone. You can also find a selection of her stories on Medium.

# Sharing Happiness, Inspiration, and Hope

Real people sharing real stories, every day, all over the world. In 2007, *USA Today* named *Chicken Soup for the Soul* one of the five most memorable books in the last quarter-century. With over 110 million books sold to date in the U.S. and Canada alone, more than 300 titles in print, and translations into nearly fifty languages, "chicken soup for the soul®" is one of the world's best-known phrases.

Today, thirty-two years after we first began sharing happiness, inspiration and hope through our books, we continue to delight our readers with new titles almost every month, but have also evolved beyond the bookshelves with super premium pet food, a podcast, adult coloring books, and licensed products that include word-search puzzle books and books for babies and preschoolers. We are busy "changing your life one story at a time®" and doing it for the whole family. Thanks for reading!